Gregory Nelson

25 January 1977

WINES
Their
Sensory Evaluation

WINES

Their
Sensory Evaluation

Maynard A. Amerine   Edward B. Roessler

University of California, Davis

W. H. Freeman and Company
San Francisco

Cartoon on page 12: By permission of William Hamilton.

Cartoon on page 89: Copyright © 1943 by James Thurber. Copyright © 1963 in Great Britain by the estate of James Thurber. Copyright © 1971 by Helen W. Thurber and Rosemary Thurber Sauers. From *Vintage Thurber* by James Thurber; Hamish Hamilton, London, 1963. Also from *Men, Women and Dogs* by James Thurber; Dodd, Mead & Company, New York, 1975. Originally printed in *The New Yorker*.

Library of Congress Cataloging in Publication Data

Amerine, Maynard Andrew, 1911–
    Wines: their sensory evaluation.

    Bibliography: p.
    Includes index.
    1. Wine tasting. I. Roessler, Edward Biffer,
1902–   joint author. II. Title.
TP548.5.A5A4   641.2′2   76-13441
ISBN 0-7167-0553-2

Printed in the United States of America

9 8 7 6 5 4 3 2

Contents

Preface

This is a short treatise on the sensory evaluation of wines. The phrase "sensory evaluation of wines" is more cumbersome than "wine tasting" but it is more accurate. Tasting is only one facet of the evaluation of wine quality, and not even the most important one. Sensory evaluation is also a better term because it emphasizes that our senses are the means by which we react to external stimuli. We hasten to admit that our sensory responses, and especially our perceptions of quality, are often modified by a variety of physiological and psychological factors and cultural influences. Both the amateur wine enthusiast and the professional wine judge are susceptible to such effects. The professional learns to avoid them as best he can, and to refine his sensory skills. The amateur can do this too; all it takes is a sensible approach, and practice.

In this book we describe what we believe is the best approach to wine evaluation. We are sure that it will be useful to wine

professionals and students. We are equally sure that it will be useful to serious amateurs—those who drink wine regularly and wish to make meaningful judgments about wine quality. Professional judges, of course, must make such decisions routinely, and the commercial consequences of their decisions are often far-reaching.

The text is divided into two parts. Part I deals with wines and their sensory examination. Part II deals with the statistical procedures used to evaluate the data obtained. These procedures are not merely useful in deriving meaningful judgments from the results of panel evaluations (whether professional or amateur)—they are essential. As you read the book, you will see why. You do not *need* to read Part II in order to profit from this book, but you will profit much more if you do, especially if you are (or want to be) a wine professional. Some of the material may look difficult to those whose exposure to mathematics ended with their school days, but it really isn't. To understand it, all one needs is a little high-school algebra and some common sense—mainly the latter.

We begin with a chapter on wine quality, a most elusive concept to define. In fact, wine quality is easier to recognize than to define. Nevertheless, many people "recognize" the wrong things, by adhering slavishly to the shibboleths of the wine snobs. We take a close look at some of these shibboleths and do not leave them (or the wine snobs) unscathed.

In the next chapter we discuss the senses that are stimulated by wines. There are six in all, including two (pain and temperature) that are not usually thought of as distinct senses but that are, in fact, physiologically distinct from the sense of touch. Examples of typical reactions to these six kinds of stimuli are given.

This is followed by a chapter on the physiological and psychological factors that affect the sensory response. Even some expert wine judges are unaware of the wide range of sensory responses—and consequent judgments—made possible by these factors. However, their long experience has usually made them aware (if only subconsciously) of the importance of these factors and taught them how to avoid their effects. We believe that the surest and fastest way to develop this talent is to understand the physiological and psychological factors from the beginning and remain fully

cognizant of them while gaining experience in sensory evaluation.

The fourth chapter deals in some detail with the best modern methods of conducting the sensory examination—from the selection of judges and tests through the setup of the experimental facilities and procedures to the critical examination of the wine in the glass. All the photographs (Plates 1–16) pertain to this chapter.

In the next chapter we discuss the composition of wines, with particular reference to those chemical compounds that most noticeably affect their sensory characteristics.

The last chapter in Part I is an outline of the major types of commercially available wines. For each type we list the most important quality factors that must be considered in the sensory evaluation.

In Part II we discuss a variety of procedures for quantitatively evaluating the differences among wines and for measuring their overall quality. The statistical procedures used to determine the significance of the results are described in some detail. We recommend these procedures to both amateurs and professionals. The former may want to apply at least the chi-square test and t-test to determine the statistical significance of the differences between two wines. Professionals will want to use analysis of variance and other statistical procedures to determine not only the significance of the results but also the relative importance of the various factors that contribute to this significance.

We do not suggest that wine consumers need to use t-tests or score cards to appreciate differences in wine quality. We are certain, however, that an understanding of such procedures will instill a healthy skepticism about the claims of quality differences that we find in the popular literature, and about the price tags that we find on some wines. Our basic premise is that wine consumers and professional enologists alike will enjoy their wines more and will make more intelligent decisions about wine quality and wine value if they understand how and why they make such decisions and how to determine, when necessary, the statistical significance of those decisions.

Part II concludes with some suggested practical exercises that are useful for refining one's sensory skills and in selecting judges for sensory evaluation panels. Following the appendixes are a

glossary (which includes a list of terms that we recommend *not* using) and an annotated bibliography.

Wine is a very complex liquid that is much more than just a dilute alcoholic solution. What makes wine so interesting is its infinite variety: its subtle nuances of color, odor, taste, flavor, and texture, all of which are determined by the chemical composition of the wine. In the proper balance, these sensory characteristics combine to stimulate the one sense that provides the most enduring pleasure and appreciation—the aesthetic sense. It is, therefore, natural to try to relate chemical composition to aesthetic quality. Such an approach need not diminish one's appreciation of wine quality. On the contrary, we believe that it will enhance appreciation.

We hope, therefore, that this book will lead to a better appreciation of the sensory and aesthetic qualities of wine, by the consumer as well as by the student and the professional. We also trust that, by more careful sensory evaluation of their wines, winemakers will make better wines.

We cannot resist the temptation to conclude with a mention of an elegant but little-known word that could be used to describe what this book is about: *degustation* (from the verb *degust*—to taste or savor appreciatively, as a connoisseur). Although its Latin derivation suggests tasting alone, it is commonly used in French, Italian, and Russian wine terminology to mean all aspects of sensory evaluation. We recommend its increasing use in English in this broad sense—the sense that Robert Louis Stevenson surely had in mind when he wrote, "Wine . . . a deity to be invoked by two or three, all fervent, hushing their talk, degusting tenderly."

April 1976   Maynard A. Amerine
                                                   Edward B. Roessler

Acknowledgments

During the past forty years we have discussed the problems of sensory evaluation with a great many people. We thank them all. Professor Rose Marie Pangborn, with whom we collaborated on a more general book on sensory evaluation, has been particularly helpful. Our colleagues, Professors George A. Baker, Harold W. Berg, James F. Guymon, Cornelius S. Ough, Vernon L. Singleton, and A. Dinsmoor Webb, have been constructively critical in this field over a long period.

Concerning this particular book we thank Professors James Gallender of Ohio State University and Ann Noble of the University of California, Davis, and Mr. Philip Wagner of Baltimore. Their criticisms and suggested changes have been most appreciated. The errors that remain are ours, not theirs.

We are indebted to Mr. Alfred A. Blaker for making the photographs of the wine glasses (Plates 7–10), the corkscrews and other openers (Plate 12), and the "tears" of wine (Plates 13 and 14; see also the footnote on page 69).

We are grateful to the literary executor of the late Sir Ronald A. Fisher, F.R.S., to Dr. Frank Yates, F.R.S., and to Longman Group Ltd., London, for permission to reprint portions of Tables III, IV, V, and VII from *Statistical Tables for Biological, Agricultural, and Medical Research*, 6th ed., 1974. We are also grateful to Professors D. B. Duncan and A. Kramer and to Dr. H. L. Harter for permission to reprint portions of various tables that they compiled.

Finally, to our editor, Fred Raab, we owe an especial debt of gratitude for his labors. He has examined every sentence for clarity and meaning. His careful work has saved us from many errors.

WINES
Their
Sensory Evaluation

I
WINES AND THEIR SENSORY EXAMINATION

1

Wine Quality

Quality in wines is much easier to recognize than to define. This is, of course, of little help to the amateur. Most amateurs readily recognize that there are important qualitative and quantitative differences among wines. What the amateur cannot know intuitively, but can learn by practice, is how to recognize the relative value of each of the factors that contribute to wine quality. It is from such knowledge, born of experience, that the aesthetics and ultimate pleasure of wine are derived. As Boileau wrote in the nineteenth century, "Drinking well makes one sage, but he who knows not what to drink knows nothing."

There are fundamentally two approaches to the sensory evaluation of wines: the subjective, emotional, intuitive, or romantic, and the objective, reasoned, analytic, or classic. There is nothing "wrong" with either point of view, but they do not necessarily lead to the same conclusions. The romantic approach is more superficial. It is perhaps the only way that intuitive individuals can

appreciate the quality of wines. Years, labels, regions, producers, etc., all of which are incidental to the wine itself, influence their judgments. By contrast the classic approach pays little attention to such external matters and seeks to discover the underlying reasons for a wine's good or bad qualities. *It is our thesis that the classic approach leads to more consistent, defensible results.* Unfortunately the popular wine literature is filled mainly with the special pleadings of the romantic approach. In any event the romanticists often do not understand what the classicists are talking about, and vice versa. We hope that this book will contribute to a better understanding of the classicists' motivations, methods, and terminology.

For a more detailed discussion of the meaning of quality see Pirsig (1974). We do not agree with Pirsig that the analytic approach to quality destroys appreciation. If anything, it should enhance appreciation. For us and for many whom we know, it certainly does.

Gale (1975) argues that wine quality judgments are based entirely on "factual" or observable, i.e., perceptual, data.* He admits, however, that these data acquire part of their meaning and all of their organization from some theory or theories that link simple perceptual judgments (beginning with sensory observations) to ever more theoretical judgments (culminating in conclusions about quality). Indeed, he says, the observations themselves must imply the theory, and it is for this reason that judgments based on such observations must be empirically either true or false. He uses the Davis wine score card (page 122) to show how a theoretical model (the score card) can be used to measure quality. Nevertheless, as we will see below, aesthetic judgments cannot be easily formalized.

Aesthetics

Aesthetics has to do with the subjective and objective appraisal of works of art: music, art, architecture, literature—and wine. The

*Harries (1973) has emphasized that food scientists now accept sensory data as objective, though perhaps not quite equivalent to instrumental data.

properties that we associate with aesthetic appreciation are symmetry, balance, harmony, complexity, etc. We believe that the full appreciation of an aesthetic object requires some degree of formal training, or at least conscious study. There is, of course, no perfect predictive equation for evaluating the relative importance of all the factors that contribute to the aesthetic quality of a work of art. Nor *can* there be any such perfect equation. The very inexplicability of the parameters of aesthetic quality is surely an integral part of the attraction of a great work of art. Nevertheless, one can obtain predictive equations, however imperfect, that may be not only useful but commercially valuable.

Wine offers a splendid field for the study of aesthetic quality. First, it has an ancient, generally recognized, and continuing tradition of quality evaluation. Second, wine has an immense range of types and of quality variations within each type. Third, new types of wines are constantly being created; this requires that existing standards of aesthetic quality be constantly refined and that new ones be established when necessary. The wide variety of old and new production methods available to the winemaker may —and often does—modify the quality of the wine. This makes it essential that the consumer continuously reevaluate his aesthetic standards for wine. Some wine judges believe that excessive use of modern filters or fining (clarifying) agents diminishes the quality of wine in subtle (and sometimes not so subtle) ways. Unfortunately, the greater the intrinsic quality of the wine, the greater the effect is likely to be. On the other hand, proper use of filters and fining agents can prevent clouding and microbial spoilage and thus enhance the quality. Also, we are skeptical that avoiding clarification always results in higher quality, even when clouding or spoilage does not occur. At least we have not found any convincing evidence in the literature or in our own experience that "natural" wines are better than wines that have been properly processed.

Everyone acknowledges that different wines give varying degrees of transitory or lasting pleasure to different individuals. The greater our understanding of the factors that affect our reactions to wines, the greater our confidence to judge them and the keener

our capacity to enjoy them. Naturally there will always be wide differences in individual preferences, and if these preferences are based on experience and considered judgment we must accept them at face value.

Our first reaction to an aesthetic object such as wine is apt to be purely subjective: we like it or dislike it. For a more lasting judgment however, we apply certain objective criteria, consciously or unconsciously. These may enhance our enjoyment of the wine or confirm our aversion to it. As we gain experience with a certain type of wine we may reverse our original judgment. Sometimes we come to enjoy a wine we originally found undesirable. Or, more likely, we may find with experience that the wine we once praised no longer pleases us. This is a part of the learning process that everyone undergoes in arriving at personal standards for evaluating the quality of any aesthetic object.

Our enjoyment of wine is thus essentially a learned response and is a complex mixture of intellectual and sensory pleasures. In addition, it has overtones of sensual pleasure and is obviously related to social customs. Our appreciation of wine is to a major extent subject to sensory skills and aesthetic principles that depend on experience. Individual preferences are, of course, important; to the individual they are all-important. All we can do is postulate that they have some rational basis and hope that some general aesthetic principles may eventually emerge for each individual.

Pitfalls. Appreciation of the quality of a wine does *not* depend on its reputation, tradition, or price. This is all the more important to remember in a world where the Madison Avenue huckster has made a fine art of touting just about anything as a superlative, "quality" product. The unwary consumer may easily be fooled as to the actual quality of a wine if he relies on Old World romance, price, region, producer, vintage, etc. Each of these, to be sure, may have some relation to quality. But it is the sensory quality of the wine in the glass that is important, not the words on the bottle label, or the price, or the excellence of the advertising.

The intelligent wine connoisseur must therefore have the sensory skill and aesthetic appreciation to be able to ignore with

confidence both the ad agencies and the wine snobs, who would often have us believe that the expensive and the imported are automatically better, and that wines from certain vineyards, producers, or vintages are always, *ipso facto*, superior. The expensive may be poor because it is too old; the imported can be inferior when it is shipped by a careless merchant; and *every* vineyard, producer, and vintage has its failures. Even in the most disastrous year some lucky producer may obtain a good or even great wine. We know of at least one California Cabernet Sauvignon of 1967 of superlative quality, although generally the wines of this variety and year in this state were not admirable. Similar examples could be cited for many Bordeaux, Burgundy, Rhine, Moselle, and other wines.

Pleasure

What is the difference between an ordinary wine and a great wine? The first principle is pleasure. But suppose the wine that greatly pleases us displeases our neighbor? Such marked variations in appreciation do occur, but usually between judges of very different degrees of experience. Differences in experience or prejudices arising from cultural, familial, or religious customs may explain many of these individual preferences or aversions. Some, of course, may be inherent in our own philosophical attitudes. Obviously each individual is the final authority on what is poor, fair, good, or superlative for him. It is also true, however, that well-trained, experienced wine judges agree rather consistently in their overall appraisals of wine quality. We base this conclusion on the results of close observation of a number of judgings, both national and international.

Disagreement almost always occurs when the panel includes a less experienced judge or judges who are less familiar with the type of wine in question. Scores or rankings of the judges also differ significantly when (1) too many wines are judged at a single session

or (2) the wines are either very similar or very different in quality or (3) some or all of the wines are atypical. The maximum number of wines that can be ranked accurately at one session may be as few as five and is certainly no more than ten to fifteen (page 65).

Finding an appreciative audience for a new wine type or for wines from a new producer or region is often difficult. The need in the wine industry is always for more consumers who will sympathetically *try* the new product and see whether it gives them pleasure. Only wine snobs arbitrarily condemn new wine types, wines from new producers or regions, or wines made by new processes. There is no substitute for personal sensory evaluation of the product in reaching a fair conclusion.

Can we agree that an adequate judgment of an aesthetic object, such as a truly fine wine, can only be made when it represents the accumulated experience of many prior judgments? Our initial judgment of a fine wine is apt to be superficial and untrustworthy unless we have had considerable experience with wines of similar character and quality. If the wine is of very limited aesthetic appeal, on the other hand, no complicated evaluation is needed or even possible.

We feel justified in rejecting a reliance on tradition or someone else's authority to form our aesthetic judgments of the quality of wines. Nevertheless, we can learn much from those with more experience. Of course, every wine critic, however experienced, has blind spots. Since aesthetic judgments are partially subjective we must ultimately make our own decisions. We either find pleasure in a given wine or we do not.

Variation in judgment, even among experts, is why we reject single-judge evaluations. A good panel should have five or more qualified judges (see page 110). We confess, however, to a certain admiration for the artist who insists on the aesthetic value of his work even when the world does not. Just consider the history of painting in the past one hundred years. Clearly, today's philistine may be tomorrow's "artist," and vice versa. Or consider wines. By and large, nineteenth-century standards for wine appreciation did

not condemn high volatile acidity (acescence), cloudiness, darkening of the color of white wines, brownish-red colors in red wines, or relatively low ethanol content. Need we add that none of these are tolerated, much less appreciated, by wine connoisseurs today?

But we emphasize again that in order to arrive at meaningful judgments a panel must have wide experience in evaluating wines of the types under study, and some common basis for judgment. Otherwise there is just a hodgepodge of personal preferences, not a vote on quality.

Complexity

Like fine art, fine wines are made by impeccable workmanship plus a clear concept of the aesthetic standards by which they will be judged. All truly fine wines produce feelings other than mere pleasure. There is a sense of awe in appreciating a fine wine—a feeling that here is a complex and superior juxtaposition of appearance, color, odor, taste, and texture. We say the wine is balanced, but in a truly great wine there is more than just balance. The components must complement one another synergistically and excite our aesthetic appreciation. A great wine should have so many facets of quality that we are continually finding new ones. It is this complexity that enables us to savor such a wine without losing our interest in it. For a great wine we cannot find enough words to describe the complexity of sensory qualities. For a simple, ordinary wine the words that come to mind seem to suffice.

Having spoken earlier of pleasure, we should add that all truly fine wines are *memorably* pleasurable. True, we also remember the characteristics of a really bad wine—but not with pleasure. Wines falling between these extremes easily drop out of mind. The wine that does not excite us enough to be remembered pleasurably can never be a great wine. This does not mean that the wine in the middle range may not be salable. Many less-than-great products of the industry sell very well indeed. Somewhere between "sales volume measures quality" and "price measures quality" there must be a middle ground. Obviously neither sales nor price alone is a measure of quality.

To summarize, fine wines have a complexity of sensory qualities that defy simple analysis. When pleasure and complexity combine to create a memorable experience we have a great wine.

Types of Consumers

In terms of the sensory evaluation of wines there are basically three types of consumers. The great majority of consumers evaluate wine in terms of their past experience, however slight, and their personal likes and dislikes. The ordinary consumer is not interested in the wine as an aesthetic object. It is just another part of the meal, and the consumer does not think about its quality any more than he thinks about the quality of the salad or beans. He consumes the wine mainly because it is the culturally acceptable table beverage, and enjoys it for perhaps the same reason, in addition to its pleasant sensory effects. But he does not attempt to analyze the reasons that he finds it pleasant.

Even at this level, however, some aesthetic judgments are made. Almost all consumers will reject (or at least resist) a variety of food or wine they find unpleasant, no matter how common that class of food or wine is in their diet. But it is not primarily the aesthetic quality of the wine that is important to such consumers, who usually choose low-priced wines with nondistinctive flavors. The sales generated by such consumers are important to the wine industry, but we do not yet know how important are the various sensory factors that affect their wine purchases (color, sugar content, etc). It is true, of course, that many people (perhaps most) can afford to buy only the relatively low-priced wines. Much potential aesthetic appreciation of wines is undoubtedly stifled by sheer economic necessity.

The production of *distinctively flavored, high-quality wines* requires expensive grapes (often grown in special regions and fermented by special techniques) and often requires (in red wines) longer aging than for ordinary wines. This accounts for their higher price. In general, inexpensive wines have innocuous sensory characteristics and more expensive wines have a greater complexity of odors and flavors. For expert judges this is the most difficult problem: to find the right balance of complexity without grotesqueness.

Fortunately not all consumers drink wine without regard to quality—otherwise all wines might as well be the same. We do not know when a consumer changes from the mere drinking of wines to introspective evaluation of the quality of each wine he consumes, but his economic status is doubtless a factor. In wine-drinking countries the typical wine consumer may normally be only a wine drinker. But on special occasions (feast days, etc., as determined by social custom) or with special friends he may be an appreciative and even critical consumer.

Our second group of consumers falls into the category of appreciative drinkers. For such consumers wine is more than just a table beverage, and wine drinking has some aspects of an aesthetic experience. Later (page 12) we will try to analyze their reactions to wine and the specific standards that they develop.

The third group includes the professional wine judges. Their task is to evaluate the sensory quality of wines *according to some agreed-upon standards.* Generally their personal preferences in wines do not come into play or are consciously ignored. This is why it is vital for the judges to have common, fixed standards for each type of wine. To achieve such standards a great deal of experience with the types of wines they are called upon to judge is absolutely essential. A professional judge may not like sweet table wines but can still be a good, dispassionate judge of their quality if he has sufficient experience with them.

Several different situations may arise in a professional wine evaluation. At competitions the standard used by the judges is often relative: the best wine of a given type—for example, the best Pinot noir. Or the judges may be required to score the wines on some absolute scale, such as 1 to 20, where a score of 20 would be

given to a "perfect" Pinot noir and a score of 1 to a hopelessly spoiled wine. Either way it is of crucial importance that all the judges have a clear, fixed, and pre-established concept of a fine-quality and a poor-quality Pinot noir wine. This is why judges in quality wine competitions *must* have wide and critical experience with the types they are asked to judge. Such experience is not so essential when the judges are required simply to rank the wines in order of merit, regardless of how good the wine ranked first may be. In this case the meaning of each rank is difficult to assess.

Another reason that experience is vital is that inexperienced judges, lacking a standard or a frame of reference, tend to drift in their sensory evaluations as a series of wines of the same type is presented. Apparently the inexperienced judge "learns" as he proceeds through the series. If all the samples are poor he may rate the best of the lot too high. Conversely, if all the samples are very good he is likely to rate some of them too low. Even a very experienced judge, when asked his opinion of a single wine, may find it difficult to rate it correctly. He is almost certain, however, to be more nearly correct in his judgment than an inexperienced judge. Statistical measures of the reliability of the judges and of their results are therefore necessary (see page 59), since these will reveal drifts in scoring.

Experienced, professional judges are also essential in winery operations. Although chemical analyses are clearly of great importance, there are times when a detailed and critical sensory analysis is indispensable, e.g., in blending, in determining how much fining agent to use, in deciding whether further barrel or cask aging is necessary, etc. Statistical measures of the significance of the differences between treatments are essential (see page 57).

One obvious difference between experienced and inexperienced judges is revealed when descriptive comments are required (page 167). The inexperienced judge lacks the full range of vocabulary to describe his impressions, and he does not use whatever vocabulary he does have consistently and meaningfully. Thus he may say the taste is "tart" one time and "green" another, or that it is "sour" when he means "bitter." Communication between judges is difficult or even impossible in such cases.

Some Shibboleths that Need to Be Questioned

We list here some popular axioms about wine. Their real meanings have often been perverted by wine snobs, who glibly use them without understanding them. In fact, the wine industry suffers enormously from wine snobs who praise the wrong wines, usually for reasons that have little to do with quality. For a short, fictional play on this subject see Amerine (1969).

1. That wine judges are *born* wine judges.

There is just enough truth in this to fool many people. If you are born into a wine-drinking family, especially one that consumes wine critically, you have a big advantage in experience. Once in a blue moon some unfortunate individual has a low sensitivity to odor and/or taste sensations. The rest of us, the overwhelming majority, have all the physical equipment we need to become excellent judges of wine quality, even if our parents drank nothing but beer. Of course, we may not *want* to become a sensitive judge of wine quality. We may be lazy or disinclined to train our senses to detect subtle differences in quality among wines. So be it.

"They were relatively nice men, Caroline. What do you suppose turned them into enophiles?"

On the other hand, if we apply ourselves we can acquire the requisite experience. With any luck at all we should be able to provide ourselves with a frame of reference that will enable us to evaluate the quality of most wines. We should not, however, underestimate the amount of experience that is necessary to become a truly reliable judge of the entire range of quality of wines of a given district or type. Few, if any, can aspire to become a qualified judge of all the different types of wines in the world.

2. That only experts can enjoy the full quality of a wine.

This is nonsense. It is a rare individual who, with even a little experience, may not enjoy drinking wine. The expert may know *why* he enjoys a certain wine but he would be presumptuous to claim that he enjoys it more than the amateur. The latter may, in fact, enjoy a certain wine more fully than the expert precisely because he does *not* have the knowledge and experience to make all the possible comparisons among wines. However, it is also demonstrable that he is generally not able to maintain his preferences as consistently as the expert.

We concede that the expert does gain a different type of pleasure from his intellectual appreciation of the complex sensory perceptions yielded by a truly fine wine.

3. That Heaven keeps some sort of order of merit for the relative quality of certain vineyards, producers, or vintages.

This is sacrilegious. Even the lowliest vineyard and the poorest year occasionally produce a glorious wine. Need we add that some of the most prestigious vineyards and producers have given us some notoriously poor wines? Consider some of the wines of Bordeaux of 1963!

But there is a germ of truth here in the opposite sense. Famous vineyards, renowned vintages, and producers of great reputation do not usually acquire their prestige unearned. The point, however, is that you should not use such prestige as your standard for judging the quality of a wine. The wine may be good or bad, but *you* are the one who should determine this—for you.

4. That small wineries produce better wines than large wineries.

Some of the worst wines we ever suffered came from small, picturesque wineries. We hasten to add that some of the best also came from small wineries. It is the standards of the producer, and a fair amount of luck, that determine the quality of the wines produced, not the size of the winery.

In theory a large winery should be able to make a more careful selection of varieties and of the lots for aging, and thus produce finer wines. This does happen, of course, but economics, marketing objectives, and other factors may interfere.

5. That wines of one area are, *ipso facto*, better than those of another area.

This presupposes that all wines are to be judged by the same standard. One cannot compare wines meaningfully if they differ from each other in a fundamental way. For example, white wines of one area have their own character and cannot be compared with white wines of another area, which have a different character. The same is true of red wines, of fortified versus nonfortified wines, of still versus sparkling wines, etc. Comparisons of quality among different types of wines are therefore usually unprofitable and often misleading.

Furthermore, people have their own preferences. There is no law that says we must prefer one kind of wine over another. Even among the wines of a given area, we may cultivate a taste for the wines of one producer over those of another.

6. That bottled wines improve with age.

This is patently untrue for many white table wines and is often untrue for red table wines. *Some* white table wines improve in quality when kept under proper conditions for a few years. Many red table wines improve with aging in the bottle for several or many years. But we can all remember wines that were at their best within a few months or years of bottling. In addition we can recall a number of wines that, judging by their odor, were bottled after too long a period in the barrel or cask.

It is true that, with aging, *some* red wines acquire nuances of bouquet that young wines lack. With still longer aging, however, they may also become oxidized in flavor and brown in color. To praise the old wine for its age and ignore its overaged characteristics is a gross error of judgment. Unless, of course, one is foolish enough to prefer age rather than quality.

7. That wines always improve if left open before serving.

It is true that some wines do improve if left open, particularly if they are decanted before serving. We can postulate several reasons for this. Overly gassy still wines lose their excess carbon dioxide. Wines with small amounts of undesirable fermentation odors are improved by this loss of carbon dioxide, particularly when such odors are present at or near the threshold level (see footnote on page 73). Wines that have off odors owing to microbial changes during aging are also improved. Wines with too much sulfur dioxide may lose some of the free sulfur dioxide and make a better odor impression.

However, the claim that leaving a wine open or decanting it results in an *increase* in the desirable odors is hard to substantiate. What chemical reaction could take place within a few minutes or a few hours that would produce enough additional desirable odors to be recognizable? There is also the possibility, even the probability, that wines may *lose* desirable odors, especially after decanting. One would have to admit that subtle losses in one odor constituent compared to others may, and probably do, change the overall odor character of the wine, sometimes favorably.

Nevertheless, it is risky to predict what will happen. For each example of an apparent improvement in the sensory impression with early opening of the bottle or decanting of the wine, we can cite examples of wines, particularly old red wines, in which the quality deteriorated rapidly. In our experience decanting is more likely to prove beneficial for young wines than for older wines. There are, of course, times when decanting is necessary to separate the clear wine from the sediment. Then we prefer to open the bottle and decant it *just* before serving.

8. That expensive wines are better than cheap wines.

Some are, many are not. Price depends on many factors that are not necessarily related to quality. Those who buy wines on a price basis deserve what they get. The law of compound interest means that old wines will always have to be sold at a higher price than corresponding young wines. But, as we have said earlier, this does not mean that they are better wines.

As usual, however, there is some truth in this shibboleth. The finest wines are made from more expensive grapes. Often they must be specially harvested, fermented, and aged. The producer must charge a higher price for his higher expenditure. But it is the quality of the wine, not the price, that is important. Some famous vineyards, secure in the knowledge that they have an established market, often charge whatever the market will bear. This means that the wines are sometimes not worth the higher price if quality alone is the criterion for selection.

9. That certain types of wines should be consumed only with certain foods.

The truth in this statement may be that we like food combinations that we are familiar with better than those with which we are not familiar. This does not explain the origins of the social custom of drinking certain wines with one food in preference to another. One can justify serving tart white wines with fish on the same basis that we serve a tart sauce with fish: the tartness represses the fishiness of the fish. But other recommendations—such as Cabernet Sauvignon or a particular château wine with lamb, and Pinot noir only with beef—appear to us to be tenuous at best. The *reductio ad absurdum* would appear to be the recommendation that a particular wine be served only with lamb chops and another wine with lamb stew.

A corollary is the prejudice *against* serving certain types of wines with certain foods. For example, red wines are not usually served with fish. Except for the advantage of the higher acidity of white wines, mentioned above, we can see no good reason for this. It

is probably not the best idea to serve a salad with a vinegary dressing with a fine wine of exceptional bouquet. Even then, however, it is our observation that most people clearly distinguish the vinegary odor of the salad from the bouquet of the wine. We certainly doubt that this odor would spoil our enjoyment of a lesser wine.

10. That one can rely on various charts to determine when a particular type of wine is ready to drink and what its quality will be.

Nonsense! At best such charts are very approximate guides. At worst they may lead one to pay an excessive price for a poor wine of a so-called great vintage year. Some good (and occasionally great) wine is produced even in a year of poor climatic conditions, and some bad wine may be made from even the finest grapes by a careless winemaker. The moral is that whatever quality a wine has is found in the wine in the glass, not in books, charts, or anything else.

Pour bien déguster, il n'est que d'avoir de bons sens et du bon sens.
—P. Poupon

De gustibus non est disputandum.

2

The Senses

Everything we know about the world around us we learn through our senses. This is, of course, true for wines and our value judgments of them. Our appreciation of a wine depends, at least initially, on our sensory impressions. The senses that are important in wine appreciation are sight (vision), smell (olfaction), taste (gustation), touch (tactile sensitivity, or feel), pain, and temperature. With experience some synthesis of sensory impressions enters into our judgment. For example, the ratio of sugar to acid seems to be important and experienced judges perceive this sugar/acid ratio separately from the sugar or acid content alone. The central nervous system can and does mediate complex interactions of sensory impressions from the various receptors.

Vision

The clarity and the tint and depth of color are the primary visual attributes of wine that must be considered, for two reasons: the pleasure that the appearance and color give us and the information about the prospective odors and tastes that these visual attributes reveal.

Color. Appreciation of color is a learned response and is highly subjective. One must admit that some wines have a more appealing color than others—red versus brown sherry, for example. Yet we do enjoy brown sherries. What we apparently appreciate most is a color that we have learned to regard as *appropriate* to the type of wine in question.

No white wines are really naturally white; they range in color from straw yellow to dark amber. White table wines are either straw yellow or yellow. As the wine ages it usually darkens in color. Only when the wine has been treated excessively with sulfur dioxide does this not occur. Wines made from very ripe white grapes contain more pigment than those that do not ripen fully. Hence wines made from grapes grown in cool regions where the grapes barely ripen are usually lighter in color. In fact, underripe grapes sometimes produce wines with a greenish tint. The ripe-grape types of wines (Chardonnay, White Burgundy, Tokay, the *Auslese* types from Germany, etc.) have more of a gold than yellow color.

When white table wines are kept in the cask or bottle for a long time (several years) they eventually turn amber or brown. Whether one appreciates brownish-colored "white" table wines is a personal matter. We consider such a preference to be an affectation of wine snobs who glory in old wines simply because they are old and expensive. If one wants a brown, sherry-like wine, why not buy brown-colored sherry—at a much lower price? Oloroso sherries, Madeiras, and many other dessert wines are rather amber in color even when young, because of the effects of processing. Their somewhat oxidized flavor also reflects this processing and aging. Curiously, most very amber wines (Marsalas, for example) *lighten*

in color during long aging in the bottle, owing to precipitation of some of the dark-colored pigments.

Rosé wines should be pink, normally without any brown, purple, orange, or tawny tint. With rare exceptions brown or tawny hues in rosé wines mean that the wine has been aged too long or processed with too much oxidation. Rosé wines made from Grenache grapes grown in a warm climate often have an orange tint. Purple tints indicate high-pH (low-acid)* wines, which sometimes result from excessive malo-lactic fermentation.

Most of the wines of the world are red, and for them there is a wide range of acceptable colors, depending on the variety of grape used and the duration of aging. Very young red wines, particularly of red-juice varieties (such as Alicante Bouschet, Rubired, and Royalty), may have a distinct purple-red color. Also, wines of high-pH grapes have a purple tint. Fortunately time reduces the purple tint but, alas, it seldom improves the flavor of these wines.

What is desired in commercial red table wines up to about five years of age is a ruby color. Red wines that are further aged in the bottle develop a more or less amber (or tawny) tint and, one hopes, the typical and desirable "bottle bouquet." A similar tint may be induced by heating the wine, but excessive heat causes a browning of the color. Furthermore, heating the wine produces a "heated" or off odor and the entrancing bottle bouquet of a bottle-aged, high-quality red wine does not develop.

If the brown color is not induced by heating and is not accompanied by an oxidized flavor, it is quite acceptable and even desirable. Taxes, growing consumer interest, and diminishing stocks of old red table wines have resulted in few tawny-colored (from long bottle aging) red table wines reaching the market. We

---

*High pH and low pH mean low active acidity and high active acidity, respectively; by definition, pH is an exact measure of active acidity. For wines it is also important to consider the total (titratable) acidity, which is the active acidity plus the potential acidity due to largely undissociated (weak) organic acids. Qualitatively, the pH of wines correlates with titratable acidity in the same way as with active acidity, i.e., high pH means low acidity and low pH means high acidity. However, pH is *not* an exact measure of titratable acidity in wines because wines contain numerous weak organic acids in varying relative concentrations and buffered by the presence of their salts.

wish to emphasize that the amber color in a red wine is tolerable only if it is not accompanied by undesirable odors.

The tint (hue) and depth of color (lightness or luminance) thus tell us a great deal about what may be wrong or right with the wine. Thus alerted, we look for certain desirable and undesirable odors and flavors in the wine. However, it is well known that spurious conclusions about wine quality are likely to be reached if color is considered independently of odor and flavor factors. Even experienced judges may be led astray when confronted with false clues in the form of nonnormal colors (e.g., when the normal color of a wine is deliberately changed in the laboratory). Nevertheless, the perceptive judge will gain considerable information about the prospective odors and flavors of the wine from its color.

The tint and depth of color are not all that the judge sees. The third parameter of color perception is *purity*, or saturation: the apparent amount of gray admixture. Inexperienced (and sometimes even experienced but colorblind) judges find it difficult to think of color as being determined by three, not two, parameters. For the color-sensitive judge, experience surely helps here, although in practice the two parameters tint and depth of color suffice for most comparisons of the colors of wines.

The human eye is most sensitive to differences in the tint of color in the yellow-green region of the spectrum. Of course, the apparent tint is greatly modified by the background color and the illumination. It is thus important, even critical, to examine wines under a constant and adequate source of illumination. If one has always examined wines by candlelight one may have learned to compensate for the low level of illumination compared with direct or reflected "northern" daylight. But as the level of illumination decreases, the ability to recognize and discriminate between degrees of color difference decreases. Modern illumination systems do not always help. For example, fluorescent lamps and mercury-arc lamps produce false or misleading tints in wines. Under low light intensity at a dinner table, wines of quite different color characteristics may appear to be of approximately the same color.

There is no easy guide for judging the appropriateness of the color in a given type of wine. With experience, however, one comes

to recognize whether the color is appropriate for the type and age of the wine and, if it is not, whether this is due to the use of poor varieties of high-pH grapes, oxidation, excess metal content, or other disorder. White wines that are high in iron may have a greenish-yellow tint. Red wines of high iron content may have an iridescent film on the surface. Both conditions are rare; they are nonexistent in wines from well-run wineries.

The practice of serving white wines in colored glasses in Germany apparently originated as a means of concealing the brown color of the wine. This was particularly true of white wines, in which an amber tint was known to be a sign of overaging or other poor winemaking practices. Serving the wine in green glasses prevented the consumer from perceiving the brown color. Modern German wine technology rarely allows brown-colored wines. We should note that consumers in some countries (Argentina, Chile, and Italy, for example) are more tolerant of brown color in white table wines.

Contradictory results on the effects of added color on taste thresholds have been reported by Maga (1974), who found that green increased sensitivity to sweetness, whereas yellow decreased sensitivity and red had no effect. For sourness both yellow and green decreased sensitivity and again red had no effect. Red did decrease sensitivity to bitterness but yellow and green had no effect. Apparently, psychological color associations do modify our responses to certain tastes. This is a compelling reason for always observing the color of wines under identical, neutral light conditions, especially in taste threshold studies.

Appearance. The other important visual aspect of wines is their clarity, or freedom from suspended material. Wines may be cloudy because of faulty treatment or microbial spoilage, or because aging has left a deposit.

The consumer finds by experience that wines that are cloudy because of faulty treatment or microbial spoilage are also usually defective in odor or flavor, or both. Even when there is only a slight haziness the critical judge will concentrate his attention on its possible causes. A floating white film may indicate the growth of aerobic microorganisms; these lead to oxidation if they are from yeasts, or vinegariness (acescence) if they are from bacteria. A flocculent deposit in a semisweet white table wine is usually a result of yeast growth. A milky cloudiness may be due to excess iron or a copper-protein reaction. Excess copper-protein cloudiness may be accompanied by a reddish-brown precipitate. In some instances a haze may signal the early stages of yeast growth. A cloudiness with a crystalline deposit can be caused by excess potassium acid tartrate or calcium tartrate.

Sometimes the texture of the wine is affected by suspended material. The growth of certain bacteria results not only in haziness but also in increased viscosity. Fortunately this condition is rare in modern commercial wines.

On the other hand, the cloudiness or deposit may be associated with normal aging. Sound white table wines usually develop a deposit only after many years. Dark amber dessert wines deposit some colored material with time. In red wines the problem is more acute. The deposition of colored material often begins with a fine, colloidal haze. Eventually this is deposited on the sides or bottom of the bottle. The amount of deposit depends on the amount of color in the original wine. The nature of the deposit varies greatly from one wine to another. Sometimes it adheres tightly to the bottle; at other times it does not adhere at all and causes problems in decanting the wine (page 15). Sometimes the deposit is heavy and granular, sometimes light and easily disturbed. With the deposition of colored material there is a gradual reduction in the amount of red color and, eventually, the appearance of more and more amber.

Odor

Our sensory appreciation of wines is due mainly to their odor. The olfactory sense is incredibly sensitive to trace amounts of odorous substances. The olfactory (odor-sensitive) region is very small and is located in the upper part of the nose. During normal breathing little air passes over this region. To detect an odor the inhaled air stream must be diverted to the olfactory region. Sniffing is the way to do this. All good judges of wine quality learn to sniff.

A quick, forceful sniff is considered best. It should not be repeated right away, however, because the olfactory sense is subject to rapid adaptation (fatigue). The best practice is to sniff the wine quickly, then remove the glass. After 15 to 30 seconds one may again sniff the wine.

Not only is the olfactory region small and located in a remote part of the nose, but the amount of air that reaches it, even with sniffing, is only a small fraction of that inhaled. Many of the odorous molecules are absorbed by the mucous membranes en route to the olfactory region. Furthermore, the olfactory slit (channel) to this region closes when the nasal passages are swollen. Moral: do not attempt to make critical decisions on the odor of wines when you have a cold. In fact, people who are prone to colds or allergies should not be selected for sensory evaluation panels.

Not all the odor comes to the olfactory region during inhalation. When wine is taken in the mouth its temperature rapidly rises to body temperature. This releases more odorous substances, which reach the olfactory region by diffusion and through exhalation. These in-mouth odors are an important part of what is called flavor. How important they are is best appreciated by recalling that when we have a cold our food seems essentially flavorless—but not tasteless, which is something else (page 38).

Normal individuals can identify a large number of different odors, and several levels of each. The number that can be identified at any one time depends on the individual's inherent ability and experience, the concentrations of the odorous constituents present, and the relative amounts of other odorous constituents. With experience one can identify 1000 or more different odors at different times, and one can detect smaller differences between the levels of a given odor. There is no shortcut for acquiring this ability. For evaluating wines one should practice as much as possible with experts who can identify the various odors. Otherwise one's training is likely to bog down on missed odors or semantic confusion in identifying the odors. To give an idea of the complexity of the problem, typical wines contain more than 300 organic compounds, of which probably 200 are more or less odorous. Of course, in a given wine many compounds are present in subthres-

hold amounts or are masked by the presence of other compounds. Nevertheless, the number of distinguishable odors is very large.

It is very rare to find anosmic individuals (those who, from accident, disease, or congenital defect, cannot smell). Of the more than one thousand individuals we have tested, only two or three were partially anosmic and only one was completely anosmic. If one is a poor judge of wine quality, it is most unlikely to be due to an inability to smell.

An odor at high concentrations may seem very different from the same odor at low concentrations. Also, when two odors are present together, one odor may mask the other, or it may add to the other, or it may have relatively little effect, or it may have a synergistic effect (the odor may appear stronger than it really is, based on its own threshold).

We will discuss three types of odors in wines: aroma, bouquet, and foreign and undesirable.

Aroma. The gamut of wine odors derived from the grape itself is called the aroma. The finest wines are produced from grape varieties that give the wine a characteristic, recognizable aroma, as we saw earlier (page 10). The unfermented grape itself may or may not have the characteristic aroma, or the aroma may be present in too small an amount to be detected. When fermented in contact with the skins, however, the wine acquires its varietal aroma or the already existing aroma is enhanced. Varieties whose *fruit*, if *fully* ripe, can be identified by its odor are Catawba, Concord, Delaware, Gewürztraminer, Ives Seedling, Muscat of Alexandria, Muscat blanc, Muscat Hamburg, Niagara, Orange Muscat, many *Vitis vinifera* × *V. labrusca* (and other interspecific) hybrids, and others. The same is usually true of Cabernet Sauvignon, Müller-Thurgau, Ruby Cabernet, Sauvignon blanc, Sémillon, Zinfandel, and others. When present in sufficient amounts the varietal aromas are readily identifiable in the wines made from these grapes.

Varieties that seldom have such a distinctive aroma in the fruit but whose wine can be easily identified (if the fruit was mature, the vines not overcropped, and the wine properly vinified) include Chardonnay, Folle Blanche, Merlot, Petite Sirah, Pinot noir,

Sylvaner, and White Riesling. Other varieties may, under special climatic and cropping conditions, produce wines with recognizable aromas: Chenin blanc, French Colombard, Mondeuse, Veltliner, Walschriesling, and others.

The amateur should have little difficulty identifying the aromas of several of the varieties mentioned above. The varieties of obvious *V. labrusca* parentage (Catawba, Concord, Delaware, Ives Seedling, Niagara, and many of the *V. vinifera* × *V. labrusca* hybrids) are characterized by a strong odor of methyl and/or ethyl anthranilate—the so-called foxy or "Welch's grape juice" odor. The odor is so distinctive that it is unpleasant to some consumers. It may be so obvious that one tires of it easily. Hybrids that do not contain *V. labrusca* do not have this odor.

The muscat family—Flora, Gewürztraminer, Gold, Malvasia bianca, Müller-Thurgau, Muscat of Alexandria, Muscat blanc, Muscat Hamburg, Orange Muscat, and many other muscats—have a pronounced odor of linalool and other related compounds. No one should find it difficult to identify this floral odor, or even the nuances of odor among different varieties. Some wines made from ripe White Riesling grapes have a distinct, muscat-like odor. Research has revealed that the ripe fruit of this variety does indeed contain linalool (Van Wyk et al., 1967).

We have had mixed experiences with Flora (a cross between Sémillon and Gewürztraminer). Commercial samples have rarely been distinctive. However, the grapes were usually from young, and probably overcropped, vines. Some experimental samples have been spicy but not as distinctive as the wines of Gewürztraminer. The Müller-Thurgau grape ripens early and is hence particularly well adapted to cool climates (Germany, New Zealand, etc.). In the best years its wines have a distinctly muscat-like odor. For many other *V. vinifera* varieties we are almost totally ignorant of the characteristic chemical compounds, but there is no doubt about the distinctiveness of their odors when the wines are produced from mature grapes of mature vines.

Chardonnay wine has an entrancing, ripe-grape aroma. It has also been characterized as fig-, apple-, or melon-like. At its best it is one of the most intriguing of all wine aromas. During aging in the cask and/or bottle its character changes from simple and fruity to very complex. The varietal character should not be over-powered by an excessively woody odor, as it too often is.

Sauvignon blanc, on the other hand, has a distinctive, somewhat spicy aroma that is easily recognized. It has some of the so-called green olive and herbaceous odor found in Cabernet Sauvignon. If the grapes are mature and yellow the wines will have this odor. This variety yields distinctively flavored wines in many regions of the world. When the grapes are grown in cooler regions their aroma may be nearly as intense as that of a muscat; in fact, Sauvignon blanc does remotely resemble a muscat in its aromatic character. Under milder climatic conditions the strong aroma is much attenuated but still easily recognized. When the vines are overcropped the fruit has a less distinctive aroma. The varietal aroma is not lost when the wine is aged in the bottle for several years.

Mature Sémillon grapes can be identified by their slightly pink blush. At this stage the fruit has a distinctive aroma that is trans-mitted to the wine. Although quite different from that of Char-donnay, its aroma has also been characterized as fig- or melon-like. Neither description seems appropriate to us. Rather than confuse the semantics we prefer to call the aroma the Sémillon aroma. It is less spicy than those of Sauvignon blanc or Chardonnay.

As we have already mentioned, White Riesling yields a wine with a fruity-floral, even muscat-like, aroma when ripe grapes are used. If White Riesling is brought to full maturity in California the berries may become brown, and in the warmer regions or seasons the acidity of the juice is too low. California producers should normally harvest the fruit before it reaches full maturity, even if the varietal aroma of the resulting wine is reduced.

Cabernet Sauvignon usually has a strong, aromatic-spicy aroma in the grape, and this is transmitted to the wine. The aroma has also been described as green olive and herbaceous. It has been identified with n-octanol and 2-methoxy-3-isobutylpyrazine (Bay-onove et al., 1975). Once recognized by the consumer it is not easily forgotten. The varietal character of the wine remains distinct even under diverse climatic and production conditions. In warm weather with irrigation the grapes are larger; the flavor of the wine is then less distinctive because of the lower surface/volume ratio

in the grapes. But even in a warm climate there will be some of the distinctive Cabernet aroma. The wine will be flat-tasting from low acidity, however.

Cabernet franc has a less distinctive aroma than Cabernet Sauvignon—at least this is true of the clone grown in California and the Soviet Union. Nevertheless, its aroma clearly places it in the Cabernet group.

Ruby Cabernet certainly has a Cabernet-like aroma. The aroma may be overpowered by an excessive malo-lactic fermentation odor, however, since the wines are very subject to this fermentation. Careful technological control should prevent the malo-lactic odor from becoming excessive.

Petite Sirah yields wines with only a moderately distinctive aroma. In fact, overcropped vines, some clones, and underripe fruit produce nondistinctive wines. The typical Petite Sirah aroma is difficult to describe—it has a fruity and ripe-grape character.

The varietal aroma of Pinot noir is one of the most elusive and difficult to characterize. The reasons are obvious. The variety does not have a strong, distinctive aroma unless the grapes are very ripe. What aroma it does have is easily affected by changes during aging and processing. Curiously, the varietal character seems to increase during the first few years of aging. Pinot noir has a mild, ripe-grape aroma that, at its best, can be described as a slightly overripe-grape aroma. It has none of the aromatic character of the wines of Cabernet Sauvignon or Sauvignon blanc, although it has been described as pepperminty.

The distinctive aroma of Zinfandel wine has been recognized and appreciated since that wine first appeared on the California market a century or more ago. It has been characterized as fruity, berry-like, raspberry-like, etc. With some experience with Zinfandel wine one should not have difficulty in identifying the aroma. Where the grapes are grown under relatively cool climatic conditions (regions II-III),* and where they ripen without bunch rot or the deleterious effects of red spider attack, they mature

---

*Region I is the coolest area where grapes can be grown and brought to maturity in California, and region V is the warmest. See Amerine and Singleton (1965) for a fuller discussion.

unevenly but adequately. Under the relatively warm conditions of regions III–IV, in a warm season, or when harvested very late, the early-ripening fruit may shrivel and raisin. When such fruit is crushed it produces wines with a characteristic flavor but with excessively high ethanol content (up to 15 or 16%). We do not enjoy this type of wine as a table wine.

A number of other varieties have recognizable aromas under favorable conditions. Folle Blanche is not usually recognized in Europe as producing a wine with a varietal aroma; indeed, in Europe it does not do so because it seldom ripens fully. In the warmer climates of California it has a characteristic, mild, apple-grapy aroma, especially when the fruit is allowed to come to full maturity.

French Colombard is a variety known as such only in California. Usually its wines are rather neutral, but under the special conditions of full maturity and normal cropping it produces wines with a distinctive aroma. The problem of the vintner is to decide when to harvest the grapes so that the aroma will not be too strong. It is a difficult aroma to characterize and not all wines labeled "French Colombard" have it—fortunately, in our opinion.

Sylvaner grapes have a mildly fruity but undistinguished aroma, and this is true of a great deal of its wine, whether produced in Europe, Australia, or California. Nevertheless, when grown in cool climates without overcropping, it can produce wines of recognizable aroma. This aroma has been described as fruity, flowery, and grapy. One can say that it is not muscat-like and only mildly distinctive.

A number of other varieties undoubtedly have distinctive varietal characters, but to a lesser degree or less regularly. Among the whites are Aligoté, Chenin blanc, and Rkatsiteli. Veltliner, Walschriesling, and a few others have recognizable aromas only under the optimum conditions of maturity, production, and fermentation. Among the reds, Carignane, Gamay, Grenache, Mondeuse (Refosco), Nebbiolo, Saperavi, and Valdepeñas appear at times to have mildly distinctive aromas, but not strong or easily recognizable ones.

Finally there are the varieties that do not impart a distinctive character to their wines. Among the whites these include Burger,

Chasselas doré, Diamant, Green Hungarian, Málaga, Palomino, Thompson Seedless, and Trebbiano (Ugni blanc, Saint-Émilion). Among the reds they include Alphonse Lavallée (Ribier), Aramon, Emperor, Mataro, Mission, Red Málaga, and Tokay.

Bouquet. Whereas odors derived from the grapes themselves are called the aroma, those derived from fermentation, processing, or aging are called the bouquet. All young wines have a yeasty, reduced fermentation bouquet. If not too pronounced, such bouquet can add to the olfactory tone of white table wines of low varietal character. Many young white wines of Switzerland, Austria, Italy, and elsewhere are pleasant for this reason. But, alas, the period during which the wines have an attractive, fresh, young odor is short—usually less than a year. (For a discussion of excess fermentation bouquet see page 36.) Normally, white and red table wines and dessert wines lose most of their fermentation bouquet before or within a few months of bottling. Wines prepared by the *macération carbonique* process (as in some Beaujolais) retain a reduced fermentation bouquet. In this process whole grapes are held under anaerobic conditions for about a week, during which they undergo an intracellular fermentation. We do not find the odor pleasant.

Processing odors are often very important, even essential. Bottle-fermented sparkling wines held on the yeast for one to four years acquire a special bouquet. Film-yeast (or submerged-culture) flor sherries have a very distinctive and desirable aldehyde bouquet plus other nuances of aged bouquet. Wines to which reduced musts are added (e.g., Marsala) have a production bouquet. Wines that have been baked (Madeira, California nonflor sherry) have a very distinctive caramel-like processing bouquet (including hydroxymethylfurfural). Wines with added grape concentrate have a similar odor.

Aging wines in wood can add a desirable bouquet if it is not too pronounced. (For a discussion of excessive woodiness see next page.) Aging wines in the bottle often leads eventually to a special bouquet, particularly in dry red table wines and ports. The nature of this bottle bouquet has not been established. It is not due to any

specific ester, although esterification is probably a part of the process. It is much easier to recognize than define. Certainly it is more subtle than most aromas. Occasionally it blends with, or may even develop from, the aroma.

Not only are there table wines (still and sparkling, flavored or not) and dessert wines (flavored or not), but within each type there are many and subtle variations. These arise from the varieties used, their composition at maturity (which depends on climate), and the method of processing and aging used. From the same grapes, harvested on the same date from the same vineyard, two wine-makers may produce two quite different wines, differing markedly in aroma (by earlier or later pressing) and bouquet (by storage at different temperatures, or for different lengths of time, or in different sizes of cooperage of varying origin).

Even after the wines are finished, one may be stored at 80°F. (27°C.) and another at 50°F. (10°C.).* After a few months the wines will be noticeably different in odor. The desirable odors may be further modified by foreign or undesirable odors that are due to spoilage or mishandling. Thus no wine connoisseur can hope to explain completely the origins of all the odorous components of a wine.

Foreign and Undesirable Odors. A major problem with wines is foreign odors. How much woody odor, for example, can be toler-ated in a white table wine? Almost all enologists would agree that a conspicuously woody odor in a white table wine is undesirable, even intolerable. Most enologists would also agree that at very low concentrations (at least in white table wines of higher ethanol content) a nonrecognizable woody odor may contribute to the complexity of the wine and thus be a positive quality factor. In between, enologists disagree, some criticizing the least trace of recognizable woody odor and others tolerating substantial amounts. We believe that if the odor is recognizably woody it is a negative quality factor.

*Throughout this book we have rounded off the Célsius equivalents of Fahrenheit temperatures to the nearest degree.

A not uncommon undesirable odor in white table wines is that of sulfur dioxide. People vary greatly in sensitivity to this compound. Furthermore, olfactory adaptation to high sulfur dioxide concentrations in wines is very rapid. The "burning-match" smell of free sulfur dioxide is easily identified and is, *ipso facto*, a negative quality factor in any wine. Fortunately sulfur dioxide is only occasionally found in wines in recognizable amounts, and normally only in white wines, especially those of low pH (as in many German wines). Aside from its intrinsic undesirability sulfur dioxide is unwanted because it masks or interferes with the desirable odors. More important, it can also affect the trigeminal nerve, causing sneezing and pain. Noticeable sulfur dioxide odor in a wine is a sure sign of poor winemaking practice. With poor-quality grapes it is at best a necessary evil.

The sulfur dioxide odor in wine is due to the free (unbound) sulfur dioxide, i.e., that which is not bound to aldehydic groups. The ratio of free to total sulfur dioxide is a function of pH—the lower the pH, the greater the proportion of free sulfur dioxide. However, this ratio is also a function of the total sulfur dioxide concentration itself: in a given wine, the higher the total concentration, the greater the proportion of the free compound. See Amerine and Joslyn (1970) for a full description of the chemical reactions. Free sulfur dioxide can be detected by some judges at concentrations of 5 to 10 mg per liter, although most individuals do not recognize the odor until somewhere between 15 and 40 mg per liter. With aging of the wine the free sulfur dioxide content decreases as it is oxidized or fixed.

The other undesirable odors can be classified as those derived from the fruit, from the fermentation and processing, and from microbial spoilage.

Among those odors probably derived from the fruit are earthy, green, raisin, stemmy, and, sometimes, moldy. Earthiness is apparently associated with the raw product because it occurs in wines made from grapes from specific localities. However, it is probably not associated with soil on the grapes because wines made from grapes that have been washed may still be earthy. Nor has the odor been identified with compounds in the fruit. Since it is

not apparent until the wine warms up in the mouth, higher-boiling substances are probably responsible. It is seldom noted in many areas. Some German wines have it; occasionally it is present in Rhône wines of France; some Rioja wines of Spain have it; and it appears in a few California wines. Our own guess is that it is associated with the microbiological flora on the grapes and perhaps also the microflora on the equipment.

The green odor is the same as or similar to a leafy odor. The six-carbon-atom alcohols and aldehydes are among the compounds responsible. Grapes grown in cool climates or seasons and grapes harvested before full maturity have this odor. It often appears in the Muscadet wines of the Loire, also in some Chablis wines and less-quality Alsatian Sylvaners, and in some German Sylvaners and White Rieslings. Southern Austrian wines have it. It is rare in California wines. It appears to be associated more with unripe grapes than with the presence of leaves. Vineyards located next to eucalyptus trees may have a eucalyptus odor from leaves that drop onto the vines and get into the containers as the grapes are harvested.

The raisin odor is found by design in the wines of Málaga and in some sweet sherries from Spain, since in these regions the fruit is partially sun-dried before crushing. (Only rarely does the fruit hang on the vine long enough to dry to the raisin or semi-raisin stage.) The resulting caramel odor is easy to recognize. It somewhat resembles the odor of grape concentrate (see page 30) but is probably not due to exactly the same compound or compounds. We have noted it, especially in hot years, in wines of several varieties: Gewürztraminer, Muscat of Alexandria, Petite Sirah, Pinot noir, Ruby Cabernet, etc.

Stemminess as an odor has largely disappeared with the almost universal use of crusher-stemmers. However, the green stems of some varieties are brittle, and if too many get into the crushed fruit they may cause a stemmy odor. It is a problem mainly with red wines. The nature of the compounds responsible is not known.

Occasionally the harvested fruit is so moldy as to impart an odor to the wine. A penicillium odor was found in some red wines made from grapes picked very late in a wet season in the Napa Valley. In

only a few other instances has this been observed in California, probably because the fruit is harvested early enough or the infected clusters are rejected by the pickers in the field. (See more on moldiness, page 36.)

Then there is a large number of off odors associated with fermentation and processing. Among these are acetic, baked, bitter almond, cooked, corked, fusel, hydrogen sulfide, mercaptan, moldy, mousy, oxidized, rubbery, sauerkraut, sophisticated, woody, and yeasty. No doubt there are many more.

A century ago the vinegary odor of ethyl acetate and acetic acid was the most common off odor of wines. By contrast, post-Pasteur wines (i.e., wines produced since Pasteur's studies of the causes of microbial spoilage) rarely have excessive amounts of these compounds. The odor may be noted from time to time in wines that are distributed in bulk (as in Spain, Italy, and Portugal). If it is recognized as vinegary it is undesirable. However, there may be a level below this obvious vinegariness at which the odors of ethyl acetate and acetic acid contribute to the fruity odor of the wine and are therefore not a negative quality factor. Apparently for this reason the addition of up to 0.4 gallon of acetic acid per 1000 gallons of wine (i.e., 0.04% by volume) is permitted in the United States. Of course, the total acetic acid content (natural plus added) must not exceed the legal limit. To prevent vinegary wines from reaching the market most countries have placed legal limits on the amount of acetic acid in commercial wines. In the United States the limits are 0.12 gram acetic acid per 100 ml of white and dessert wines, and 0.14 for reds. The more stringent limits adopted by California are 0.11 and 0.12 gram per 100 ml, respectively. Similar but somewhat higher limits are prevalent in other countries. Expert wine judges usually begin to detect acetic acid at 0.07 gram per 100 ml. Even this level is seldom reached in California, where wines are not sold to the consumer from bulk containers.

Madeiras and some California sherries are baked at 120° to 140°F. (49° to 60°C.) during processing to achieve a caramel odor, which is considered desirable. Hydroxymethylfurfural and other compounds are formed. On the other hand, some sweet table wines are baked for stability. If a distinct caramel odor is produced in

such wines it is considered a negative quality factor. The same is also true of ports and other dessert wines that are baked to hasten maturation.

A cooked odor is not the same as a baked odor. High fermentation temperatures may give some red wines such an odor. It was formerly noted in some California table wines made in the warmer regions, but now that adequate cooling equipment and processes are used we seldom find it.

In a few European countries potassium ferrocyanide is used to remove excess amounts of iron and copper. The practice is called *blue fining* and is not used in the United States. A blue precipitate forms, which is usually completely removed by filtration. If the filtration is poorly done, however, some of the blue precipitate (a ferrocyanide complex) may get into the bottle. With time, traces of hydrogen cyanide will develop from the decomposition of the complex and the wine will acquire a characteristic bitter almond odor. We have rarely observed this odor, and then only in imported wines.

Corked is an odor that can develop in wines in cork-finished bottles. Contrary to common belief it may occasionally develop within a year or two of bottling, although it is usually found only in older wines. The odor is almost always associated with porous corks into which the wine can penetrate. Very porous corks apparently contain mold growth, most often of *Penicillium*. Although the odor is associated with a mold it is different from the odor due to moldy grapes. Once recognized, this unpleasant odor is never forgotten. Fortunately it is not common, although we have seen most of an entire bottling with poor corks contaminated by it. In buying wines never select a bottle that shows evidence of leakage (ullage).

The higher-boiling alcohols (commonly called fusel oils, from the German *Fusel*, bad liquor) produce a distinctive off odor called the fusel odor, particularly in some dessert wines. A wine having this foreign odor would surely be penalized in any judging. At lower concentrations the odor undoubtedly contributes to the complexity of the wine and may then be a positive quality factor. One exception to the undesirability of this odor is found in ports from

Portugal. There, by long usage, a recognizable odor of fusel oils is tolerated and even expected in many ports. But this is not condoned elsewhere for sweet red wines or any other type of wine. The odor threshold for mixed fusel oils in wines appears to be about 300 mg per liter.

Between the frankly yeasty and the obviously mercaptan there is a range of odors that resemble each other. All very young wines have a yeasty, beer-like odor that usually disappears after the first racking. It is probably due mainly to hydrogen sulfide in concentrations near the absolute threshold of detection (about 2 parts per billion). If the odor remains after the first racking it is usually hydrogen sulfide and is certainly a negative quality factor. Sometimes mercaptans are formed. This is even more serious because they are difficult to remove, owing to their relatively high boiling points.

Moldiness from the fruit has already been noted. Mold growth can also develop in poorly cleaned or drained wooden cooperage, especially under warm storage conditions. Unless the mold is removed before the containers are filled with wine, a moldy odor may be picked up by the wine. One of the reasons some European wineries favor new cooperage annually, despite the cost, is the desire to avoid such foreign odors. If the wood containers are filled with water, bacterial and fungal growth may occur in the water and may transmit a moldy odor to the wine unless the container is thoroughly cleaned. This is sometimes called the waterlogged odor; fortunately it is rare.

One of the oldest off-bacterial odors found in wines is the sauerkraut odor (lactic acid and some other compounds), which results from the excessive growth of lactic acid bacteria. It is found in table wines produced by pressure fermentation, warm storage, or late racking, especially when high-pH musts are used. In pressure fermentations the long, slow fermentation in the presence of sugar sometimes promotes bacterial growth and accumulation of this particularly odious odor. Control is not difficult if sulfur dioxide is used (*Lactobacillus* is very sensitive to sulfur dioxide), along with low storage temperatures, early racking, etc. The sauerkraut odor is uncommon in California wines.

In dessert wines, especially baked types of relatively low ethanol content (17%) and high pH, a mousy odor may develop. When this odor is suspected a simple method of identifying it is to place a few drops of the wine in the palm of one hand, rub the hands together, and then sniff them. Appropriate amounts of sulfur dioxide and careful technological control should prevent the problem. We have also noted mousiness in a few high-pH table wines.

The oxidized odor is not difficult to recognize; in fact, experienced enologists can identify it even when the acetaldehyde level is very low. The so-called bottle-sickness odor following bottling is really an oxidized odor. When low-sulfur dioxide white table wines are bottled they often acquire this odor, which may persist for several weeks; it then disappears.

As wines age for several years to many years the acetaldehyde odor develops, whether in the bottle or the cask. This is undesirable in table wines. In dessert wines it may be desirable (as in dry sherries), tolerable (as in sweet sherries), or undesirable (as in sweet red wines such as ports).*

The rubbery odor is of unknown composition. However, Brown (1950) definitely associated it with wines made from the fermentation of high-pH grapes in the San Joaquin Valley and hence called it the Fresno odor. (It is also known in the industry as the rubber boot odor; see page 201.) We feel that it probably results from bacterial growth in high-pH musts; its origins may thus be similar to those of the mousy odor.

The term *sophisticated* refers to all foreign odors, other than those discussed above, that are intentionally or unintentionally added to wines. In France herbs are sometimes used to give wines a muscat-like character. Some years ago a sparkling red wine with some blackberry essence added was produced in California. Unintentional odors occur when a tank containing vermouth is not thoroughly cleaned before being filled with a nonvermouth wine, or when grape and fruit wines become mixed.

---

*A curious exception to the latter example is the old red dessert wines of Priorato in northeastern Spain, where these high-aldehyde, rancio-flavored, tawny-colored wines are appreciated.

Taste

The sense of taste is almost entirely localized on the tongue. Tastes are those nontactile sensations that are perceived when a food, e.g., wine, is taken in the mouth. As we have already noted, many of the so-called tastes of wine are really odors. They are usually identified as flavors perceived in the mouth. If the nose is closed very tightly, any sensations are from taste receptors on the tongue or in the mouth.

In judging wines, taste is usually considered to be less important than odor. However, if the taste characteristics are poorly balanced —too bitter, too sweet, too acid, too sweet for the acidity, etc.— then taste may be the sensory characteristic that leads to rejection of the wine. Low titratable acidity and high pH (see footnote on page 20) may be accompanied by undesirable odor characteristics. This often simplifies the judge's task. A balance of tastes that is appropriate to the type of wine is certainly essential. As paradoxical as it sounds, taste must not be neglected in judging wines. Indeed, it may need more emphasis than it is commonly given.

We have seen that the olfactory sense detects minute quantities of many compounds and undergoes rapid adaptation. Physical loss of the odorous substances by evaporation to a level below the olfactory threshold is a major problem. With taste we are dealing with compounds at much higher molecular concentrations. Adaptation is still a problem but loss of taste due to evaporation does not occur unless the evaporation unduly concentrates one taste characteristic, e.g., the sourness (acidity).

There are basically only three tastes that are important in wines: sweetness, sourness, and bitterness. The fourth taste that we are capable of perceiving, saltiness, is seldom noted in wines, although it may be a factor in some very dry sherries. The sweetness/sourness balance seems to be a separate factor from sweetness and sourness considered individually. McBurney (1974) has recently summarized eleven lines of evidence that there are indeed four primary tastes. He indicates that there may be four separate physiological systems for coding taste information.

Sweetness. Sweetness in wines is due primarily to the reducing sugars glucose and fructose, and to a lesser extent to glycerol and ethanol. The average threshold for detecting sweetness in wines is about 1.0% by weight (as reducing sugar), although individuals differ widely in their sensitivity to sweetness. We have found individuals who can regularly detect about 0.5% sugar in wines and some who fail to detect as much as 2.5%.

We are more sensitive to fructose than to glucose, but by a factor that depends on the fructose concentration itself: we are about 50% more sensitive up to about 5% fructose, and about 35% more sensitive between 5 and 15% fructose. Variation in the fructose/glucose ratio may thus account for some of the differences in the reported sugar thresholds in wines. Wines of different maturity and wines fermented with different yeasts do have different fructose/glucose ratios. Most sweet wines, however, contain about equal percentages of these sugars. For a detailed discussion of this subject see Amerine et al. (1965a).

The sweetness of glycerol in wines has not been adequately studied. Normal table wines contain 0.5 to 1.5% by weight of glycerol (Amerine and Joslyn, 1970). The threshold for detecting glycerol in wines is about 1.5%. Compared to glucose and fructose its sweetness is thus significant in only a limited number of wines. Small amounts of 2,3-butanediol are also present in wines and may add to the sweetness. It can also be shown that ethanol has a "sweet" parameter. In fact, ethanol enhances the apparent sweetness of sugar solutions. Tannins, on the other hand, seem to reduce sweetness—at least they increase the threshold for detecting sweetness and also increase the minimum detectable difference between two degrees of sweetness (Berg et al., 1955b). One important characteristic of sweet compounds is that for many people they reduce the sourness due to the acidity. This is not universally true, however, especially among experienced judges.

People differ not only in their ability to detect sweetness but also, to an enormous degree, in their preference for or aversion to sweetness. Even for such a typically dry wine as Zinfandel, samples on the sweet side are occasionally found. We confess that we see no

great harm in this, although it does confuse and annoy the consumer who prefers a dry Zinfandel and unexpectedly gets a sweet one. Possibly some labeling requirement for sugar content would be useful, especially for rosés, Chenin blanc, dry sherry, and sparkling wines labeled *brut*, of which both sweet and dry types are common. Some winemakers might wish to state the sugar content on a voluntary basis.

Table wines with an inappropriate degree of sweetness, particularly in relation to the acidity, have an undesirable *sweetish* taste. We find this a useful term. On the positive side, the *sweet* taste appears to round out and blend with some flavor components. In addition there is a definite, pleasant mouth-feel effect at high (but not too high) sugar concentrations.

For fruit juices at higher sucrose levels the bitter, sour, astringent (puckery), and vinegary sensory responses are reduced, causing the odor notes of such juices to seem more pleasant. Von Sydow et al. (1974) concluded that increased sweetness "appears to enhance desirable aroma by reducing the harsh taste of some beverages, on a psychological level, rather than acting upon any chemical constituents and thus modifying the vapor composition," Thus the milder, more acceptable taste impression enables the judge not to be distracted "by harsh taste impressions and to focus on the interplay of aroma attributes. In this respect, oversweetening the juice would be as disastrous as undersweetening." How the sensory responses of knowledgable wine consumers judging traditionally dry types of wine would be affected by oversweetening is not clear. Also, with vinegariness oversweetening appears to be as objectionable in sweet dessert wines as in dry table wines.

Sourness. Sourness is the tart taste of wines. Unfortunately, in the wine industry vernacular, sourness means wines of high ethyl acetate and acetic acid content, i.e., wines that are vinegary. This is *not* sourness in the psychological-physiological sense that we will be using here. By sourness we mean the acid taste in the mouth.

Sourness is a function of the titratable acidity and the pH of the wine. Theoretically the sourness of a wine should be highly negatively correlated with its pH because it is the hydrogen ion (more correctly, the hydronium ion) that stimulates the sour-sensitive taste buds on the tongue. In reality the sourness appears to be some function of both pH and titratable acidity. Furthermore, the buffering capacity of the wine and of the person's saliva, the sweetness of the wine, the particular balance of different acids, and other factors all appear to have some effect on the degree of sourness. The order of decreasing sourness of the principal organic acids of wine (based on their pK_a values—a measure of acid strength) should be tartaric, citric, malic, and lactic. In fact, the order in wines is probably malic, tartaric, citric, and lactic if the titratable acidity is the same for all the acids, according to Amerine et al. (1965b). The actual sour taste of a wine is thus a complex function of numerous factors. Certainly wines with a pH less than 3.1 or a titratable acidity of more than 0.9% will taste sour, whereas those with a pH greater than 3.75 or a titratable acidity of less than 0.5% will taste flat.

Because sourness has a special meaning (acetic acid) in the wine industry and to much of the public, we propose that the terms low, normal, and high total acidity be used in judging wines, even though we would prefer to use the terms low, normal, and high sourness. The terms green and unripe for high-acid wines (particularly white wines) seem useful to us, although green also refers to a specific odor (page 33). Tart also appears unequivocal as a term for too much acidity. Fruity, however, could have odor implications. Although it seems to be associated with moderate acidity it should probably be avoided unless a true fruit-like odor is present and is associated with a moderately high sour taste, i.e., a true fruity flavor. Acidulous is a term that denotes excessive total acidity (particularly in wines of low ethanol content). Flat is the term used for wines of insufficient total acidity.

Bitterness. Bitterness is a taste that the inexperienced judge finds most difficult to evaluate uniformly, either positively or negatively. Most inexperienced judges find a noticeably bitter taste unpleasant. Experienced connoisseurs, however, find some bitterness in red wines to be pleasant. It is a true taste because it is experienced in the mouth. However, it is often confused with the

tactile sensation of astringency, even by some experienced wine judges. We believe that bitterness and astringency are two separate sensations and that with adequate training they can be distinguished.

The discussion in Amerine et al. (1959) is misleading on this subject (see their pages 505 and 507). For both bitterness and astringency people show wide variations in sensitivity and in their understanding of the terms. For bitterness we now prefer descriptive terms such as not bitter, slightly bitter, moderately bitter, and highly bitter. We no longer favor the terms smooth, slightly rough, étc., because it is not clear whether they refer to the bitter taste or to the tactile sensation of astringency.

Polyphenolic compounds (especially the tannins) have two sensory characteristics: true taste bitterness and tactile astringency. Excessive bitterness or astringency can overstimulate the free nerve endings and result in mild pain sensations (as with bitter coffee). We will discuss the pain response shortly.

Neither bitterness nor astringency is normally a problem with white wines because the polyphenolic content of white wines is low. However, a few white table wines of low tannin content do have a true bitter aftertaste. We do not know how to account for this, unless it is due to bitter products of some bacterial activity. Very dry white wines with high acidity may *appear* to have a bitter taste. This is sensory confusion, a problem that seldom afflicts experienced judges.

Red wines of high polyphenolic content age better than those of low polyphenolic content. In this sense a degree of bitterness or astringency in young red table wines may be associated with eventual wine quality. The tannin content decreases as wines are aged, hence old red wines are less bitter and astringent. Nevertheless, excessively bitter or astringent wines are (and should be) criticized.

Finally, probably because of less semantic confusion about bitterness and astringency, experienced judges are able to distinguish lower levels of polyphenolic compounds than inexperienced judges (Berg et al., 1955a). Surprisingly, sweetness in a wine does not appear to interfere appreciably with one's ability to differentiate various levels of bitterness, although more data on this are needed.

Special bitter tastes are occasionally noted. Wines of high sulfate content have a specific and objectionable bitter taste. White wines that have been fermented on the skins may also be undesirably bitter. There are undoubtedly other examples.

Touch

Foods and beverages give a variety of tactile (feel) sensations in the mouth: astringent, thin, full, etc. It is important that taste sensations be distinguished from the tactile sensations—those of touch.

We have seen that astringency (the puckery feel) is different from bitterness (true taste). Singleton et al. (1975) indicate that the only astringent substances normally found in wines are the polyphenolic compounds, especially the tannins. Their panel was able to differentiate astringency from bitterness. They noted, however, that high astringency tended to mask bitterness. Arnold et al. (1976) came to a similar conclusion. The condensed tannin fraction appeared to be the most astringent and bitter. The catechins were shown to be the least astringent and bitter.

For increasing astringency the terms not astringent, slightly astringent, moderately astringent, and highly astringent are appropriate. We know of no definitive experiment that includes threshold-level responses, but astringency appears almost always to be a negative quality factor in white table wines and probably in other types of wines as well. The astringency of young red table wines decreases during aging.

The viscosity of dry wines is due primarily to ethanol, although other compounds have an effect. Wines of very low ethanol content are thin in body, whereas table wines of high ethanol content are full in body. The sugar content also affects the feel of the wine. For example, a wine of 10% sugar and 10% ethanol does not give

the sensation of thinness, despite the low ethanol content. One thing is certain: the body of the wine is not due exclusively or even primarily to the glycerol content. Glycerol does have a high viscosity but its maximum concentration in most wines is only about 1.5% by weight. The tactile sensation due to this amount of glycerol is minimal, especially in the presence of ten times as much ethanol. Since glycerol is a normal byproduct of alcoholic fermentation, high-ethanol wines are also high in glycerol. But it is our opinion that the ethanol, not the glycerol, gives the wine its body. The addition of glycerol to wines has been practiced in some areas but we do not feel it is justified.

It is not known whether several other compounds stimulate tactile or pain receptors. The burning sensation associated with high ethanol content may be the result of stimulation of both types of receptors. Iron and copper have an astringent character when present in unusually high concentrations (about 20 and 2 mg per liter, respectively). The prickly, in-mouth sensation of wines containing excess carbon dioxide (more than about 0.3 gram per 100 ml) is no doubt tactile in origin. Overly sweet wines (more than about 15% sugar), such as cream sherries, white port, etc. have an unctuous texture.

Pain

Pain sensations result from overstimulation of sensory receptors, as anyone who eats chili peppers can attest. It is rare for a wine to be so acid as to give genuine pain, although some cold-year German and southern Austrian wines and Portuguese *vinho verde* wines approach it. A *little* pain may not be objectionable. Some people tolerate, even prefer, more than others—for example, in their chilis or hot curries.

The effect of excessive sulfur dioxide in overstimulating the trigeminal nerve endings in the nose (resulting in sneezing) is a pain reaction. High ethanol concentrations (particularly in the absence of sugar) can result in pain. It is usually the high ethanol content that is responsible, but ethanol *per se* cannot account for the burning sensation in some dessert wines and brandies. We have little evidence regarding the pain-inducing syndrome.

The following factors seem to be associated with pain reactions from wines or brandies: excessive amounts of some component, notably ethanol in brandy or ethanol in the absence of sugar (particularly at high acidity); high ethanol/high aldehyde (as in some sherries); very high total acidity (low pH); high acidity/low ethanol; high acidity/low sugar/low ethanol (as in some German wines); high acidity/low sugar/low ethanol/high carbon dioxide (as in some sparkling wines); high polyphenolic content (as in young red wines); high polyphenolic content/low sugar; sulfur dioxide (particularly in low-pH white table wines). There are undoubtedly others.

Temperature

Temperature is important in wine evaluation—first because of the warm and cold sensations themselves, and second because of the effects of temperature on the senses of smell, taste, touch, and pain.

The cold sensation is intrinsically pleasant in white and sparkling wines. It is also valuable because at low temperatures wines retain their carbon dioxide better. With dry white table wines there are relatively few points of sensory interest to begin with, so the cold sensation adds to our interest in such wines. Furthermore, white wines are more often high in sulfur dioxide and the low temperature reduces the volatility of this compound.

With respect to taste, the effect of temperature is not clearly established. Some experiments (see Amerine et al., 1965a) indicate that the palate is more sensitive to sweetness and sourness at higher temperatures (about 95°F., or 35°C.) and more sensitive to bitterness at lower temperatures (about 50°F., or 10°C.). However, these results may be artifacts of practice or experience and one should be cautious in viewing them as significant.

It is surely true that odorous compounds are more volatile at higher temperatures. Just how high the temperature should be for

optimum taste and odor is not clearly established. Perhaps we prefer our white wines chilled because the sulfur dioxide odor is less pronounced at lower temperatures and because the low temperature is desirable for its own sake. (The greater retention of carbon dioxide at lower temperatures is also a positive factor.) But this could be a conditioned response, i.e., we could prefer white wines chilled simply because we are accustomed to it.

On the other hand, perhaps we prefer a warmer temperature for red wines because that results in greater volatility of desirable odors. But that preference might be a conditioned response also. The question is, why did we become accustomed to serving wines at certain temperatures?

Interrelation of the Senses

There is undoubtedly some interaction between the senses. For example, consider a cloudy wine. The odor is almost always perceived as less pleasant and less distinctive than if the wine is brilliantly clear. This is a stimulus error (see page 52). Similarly, if a wine has a very distinctive varietal aroma most judges are less apt to recognize taste deficiencies after smelling the wine. In fact, Ribéreau-Gayon (1973) notes that odors do interfere with judgments on taste. Doubtless other interactions also exist. Puisais et al. (1974) list several other possible interactions: the effect of music on color and pleasantness of the wine, the effect of light on pleasantness and odor, the effect of color on taste and odor, etc. Unfortunately no data are given to substantiate the observations.

Interpretation of Words. Ribéreau-Gayon (1973) and Vedel et al. (1972) have published lists of words expressing gradations in taste or odor characteristics. Ribéreau-Gayon uses the series *plat* (flat), *lavé* (washed), and *aqueux* (watery) for the sweet taste in a series of wines of decreasing ethanol content. For the same ethanol content with decreasing sugar content, the sweet taste is expressed by the terms *moelleux* (mellow), *mou* (soft), and *alcalin* or *salé* (alkaline or salty). For decreasing acid content he suggests *vert*

(green), *acide* (acid), *dur* (hard), *mordant* (biting), *sec* (drying), *creux* (gaunt), and *maigre* (meager). For decreasing bitterness (*amertume*) he uses *astringent* (astringent), *âpre* (bitter), *ferme* (harsh), and *dur* (hard). Obviously he does not distinguish between bitterness and astringency, nor between the hardness due to sourness and that due to bitterness. For a balanced wine (sugar and acid) the terms he uses for decreasing ethanol content are *spiritueux* (spirituous), *chaud* (hot), *vineux* (vinous), *léger* (light), *faible* (feeble), and *petit* (slight).

If the terms are well-understood by all the judges they are appropriate. However, we know that even experienced judges (particularly from different regions) are apt to have very different concepts about the subjective sensory terms used above. In Vedel et al. (1972) the series *charpenté* (structured), *tannique* (tannic), *rude* (rough), *rêche* (harsh), and *astringent* (astringent) is used. In our experience different judges have very different conceptions of the meanings of these terms and especially of their relations to each other. (See also the discussions of bitterness and astringency, pages 41–43.)

Ribéreau-Gayon (1973) has made the useful observation that the meaning of terms may change with time. Wines that were formerly considered *souple* (supple or soft) would not be so graded today. Also, preferences change with time. There are many historical examples of this. Really dry wines predominated in Germany in the last century; today it is difficult to find a truly dry German white wine. Bordeaux wines of high volatile acidity were not damned at the turn of the century; today they are rare.

See the Glossary (page 193) for more on appropriate and inappropriate terms for describing the sensory characteristics of wines.

The art of appreciative tasting depends on the union of sight, scent, and palate.
—P. M. Shand

Smell is the essential sense for degustation.

3

Factors Affecting Sensory Response

We all have different inherent sensitivities to sensory stimuli. These inherent differences are modified by the effects of experience. For example, an individual who has been regularly exposed to a certain odor is more likely to recognize it, and at a lower threshold, than one who has not. Unfortunately not all people respond equally to training. Some learn rapidly and others slowly, but everyone *can* learn to refine his sensory abilities.

Physiological Factors

For each of the senses human sensitivity varies over a wide range in very complex ways. Thus some people are more sensitive to color differences than others (about 25% of males are color-blind to varying degrees). Some are more sensitive or less sensitive

to sweetness, sourness, bitterness, various odors, pain, temperature, etc. A given individual may differ markedly in his sensory responses to various types of compounds. For example, a person may be ultrasensitive to sourness and relatively insensitive to sweetness, or vice versa.

Physiologically we change in sensitivity with age (with experience as a complicating factor). We are apparently more sensitive, especially to sweet, bitter, and salty tastes, at 20 to 40 years of age than at 40 to 60. It appears that age has little effect on sensitivity to sourness. Again, individuals vary markedly. An inexperienced judge of 20 may be less sensitive to odors or tastes than an experienced judge of 50 or 60.

No final evidence of any effect of tobacco on the ability to judge wines appears in the literature. Generally little or no difference is found between smokers and nonsmokers. For example, McBurney and Moskat (1975) found no significant difference between college-age smokers and nonsmokers in taste thresholds for the detection or recognition of sweetness and saltiness. However, some non-smokers judging wines are disturbed by the odor of tobacco smoke. We recommend that smokers abstain from smoking for an hour before attempting to judge wines. Of course, smoking should never be permitted in the room where the wines are judged.

Disease or accident may result in altered, diminished, or lost sensory response. Fortunately these aberrations are relatively rare. Much more common are cases of specific taste blindness. For example, about one-third of the American population is insensitive to the bitter taste of phenylthiourea (a compound that is not known to occur in wines). Other types of taste blindness are also known. None of them are believed to affect the ability to judge the quality of wine or any other food, but the possibility does exist.

Sensitivity to odors and tastes varies during the day—differently for different individuals, it seems. Most enologists believe that their sensitivity is greatest just before a meal, i.e., when they are hungry. If wines are to be tasted after a meal it is recommended that the meal be light and not spicy.

Psychological Factors

There are also many factors that can be classified as psychological. They include motivation, concentration, memory, and the following errors: time-order, contrast, stimulus, logical, leniency, proximity, association, and central tendency. We will discuss each of these in turn, in this section and the next section.

Proper *motivation* improves sensory performance. This is called the payoff function because some form of reward helps to maintain interest. The reward may take the form of time off from work, money, prizes, public recognition of one's ability, etc. Interest in making the correct judgment increases the chance of doing just that. Knowledge of the results is thus an essential motivating factor. It shows the judge where his mistakes were and thus alerts him not to make them again. It also shows him how he performed within the group. Everyone wants to do well in making aesthetic judgments. Knowing that one's ratings or ranking of the various wines will be openly compared with those of other individuals and the group averages is thus a powerful stimulus to careful evaluation.

Good powers of *concentration* are obviously an advantage for any judge of wine quality. First, it is believed that by concentrating on a specific sense the threshold for that sense will be lowered, i.e., sensitivity will be increased. Second, by concentrating on each sense separately the judge is less likely to overlook any important negative or positive factors affecting quality. People differ markedly in their ability to concentrate. By conscious practice one can improve one's own ability. Lack of distractions (extraneous noise, etc.) probably aids concentration more than anything else.

Memory is aided by concentration. The ability to recognize sensory characteristics quickly is obviously important: it saves time. This should result in less sensory adaptation, better results, and more time for judging more samples. Experience is the obvious prerequisite for memory. One cannot remember, much less identify, an odor that one has not experienced previously. Theoretically a good memory should help us distinguish more levels of quality or at least repeat our quality judgments more consistently. This has not been demonstrated with wines but we believe it is a fact.

Psychological Errors

The psychological errors are no less real for being psychological. They can and do introduce biases in sensory judgments—biases that are often very difficult to detect.

Time-Order and Contrast. Perhaps the most common error is that of *time-order*, i.e., the prejudicial selection of one sample over the others on the basis of its place in the order of presentation. In practice the first sample presented tends to be preferred. A probable reason for this is that in making the quality judgment on the first sample one has no immediate frame of reference for purposes of comparison. The second sample, however, has the first sample for comparison. Another reason is simply that one is apt to be less critical with the first sample. The time-order error is made for any series of wines, whether of the same type or not. It is impossible to avoid this error when two or three different types of wines are being served sequentially with a meal. In laboratory tests in which several wines of the same type are served simultaneously it is possible to minimize the effects of the error by having each judge start with a different wine.

The *contrast* error appears simple but is by no means simple to interpret. It has some aspects of the time-order error, and may take different forms. For example, a wine of exceptional quality is served first, followed immediately by a wine of much lower quality. Is the second wine rated lower than it should be because of the effective contrast with the high quality of the first wine? Conversely, a very poor wine may be served first, followed by a fine wine. Is the appraisal of the second wine more favorable than it should be because of the effective contrast with the low quality of the first wine? In other words, effective contrast leads to more favorable sensory impressions when a pleasant, although perhaps

merely ordinary, sample follows an unpleasant one. The opposite effect occurs when an unpleasant sample follows a pleasant one, i.e., the latter seems more unpleasant than it really is.

In tests with foods the first contrast error (i.e., better after poorer appears better) seems to prevail. The opposite error has not been substantiated. Tests have also shown that if a series of *equally* poor samples are presented the quality of successive samples appears to deteriorate. This is not true, however, if a good sample is presented somewhere in the series. Due attention to these errors should be given in tests with amateurs. The means of avoiding them is clear: present the samples in a random order so that, statistically, good samples follow poor samples as often as they precede them.

Stimulus and Related Errors.   The *stimulus* error is also common. It occurs when the judge uses irrelevant criteria in making his judgment. For example, knowing that one wine is from a bottle with a screw-cap closure and another is from a bottle with a cork stopper may prejudice the judge in favor of the latter wine. It is true that the less-fine wines are generally sold in bottles with screw-cap closures, but this is no guarantee that a good wine may not be found in such a bottle, or that a poor wine may not be found in a cork-stoppered bottle. To give a wine a low or high rating automatically because of the type of closure or other irrelevant factor is a stimulus error. To eliminate this error the wines should be served in identical glasses without any identification except a number and, if appropriate, an idea as to the type. It is surprising how many so-called wine experts are "label drinkers." Their sensory judgment is based on the source or reputation of the wine, or its producer, or the year of production. But none of these are guarantees of the quality of the wine *in the bottle*. Perhaps the wine was opened or decanted too early, or was inadvertently shaken or heated or frozen. Thus, although other bottles of the wine of that vineyard, producer, and year may be splendid, this one may be inferior—or vice versa.

We admit, however, that at home or in a restaurant we like to see the bottle, preferably before the cork is drawn! Aside from normal curiosity about what we are about to drink, knowing that a certain wine is to be served alerts us about what to expect. We recall the last time we had the wine. We know what level of color or acidity or sweetness to expect. We apparently put ourselves in a mood to enjoy this particular wine. And our chances of really enjoying it are greater, perhaps partly because of the stimulus error. Can this be wrong, since we are drinking the wine for pleasure?

The *logical* error occurs when a judge associates two characteristics of a wine or food because they are logically related. Of course, in the specific wine in question they may *not* be related, and a form of stimulus error occurs. For example, it is usually true that a slightly amber white table wine is too old or has been exposed to air, and will have an oxidized odor. But it is quite possible for a slightly amber white wine to be young and fresh. White wine made from red grapes is an example. Just because amber color and oxidized odor are logically related does not mean that they *must* occur simultaneously.

Leniency is another form of the stimulus error. One is apt to make overly lenient judgments on wine quality in the presence of the winemaker or in the home of one's best friend. Although we have not observed it, the opposite error may also occur: downgrading a wine precisely because we do not know the winemaker or the host. The insidious thing about this and other types of psychological errors is that they occur without our knowing it.

The *proximity* error is also a form of the stimulus error, and is associated with the use of scoring scales. For example, a wine rates high in one characteristic, say, color. This favorable appraisal then influences the judge to have more favorable impressions of related (proximate) characteristics—taste, odor, etc. It is difficult to avoid this error.

Yet another form of the stimulus error is the *association* error, the tendency to repeat previous impressions. This is somewhat of a

contradiction of the example given earlier for a succession of equally poor samples apparently getting worse under the contrast error. However, inexperienced judges do tend to repeat previous impressions. Possibly it is a combination of the central tendency error (see below) and lack of concentration.

Central Tendency. The error of *central tendency* is committed by timid or inexperienced judges who are fearful of making the wrong judgment. Suppose the judge has four commercial Cabernet Sauvignons to score (see page 122) on a 20-point scale, with 13 being the break-even point for commercial acceptability. The judge knows that his score must be at least 13 and cannot be more than 20. He is thus likely to make the least error by giving scores in the middle of the acceptable scale, i.e., from about 15 to 17. If he is timid or lacks experience with Cabernet Sauvignons he may subconsciously take the safest course by giving such scores. This is again a form of stimulus error, in that his judgment is the result of factors not related to the quality of the wine.

Inexperienced judges also sometimes give wildly erratic quality judgments, in both directions. As the judge becomes more experienced his confidence in his ability increases and errors of central tendency occur less frequently. We should add that some people do not seem to be subject to the error of central tendency. They simply don't care what others think of their quality judgments.

This wine is full of gases which are to me offensive;
It pleases all you asses because it is expensive.
                                                                     —A. P. Herbert

The dearest wine is not always the best.

4

The Sensory
Examination

There is a good deal of difference between sampling two red table wines at the dinner table and evaluating the same two wines in an international competition to decide which is the better. Of course, the same physiological limitations and psychological errors (Chapter 3) still plague both situations. Certain aspects of the sensory examination remain unaltered whether in the home or in a well-equipped sensory laboratory. In either place one must evaluate the appearance and color of the wine. Unless the dining room is very dimly lit, a fairly good appraisal of the appearance can be made there. But it is practically impossible to make a reliable judgment of wine color in the normal dining room. The usual illumination casts a brownish tint on the wines, which distorts their true color and makes them look older than they really are. The more dimly lit the room, the more difficult it is to distinguish small differences in hue.

Furthermore, wine evaluation in the dining room suffers from extraneous food odors and the contrasting tastes of various foods. To which the consumer may respond that that is just how most wines are consumed. But that misses the point: wine consumption at home is based on a preference decision, whereas wine evaluation in the laboratory is based on a difference decision or a difference-preference decision. The latter are expressed in terms of some sort of scale, often as a rating of the intensity of some attribute.

There are other differences between the home and the laboratory. The normal dining room is not set up for serving wines "blind" in coded, identical glasses. This is just as well, because to do so would probably spoil the enjoyment of the wines, if not the whole meal. A dinner is a dinner, but a sensory examination of wines is something else. The number of possible psychological errors and the problem of adaptation make it extremely difficult to conduct a valid sensory examination of wines at the normal home dinner. In fact, competitive judgings at home are now sensibly done before sitting down to the dinner. There is the additional problem that some participants in a home wine judging do not arrive entirely free of alcohol, or they may insist on drinking the wines. At some point during the judging, critical appraisal becomes unreliable. For pure enjoyment of the wines this may be normal. But for close evaluation of relative quality with maximum efficiency, the sensory examination should be conducted under specially prepared conditions.

Basic Considerations

The following questions need to be answered in any sensory quality examination: Where? With what? How many? How coded? Order of sampling? Time of day? Number of judges? Technique to be used? Possible and necessary statistical analysis of the results?

Table I. Five wines ranked by 5 judges. The best ranking is 1.

			Wine		
Judge	X	Y	Z	R	S
1	3	4	5	1	2
2	4	2	5	3	1
3	5	4	1	3	2
4	2	5	3	1	4
5	5	2	3	1	4
Rank total	19	17	17	9	13

Under private or commercial conditions, expert sensory evaluation is expensive because trained persons are required. In addition, carrying out the statistical analyses of the results may be time-consuming. Why is statistical analysis necessary? First of all, without proper statistical analysis incorrect conclusions may be drawn from the data. Recently there has been a plethora of "comparative" tastings of wines. For example, five judges rank five wines for relative quality. Suppose the results are as shown in Table I.

From these results one might conclude that wine R is the best, followed by wines S, Y or Z, and X. But is this a valid judgment and is it repeatable? Quite the contrary. As we will see from the discussion of ranking (page 164), there are, according to accepted levels of statistical significance, no differences among the five rankings. The statistical treatment indicates that the judges do not exhibit a noticeable degree of agreement in their rankings, and it is therefore not appropriate to estimate an overall ranking for the wines.

Or consider the results of recent, widely publicized "judging." Fifteen judges scored five wines on a 20-point scale, with the results shown in Table II.

Table II. Five wines scored by 15 judges. The best score is 20.

	WINE				
JUDGE	H	I	J	K	L
1	17	13	14	13	18
2	12	15	15	12	19
3	19	18	15	13	17
4	14	16	12	13	14
5	19	18	20	14	18
6	15	16	18	14	15
7	17	19	17	16	20
8	12	15	13	14	15
9	13	17	18	17	19
10	14	16	17	14	16
11	19	20	18	15	17
12	15	19	17	18	19
13	14	16	14	17	13
14	18	18	13	19	16
15	10	18	12	16	15
Total	228	254	233	225	251
Mean	15.2	16.9	15.5	15.0	16.7

The press release says that wine I is the winner, so the public rushes off to buy it. But is it significantly better than wine L? No. It can be shown by statistical analysis (page 143) that wines I and L are not significantly different from each other, i.e., that they could not be distinguished on the basis of their scores, by this panel. It can also be shown that wines H, J, and K are significantly poorer than wines I and L, but that they are not significantly different from each other.

A statistical approach must always be employed in the analysis of sensory data because of the inherent variability of aesthetic judgments. (See also pages 11 and 101.) The *only* way to evaluate the results and reach reliable conclusions is by the use of appropriate statistical procedures.

It is therefore essential that the sensory examination be set up in such a way that we can obtain the required information with the greatest degree of statistical, physiological, and psychological confidence. We also wish to accomplish this with the fewest replications. Statistical confidence relates to the control of errors of the first and second kind (page 104); physiological and psychological confidence relate to the avoidance of sensory adaptation, psychological errors (Chapter 3), etc.

Judges. In the home there is nothing that one can do to qualify the judges. They are guests and, as such, deserve the assumption that they are all equally qualified to judge the wines presented. The results, however, must be taken with a certain healthy skepticism. The group is likely to have varying degrees of competence for the wines served. This introduces a variable that increases the differences in response among the judges and reduces the reliability of the average results. The average results of five qualified wine judges can be accepted with a great deal more confidence than those of five wine dilettantes, however interested and good-willed they may be.

No one should make critical sensory evaluations unless he is in good physical and mental condition. It is essential that the judge not feel rushed or under pressure. As much as possible, he should concentrate on the task at hand and be free of extraneous problems or distractions.

The recent research of Kare (1975) casts doubt on the reported decrease in taste discrimination in older persons (80–85) compared to younger persons (40–45). We have observed excellent judges over 70 years of age who were better than many younger judges.

Tests. Under laboratory conditions it is possible to identify the judge who is "off" by comparing his results on successive samples with those of the rest of the panel. But in the home this is very

difficult; if the test is not replicated, it is impossible. Therefore, if the test is to have commercial importance, it must be conducted under laboratory conditions and it is necessary to attempt to qualify the judges.

To qualify a judge unequivocally for the sensory evaluation of wines is probably impossible. As we said, he must be in good physical and mental condition. Some internal test to determine when he is "off" is desirable, but how to judge his inherent ability is most difficult. Nevertheless, some basic hurdles can be erected to eliminate at least the grossly inadequate judge. First of all, we want to know what experience he has had in judging wines, particularly those of the type in question. Ask him!

One of the biggest faults in wine judgings is that people with inadequate experience are thrust into situations in which they are asked to make quality judgments on types of wines for which they are unqualified. Rather than bow out gracefully and risk a certain loss of face, they blunder ahead. Perhaps they are not even aware of their limitations. There is, of course, no perfectly qualified judge of all wines because no one can possibly have experienced all wines, much less developed critical judgment of them. However, the truly experienced wine judge can, to a certain extent, extrapolate his experience with known wines to *similar* types of wines. But such extrapolation is surely limited and is no substitute for experience with each type of wine being judged.

One of us (M.A.A.) has seen judges in international competitions who were well qualified for judging European table wines but who made colossal errors in judging Portuguese ports, Spanish sherries, and Eastern United States wines, precisely because they had limited or biased experience with these types.

The following few simple tests are not infallible. Everyone has an off day or an off test. Giving a test just before a judging puts a great deal of pressure on the judge, not to speak of embarrassment if he is disqualified. The best qualification tests (perhaps the only ones) were used for qualifying judges for the California State Fair some years ago (see Amerine and Ough, 1964).

The tests required that wines of known composition be placed in proper order: sugar (base wine—0.2, 0.5, 1.0, 1.75, and 2.5%); acidity (base wine—0.5, 0.55, 0.65, 0.8, and 1.0%); sulfur dioxide (base wine—50, 100, 150, 225, and 300 mg per liter); etc. Tests of varietal dilution were also given: muscat (100, 80, 60, 40, 20, and 0%); Cabernet Sauvignon (100, 80, 60, 40, 20, and 0%). Sauvignon blanc, Gewürztraminer, and Zinfandel could also be used for dilution tests.

Identification of varietal aromas is also a useful test, but one must be *sure* that the wines do have distinguishable and typical varietal aromas. Amateurs cannot be expected to do well in such a test. Irrelevant differences in appearance or color can interfere with the aroma examination, but this problem can be overcome by using wine glasses that are painted black on the outside (see Plate 1). For white wines, a series of Chardonnay, Chenin blanc, Sauvignon blanc, Sémillon, and White Riesling could be used. For red wines, Cabernet Sauvignon, Gamay, Petite Sirah, Pinot noir, and Zinfandel would be within the competence of satisfactory judges. In the California State Fair tests, each reversal or error was a demerit. The judges with the least number of demerits were selected. The selection process took place two months before the actual judging.

Wines for such qualifying tests should be of generally recognized commercial quality. Finding such wines is not always as simple as it sounds. Certainly the wines should not be selected on the basis of price or popular reputation.

Variations of these tests could be used for international judgings, but the costs of arranging such a qualifying process would probably be prohibitive. In lieu of this, experience and reputation are used as criteria for the selection of judges. This practice has obvious deficiencies. A judge's reputation is not always based on accuracy and consistency. And even the most experienced judges for one type of wine may be inexperienced with other types. About all the selection committee can do is be sure that at least one judge is qualified for each type of wine and that the judges have some

respect for each other's abilities concerning the types they are qualified to judge.

We admit that qualification tests for the selection of judges are usually impracticable and often impolitic. The solution is to use appropriate analytical procedures to determine statistical significance based on the combined assessments of the judges. In our experience this sometimes reveals that the combined scores of a panel of judges indicate no significant differences among the wines. This may be disappointing to the judges and those conducting the test, but it is far better to publish results that are dull but meaningful than results that are interesting but meaningless. The results may also reveal the anomalous data of one or two judges. Such judges need not be included in later judgings.

Locale and Equipment

The best locale for judging wines is an area free of extraneous odors, colors, and sounds. Outdoor settings fail on all three counts. Normal temperature for sensory evaluation rooms is about 70°F. (21°C.). Food technologists find a gray background best, and so do we. Certainly red and brown colors should be avoided. The room should be well-lighted; natural northern light or its equivalent is preferred. Artificial light of the daylight type is satisfactory but fluorescent lamps and mercury-arc lamps are not.

To prevent the accumulation of odors, dentist-type spittoons are recommended. Air conditioning is also desirable to remove odors and to provide comfortable temperature and humidity. For judgings extending over several hours or days, physical comfort is an important factor. Naturally, the judges should not be able to see each other's score cards during the judging.

A lazy susan serving table in a modern wine-examination room is shown in Plate 2. Various aspects of separate booths for the sensory examination of wines are shown in Plates 3 through 6.

Glasses.   The 8-oz.-capacity (235 ml) tulip-shaped glass is preferred for comparative testings. In fact, for home use we find it

better than the tiny glasses commonly used for sherry, the colored glasses sometimes used for German wines, the gigantic monstrosities recommended for Burgundy in some fancy restaurants, and other such aberrations. The tulip-shaped glass is also appropriate for sparkling wines, provided that a small, rough cross is scratched in the bottom of the glass to provide a site for the formation of bubbles. This can be done (not always with ease) with a steel file or, better yet, a scriber. The hollow-stem glass also gives a steady release of bubbles from the warmth of the hand on the hollow stem. The fluted glass is favored by some. It too works better if a small, rough cross is made in the bottom of the glass. An "ideal" glass has recently been recommended (Anon., 1973). It is shaped like a truncated, elongated egg and holds 215 ml. Four typical glasses used in wine evaluation are shown in Plates 7 through 10.

The thinner the glass, the faster the wine warms up when the glass is held in the palm of the hand. The thinness of the glass is not a critical use factor, and thin glasses can be expensive. (They also break more easily.) The silver cup, much favored in Burgundy, does not seem to have much merit except as a means of detecting small differences in color (by reflections from the polished surface). Glasses, if always filled to the same level, serve this purpose equally well or better.

If traces of detergent are left in glasses after washing, they may impart a foreign odor and taste to the wines. We recommend *thorough* rinsing in hot, soft water. If a towel is used for drying, it must be specially washed so as to remove all detergent and sizing odors. Glasses stored in odorous surroundings (e.g., a new pine cupboard) will acquire the odor, especially if they stand upside down on a wood surface. The acquired odor may then be imparted to the wines. This problem can be avoided by hanging the glasses upside down (see Plate 11).

Corkscrews and Other Openers. First the metal capsule must be removed. We recommend that it be cut off well below the rim of the bottle. The neck of the bottle and the top of the cork should then be carefully cleaned, preferably with a wet cloth followed by

a dry cloth. This is so none of the surface material gets into the wine.

Removing the cork can be a serious problem. Just after corking, the closure is rather hard and, unless paraffined, it may stick. Corks that have been in bottles for many years may become spongy in the center and stick to the sides.

There are dozens of different types of openers; four basic types are shown in Plate 12. We prefer a corkscrew with a long (2-inch) screw that has a wide, flat (not round) surface. Corkscrews that work by some form of leverage are best, though with experience even a direct-pull corkscrew can be used. If the cork is very spongy the hollow-needle pump opener is useful. The needle is pushed through the cork and air is pumped into the space between the cork and the wine. Only a few strokes of the pump should be used. If the cork does not move, use a corkscrew. We do not recommend hollow-needle openers with carbon dioxide cylinders. If the cork is stuck and too much carbon dioxide is released, the bottle may explode.

Some people prefer the U-shaped puller. This consists of two flat, springy prongs that are pushed between the bottle and the cork. If the cork is good it is then easily withdrawn. However, if the cork is loose it may be pushed into the bottle.

Temperature

We recommend that red table wines be served at or near 68°F. (20°C.), which is slightly less than normal room temperature in the United States. For white table wines about 60°F. (16°C.) is low enough to give the desired cool sensation and high enough to allow detection of most of the desirable (and undesirable) odors. For sparkling wines about 55°F. (13°C.) is ideal. This again is high enough to allow detection of the bouquet. Most restaurants and many people at home serve white table wines and sparkling wines too cold. In the sparkling wines this restricts the loss of carbon dioxide, and some odors (good and bad) cannot be detected. For dessert wines about 65°F. (18°C.) seems to be a good compromise. At higher temperatures dessert wines appear too alcoholic. On the other hand, dry sherries are certainly more appealing at 60–65°F. (16–18°C.) than at higher temperatures.

People differ in their reactions to the temperatures at which wines are served. If one is accustomed to testing wines at 60°F. (16°C.) it is probably best to stick with that temperature because some bias will surely be introduced if a significantly higher or lower temperature is used. However, we believe that pre-testing conditioning is justified so that all the judges are accustomed to testing at a certain temperature.

Number of Samples

We recommend not more than five samples, or ten if the differences between samples are large. The problem varies according to the nature of the test. If the test is simply to eliminate poor samples, a careful judge can test 20 to 50 samples without undue fatigue. This is because this particular task is comparatively easy. In establishing preference or relative preference, many comparisons are required and the task is more complex and time-consuming. Adaptation is then a constant problem and severe restriction of the number of samples is essential.

The number of samples can be increased if a wide variety of characteristics are represented, as, e.g., in three dry white table wines, three sweet table wines, three rosés, three dry red table wines, three sherries, and three ports. Judges of normal competence and experience should be able to evaluate these 18 wines in about two hours. If all the wines are of the same type and of approximately the same quality, no more than five to ten samples should be judged at one time. If the wines are to be compared, the smaller number is preferable. If each sample is to be judged separately and only once, the larger number should cause no problems.

When as many as 20 samples of the same type must be evaluated at one judging, either of two simplifying procedures can be adopted. The judges could first identify and eliminate those samples that they all agreed were poor or non-type-conforming. With luck, this would reduce the number of samples deemed worthy of detailed evaluation. Or, the judges could examine the samples in incomplete block arrangements (page 154).

The problems of having too many samples are often underestimated. Adaptation is a constant threat to accuracy. As the number of samples increases, psychological confusion due to an inability to remember the sensory impressions of previous samples becomes a major problem. If each sample is compared with every other sample one time, the numbers of necessary comparisons are as follows:

NUMBER OF SAMPLES	NUMBER OF COMPARISONS
2	1
3	3
4	6
5	10
6	15

This is for one order of comparison only (i.e., sample 1 then sample 2, or vice versa, but not both). If the comparisons are to be made in *both* orders (i.e., sample 1 then sample 2 *and* vice versa), a judging of five samples would require at least 20 comparisons. If some of the samples are very similar many more comparisons may be needed. The problems of physiological adaptation and psychological confusion then become severe and make it difficult to obtain meaningful results.

In large, formal judgings some compromise has to be made unless the examination is to take an inordinate amount of time. One possibility is to have a preliminary judging solely for eliminating the poorer samples. (The judges must be careful not to eliminate any acceptable samples.) At subsequent sessions scoring or ranking can be used on the wines that remain. This reduces the number of comparisons and increases the accuracy. In any event the judges should not be kept at their task for more than about one hour at a time, with generous breaks (15 minutes) in between.

Klenk (1972) says that German wine judges can and do evaluate 150 to 200 wines in a day. He estimates this as equivalent to drinking a bottle of wine per day even if most of each sample is not swallowed. In fact, he believes that, if the judge is careful not to swallow any of the wine, up to 300 wines can be evaluated in a day! No statistical evidence for the validity of this belief is given, and our observations indicate that errors will occur, more often in the afternoon than in the morning. Klenk also allows judges to evaluate up to 50 sparkling wines or brandies per day. He is right that sparkling wines and brandies are very fatiguing, but even 50 of them seems excessive to us, if they are to be ranked in order of relative preference.

Procedures

Coding.   As we have already noted, knowing the identity of the wine has real advantages for appreciation. But when objective comparisons of wines are to be made (whether by difference or preference) it is necessary to eliminate, or at least minimize, all biases.

Thus it is essential to conceal the identity of the wines. Some form of coding must be used. In contrast to our previous recommendation (Amerine et al., 1959) we now prefer two-digit numbers from 14 to 99. If the number of samples is small, one can choose the code by pointing at random at a list of numbers from 14 to 99. However, in some complicated block designs entailing many samples, a preprinted list of random numbers should be used to avoid duplications. The code numbers used should not suggest any particular order or quality to the panel.

Systematics.   Inexperienced judges often attempt to do too many things at once in sensory evaluation. Important sensory qualities are often missed in this pell-mell examination. Professionals proceed systematically (and usually slowly).

The best system is to begin by observing the appearance. This may give valuable clues about possible defects in the wine. For example, the type of cloudiness may reveal the nature of the defect (page 22). Note also whether bubbles are present—they are usually evident as tiny bubbles at the glass/wine interface. This indicates excess carbon dioxide. In sparkling wines the bubbles are larger, and they rise freely. The smaller the bubbles, however, the longer the wine will stay sparkling. If the bubbles are very large (usually in rapidly fermented or poorly carbonated sparkling wines) the wine may go flat in a few minutes.

Some judges pay a good deal of attention to the "tears" of the wine. If a clean wine glass is half-filled with wine, one observes that a liquid film creeps slowly up the side of the glass. After a few minutes some of the liquid at the ascending interface begins to form drops, which roll back down the glass in irregular columns. Thus the wine is said to be weeping, and the drops are its tears. (In Great Britain they are called "legs"; in the technical literature they are called "arches.")

The phenomenon is due to the Marangoni effects, but it was not first explained by Marangoni. Scriven and Sternling (1960) have given a history of the pertinent studies. They credit the British engineer and physicist James Thomson (the brother of Lord Kelvin) with the first correct explanation, in 1855. Briefly, the preferential evaporation of ethanol at the surface of the wine causes the surface film to be more aqueous than the liquid below. The maximum rate of ethanol evaporation is in the region of the air/liquid/glass interface at the top of the meniscus. Therefore the water concentration is a maximum in this region, and so is the surface tension. The vertical gradient in the surface tension causes the liquid film to creep up the side of the glass until it can no longer overcome the effect of gravity. As more liquid is dragged up the side of the glass by this "surface tension pump," it coalesces into drops (tears) at the top of the film, and flows back down again.

It is clear that the tears of wine are primarily water. The greater the ethanol content of the wine, the more tears there are. For the

tears in 12% and 18% solutions of ethanol in water, see Plates 13 and 14.* The idea, still put forth in some popular texts, that the tears of wine are glycerol is obviously erroneous. The boiling point of glycerol is 554°F. (290°C.), and its vapor pressure above the wine is negligibly low.

A careful consideration of the color and its appropriateness for the type of wine should follow the examination of the appearance. Abnormal colors may suggest defects in the wine. A brown-colored wine may be oxidized or unduly bitter (page 19). Of course, one must be wary of stimulus errors. A bluish-colored wine *may* have an undesirably high pH but it could be a very young wine of certain varieties that is basically sound. Reducing the pH or fining and filtering the wine usually removes the bluish tint.

When finished wines are being considered for purchase, their appearance and color may be of critical importance (see Plate 15). At the present time no one can sell a cloudy wine in the United States, much less a wine of abnormal color. The experienced judge sets cloudy and off-color wines aside, thus saving his palate for wines without these defects. Of course, when a sensory examination of young wines is made in the winery to determine the appropriate finishing techniques, the appearance is of only secondary importance, since the finishing will surely eliminate any cloudiness. Slight defects in color are often corrected by appropriate aging, finishing, or blending.

Following the visual inspection a careful olfactory examination should be made. This too should be done systematically. The wine in the glass should be swirled rather vigorously (three or four

*Photographers will be interested in how these technically very difficult photographs were obtained. They were taken with an 8 × 10-inch view camera mounting a 12-inch focal length lens. The optimal background consisted of an out-of-focus, black grid on a gray card, to provide visual edge refractions in the otherwise virtually invisible tears. This grid was placed 12 inches behind the principal plane of focus of the subject. The lens was closed down to f/11. Exposure was by flash, to freeze the motion. To obtain adequate contrast it was necessary to print on ultrahigh-contrast Brovira #6 enlarging paper. The developer was heated to further increase the print contrast.

swirls should be enough) and then the glass brought quickly to the nose and sniffed. The purpose of the swirling is to expose as large a surface area of wine as possible so that evaporation of the volatile substances is enhanced. The released odors are concentrated by the tulip shape of the glass, with the more volatile components being lost first. If the swirling is too prolonged, more of the more volatile odors (both desirable and undesirable) will be lost, perhaps to below their absolute thresholds, and the character of the odor will change. We recommend a quick, strong sniff with full mental concentration on possible off odors, which are usually identified first. Successive swirlings and sniffs follow only after a brief pause (15 to 30 seconds), to forestall the effects of adaptation, and should be directed to the aroma and bouquet and their appropriateness for the type. If more than three or four such examination cycles are desired one should empty the glass, pour some fresh wine, and repeat the process. Experienced judges try to quantify their impression at each stage—both for off odors and the desirable aroma and bouquet.

Finally, some wine (about 10 ml, or ⅓ ounce) is placed on the tongue and spread over its entire surface so as to make contact with as many taste buds as possible (see Plate 16). It is wise to try to identify each of the basic tastes successively. We prefer to evaluate the degree of sweetness first, followed by sourness and bitterness. Many other judges look for the degree of sourness first, followed by sweetness and bitterness. As already indicated (page 42), bitterness should not be confused with astringency, which is a tactile sensation. The degree of each taste should be noted, preferably in writing.

During the actual tasting, more odors are being released as the wine warms up in the mouth. These odors are often called *flavor*, and they should be looked for consciously.

How much wine, if any, should be swallowed? At home we drink the wine. But in a judging of five to twenty wines this is inadvisable, to say the least. Nevertheless, experienced judges consciously or unconsciously swallow a little wine to savor the aftertaste. We

doubt that there are enough taste buds in the throat to make this worthwhile. But if a judge thinks this is important it is probably wise to allow him to continue, provided he doesn't swallow too much!

The texture of the wine must also be noted. The tactile sensations of astringency and the thinness (alcoholicity) or thickness (related to sweetness) are easiest to recognize.

Theoretically, all of the sensory impressions should now be complete, except perhaps those of temperature. However, as the score cards indicate (page 122), there is one more attribute that must be taken into account. Apparently the sensory reactions together mediate a combined response, which we call general quality. This requires experience. General quality should not be used by the judge as a means of adjusting his quality score to what he considers "correct." General quality is a separate and distinctive factor. We have taught our students that it is the memorableness of the character of the wine, or its lasting come-hither appeal.

A bottle of good wine, like a good act, shines ever in the retrospect.
—R. L. Stevenson

The wine which demands a second, third, . . . glass can never be a bad wine. The wine of which you cannot finish one glass can never be a great wine.
—E. Gallo

5

Composition
of Wines

The major component of wine is water, the amount of which varies from about 70 to 90% by volume. Pure water has no color, odor, or taste. It does, of course, produce certain tactile sensations but, like the absence of color, odor, and taste, these are merely standards for comparison, not inherently meaningful characteristics. It is only the deviations from the feel of pure water caused by the presence of the *other* components of wines—primarily ethanol, sugars, and tannins—that are meaningful in terms of the concept "wine." The same is true (for different classes of dissolved components) with regard to deviations from the lack of color, odor, and taste. Thus our perception of wine is a complex of sensory responses that deviate, in certain ways and within certain ranges, from those that we associate with water. The same could be said of beer, milk, orange juice, etc.

Ethanol

The second most important component of wines is ethanol. Some odd types of wine have only 5 to 9% ethanol by volume. Commercial table wines have 9 to 14% and dessert wines range from 14 to 21%. The question of what is a table wine is normally determined by government regulations, as in the United States. However, the specific regulations of various countries differ. In terms of wine production, most (but by no means all) wines with more than 14% ethanol have had wine spirits added, i.e., have been fortified.

Ethanol (ethyl alcohol or often just "alcohol") has a distinctive odor, taste, and feel. For solutions of ethanol in water, Parker (1922) reported absolute thresholds* of 0.55% (by volume) for odor, 17.5% for taste, and 32.3% for pain. These figures, especially the one for taste, need to be reinvestigated. In addition the wide variations among individuals, the effects of their experience, and the known effects of the method of testing should be taken into account. Wilson (1972), for example, reported a taste threshold of 4.2 ± 0.2% for ethanol in water and a pain threshold of 21.2 ± 1.2%.

The difference threshold† for ethanol in water varies with the

*The word threshold need not disturb the nontechnical reader. The *absolute threshold* for a given compound (e.g., salt) is the minimum concentration that a person can correctly identify. At concentrations below the absolute threshold the compound is not identified, although its presence may sometimes be perceived in some unspecifiable way. Since different people have different thresholds (and the same person has different thresholds at different times) some statistical measure of absolute threshold must be defined. Usually we define it as that minimum concentration that 50% of the population can correctly identify.

†The *difference threshold* for a given compound at a given concentration (above the absolute threshold) is the minimum difference that can be detected between that concentration and another. The higher the concentration of the compound in the solution, the greater the difference threshold. In other words, at low concentrations one can detect smaller differences in concentration between two samples than at high concentrations. This is hardly surprising, because a difference in concentration of, say, 1% at a 5% concentration level is proportionally greater than a difference of 1% at a 20% concentration level. A given difference between two small numbers is always more significant than the same difference between two large numbers. Like the absolute threshold, the difference threshold is usually defined on a statistical basis, namely, as that minimum difference in concentration that 50% of the population can detect.

ethanol concentration (Berg et al., 1955b). At low ethanol concentrations (about 5% by volume) this threshold is about 1%. In other words, 50% of the population can distinguish between 4%· and 5% ethanol or between 5% and 6%. At 10% ethanol the difference threshold is about 2.0%; at 14% ethanol it is about 3.0%; and at 19% ethanol it is about 3.5%. In red and white table wines of 12% and 11% ethanol the difference threshold for ethanol was 4% in the studies of Hinreiner et al. (1955a), i.e., it was almost twice as great as the difference threshold for ethanol in water.

It is also of some interest to know that adding sugar to an ethanol-water solution increases the absolute threshold for ethanol. The more sugar is added, the greater the absolute threshold becomes. Sweetening wines does not increase the difference threshold for ethanol. It can also be shown that the increase in the absolute threshold for ethanol at higher sugar levels is somewhat suppressed by acids.

Ethanol has some effects on the acid taste of wines. If a wine is carefully dealcoholized and then brought back to the original volume with water it will taste much more acidulous and unbalanced than the original wine. This is because ethanol has a slightly sweet taste. But the ethanol also undoubtedly affects the activity of the acids. Furthermore, it determines the viscosity (body) of the wine, which affects the degree of acid taste.

Other Alcohols.   A number of aliphatic alcohols with more than two carbon atoms exist in musts or are produced during alcoholic fermentation, and are found in wines. If the wines are fortified with wine spirits these may be a supplemental source of higher alcohols. The most important aliphatic alcohols in wines and wine spirits are 3-methyl-1-butanol (isoamyl alcohol), 2-methyl-1-butanol (active amyl alcohol), and 2-methyl-1-propanol (isobutyl alcohol). Small amounts of 1-propanol, 1-butanol, and 1-pentanol (n-propyl, n-butyl, and n-amyl alcohols, respectively) are also found. These all have more or less of the fusel oil odor. At high concentrations they are a negative quality factor but at low concentrations they may add desirable complexity to the odor.

Odors

There are more than 300 organic compounds found in varying concentrations in wines. Most are found in subliminal (below threshold) concentrations. Still, they may have additive, masking, or synergistic effects. About 100 are odorless. A few besides the alcohols mentioned above can be recognized in wines: acetaldehyde (in sherries), vanillin (in wines and brandies stored in American oak), acetal (possibly in old wines and oxidized table wines and brandies), linalool (in muscatels and other wines with a floral note), ethyl and methyl anthranilates (in *V. labrusca* varieties and some of their hybrids), 2-phenylethanol (in table wines with a floral note), *n*-hexanol (in some wines of low ethanol concentration), ethyl acetate (in spoiling wines), ethyl laurate (a part of the ubiquitous vinous odor), biacetyl (in certain oxidized wines, especially red table wines), hydroxymethylfurfural (in baked wines), etc. Of course, the actual, perceived odor of a wine is a mixture of numerous odorous constituents. For example, linalool alone is not the muscat odor. The odor appears to be a balance of small amounts of α-terpineol, nerol, and geraniol, as well as linalool and probably other compounds.

Many off odors are due to known specific compounds, such as sulfur dioxide, hydrogen sulfide, various mercaptans, and various breakdown products of sorbic acid and of excessive malo-lactic fermentations.

Tastes

Sweet. The most important sweet compounds in wines are the sugars glucose and fructose. Their absolute thresholds in wines are below 1%. Of the two, fructose has the lower threshold because it is about twice as sweet as glucose at very low concentrations. At high concentrations the difference in sweetness is less (page 39). Ethanol increases the apparent sweetness of sweet wines, i.e., it decreases the absolute thresholds of the sugars. Tannins, however, increase the absolute and difference thresholds of sugars, according to Berg et al. (1955*b*).

Glycerol is found in all wines, in concentrations from about 0.5% to over 1.5% by weight, the higher concentrations being found in wines made from botrytised grapes (those attacked by *Botrytis cinerea*). Glycerol has a sweet taste; the absolute threshold is about 1.5% (for some individuals it is much higher). In wines containing residual sugar, such as most of those made from botrytised grapes, the sweetness of the glycerol is masked by the sweetness of the sugars. The glycerol threshold is higher with higher acidity and ethanol concentration. Other compounds may also add a little sweetness to wines, e.g., 2,3-butanediol, pentoses, and amino acids.

Bitter. For the reasons discussed previously (pages 41–43), the role of polyphenolic compounds in bitterness (taste) and astringency (feel) is unquestioned but semantically confusing. According to Berg et al. (1955*a*), if the total phenolic content in aqueous solution is less than 0.02% by weight, as in white table wines, there is little bitterness or astringency. Vedel et al. (1972) and Ribéreau-Gayon (1973) emphasize that the actual bitter taste impression is due not only to bitter-tasting compounds but also to the interaction of bitter, sour, and sweet tastes, and to the ethanol content.

When permanganate oxidation is used as a measure of total phenols and colored substances it is found that the higher the value, the more bitter the wine. An index of lack of astringency (and bitterness?) in red wines has been proposed by Ribéreau-Gayon (1973). It is calculated by subtracting the sum of the acidity and the polyphenolic content from the ethanol concentration. Wines with an index of 6 or more are less astringent than those with an index of 3 to 5. Thus, the higher the ethanol concentration, the less astringent the wine, all else being equal. A statistical analysis of such data to determine the usefulness of this index is needed.

Acids. Important organic acids found in wines are tartaric, malic, succinic, and lactic. Small amounts of acetic, citric, formic, gluconic, glucuronic, oxalic, phosphoric, sulfurous, and other acids are also found. The actual sour (acid) taste of a wine depends on the absolute and relative amounts of the various acids (the total acidity), the proportion of acids present in undissociated form or as acid salts (factors that affect the pH of the wine), the sugar and ethanol concentrations, and other factors. If the acids are tested separately in water, tartaric acid is the sourest, but in wines malic acid appears to be the sourest. (See also pages 40–41.)

The difference threshold for the total (titratable) acidity in table wines varies from 0.02% to 0.05% (Amerine et al., 1965*b*). At the same time in the same wines, a difference of only 0.05 pH unit could be distinguished. Ethanol increases the difference threshold for total acidity, all the more so if sugar is present. Tannins also increase the difference threshold for total acidity. However, the presence of sugar minimizes the tannin effect.

Salts. The salty sensation is rare in wines. Wines that are high in potassium sulfate as a result of treatment of the musts with calcium sulfate (i.e., wines that are "plastered") have a slightly salty taste. Some wines made from grapes grown near the sea occasionally have a salty taste; so do a few very dry sherries. Wines overtreated in sodium-ion-exchangers may also have a salty taste.

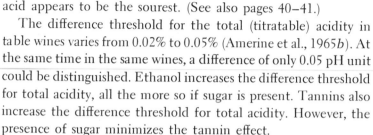

Music and wine are one.
—R. W. Emerson

On the tongue the wine speaks.
—P. Poupon

6

Types of Wines

In this chapter we attempt to distinguish the many basic types of wines, in outline style. For each type we list the most important (but by no means all) quality factors that must be considered in the sensory evaluation. Because the outline is rather detailed and extends through the entire chapter, it is helpful to get an overview of the material by seeing a condensed form (no text) of the outline. This is shown on the following page.

The types of wines named are primarily those produced in or imported to the United States. The name of a wine is capitalized when it is that of a specific grape variety or the geographic region in which the wine was actually made, or when it is proprietary (trademarked).

Wines with No Added Flavors

Wine was originally just fermented grape juice, i.e., no flavors were added. The most numerous and important types of commercial wines still fall in this category. Our discussion of them constitutes the bulk of this chapter.

I. Wines having excess carbon dioxide (sparkling and carbonated wines)

A. Champagne (*Sekt, spumante,* etc.)

Champagnes produced by bottle fermentation should be light yellow, the exact tint of which will vary depending on whether the base wine was made from white grapes or from a blend of white musts from white and red grapes. (Wines made from the blend will be slightly darker.) The varietal character should be subdued but there must be an appreciable bouquet due to bottle aging in contact with the yeast. The wine must have enough acid that the secondary fermentation in the bottle is free of bacterial growth, but it should not be too acidulous.

From the standpoint of marketing, the finer the quality (aroma, bouquet, taste, and flavor) of the champagne, the drier it may be. Since the base cuvée is always a blend, the winemaker has the opportunity to introduce complexity and individuality by selecting wines of varying composition and character. The more common problems of bottle-fermented champagnes are a yeasty odor when they are disgorged too soon after fermentation, excess acidity due to the use of unripe grapes, and too obvious a varietal flavor. Complexity of character with a fruity flavor should be looked for.

Champagnes made by the bulk or tank process or by the transfer process can and do differ in character from those produced by the bottle process. There are two reasons for this: the former wines are not normally aged on the yeast, and there is some oxidation associated with transfer of the wine or with filtration. Such wines have appreciably more

acetaldehyde; to prevent the early development of an oxidized odor some sulfur dioxide is often added to fix the acetaldehyde. Again the best champagnes are usually the driest, but sweeter types are available for those who prefer them. Although "brut" is the driest type, the "brut" of some producers is much sweeter than it should be. Sparkling wines labeled "brut" should have less than 1.5% sugar. "Extra dry" wines should not have more than 3% sugar. The distinction between "extra dry" and "sec" is not clearly maintained in practice. Perhaps one or the other of these designations would suffice.

Important problems with champagnes are lack of pressure, rapid loss of gassiness (the bubbles are then large), oxidation (often accompanied by early darkening of the color), lack of acidity, and a yeasty or sulfide odor (often due to the use of too much yeast and/or too high a fermentation temperature).

B. Pink (or rosé) champagne

A pink color without amber, orange, or purple is desired. Of course, the finished product should be brilliantly clear. The best pink champagnes, in our opinion, are those that have a tart, fruity flavor and that have been finished with less than about 2% sugar. Nevertheless, a few commercial products are low in acid, flat-tasting, and contain 3% sugar or more.*

C. Sparkling burgundy and cold duck

A sparkling red wine called sparkling burgundy has been marketed for many years. In recent years some sparkling red wines have been labeled cold duck. We have been unable to find any consistent chemical or flavor differences between the two types. Cold duck seems more often to have some Concord flavor, but sparkling burgundy with a

*For these and other wines we wish that the producers would use appropriate labeling to enable the purchaser to distinguish the dry wines from the sweet wines.

Concord flavor has been made in New York and Ohio since before Prohibition.

Most sparkling red wines contain about 5% sugar. Such wines have a bitter and astringent character due to the relatively high tannin content in the presence of carbon dioxide. This is objectionable to the consumer. Adding sugar covers the bitterness and astringency. If there were a demand for higher-quality sparkling red wines, we believe more attention would be paid to making the blend and reducing the sweetness.

D. Sparkling muscat

Only a few wines of this type are produced; most of those on the United States market are from Italy. The reason there are so few is that the muscat flavor is very strong and distinctive and the palate soon tires of it. Such wines usually contain 8 to 11% ethanol. They are always made very sweet because muscat-flavored wines without sugar are almost always flat and bitter-tasting. A high sugar content overcomes these defects but also tires the palate.

Because the muscat grapes are harvested when fully ripe (to secure good flavor and sugar) the color tends to be yellow-gold. With aging, of course, it darkens. One accepts this unless the flavor is frankly oxidized (sherry-like).

E. Carbonated and similar wines

A wide variety of wines of this type are now produced. The "pearl" wines, which originated in Germany, are tank-fermented wines. They have only one to two atmospheres of pressure and are more often than not on the sweet side. Some are higher in sulfur dioxide than others.

Because fully carbonated wines are heavily taxed in the United States they are almost as expensive as regular sparkling wines. Recent (1974) changes in United States regulations, however, permit a relatively high degree of carbonation without incurring the excessive tax of a fully carbonated wine. Fully carbonated wines are now seldom produced in the United States. Some have a fruit/grape wine base. Unfortunately some are too sweet, in our opinion. We suspect that they are often served over ice as an inexpensive substitute for a cocktail (with or without the addition of bitters).

One variant is the low-ethanol, low-carbon dioxide moscato amabile of the L. M. Martini winery in California. The muscat must is fermented at very low temperature —about 32°F. (0°C.)—for a year or more. When the fermentation slows down or "sticks," the wine is bottled. Enough carbon dioxide remains to give the wine perceptible gassiness. The ethanol content may be only 8% and the sugar content up to 10%. The wine is not only strong in muscat flavor but also retains much of its fermentation (yeasty) odor. As with all strong-flavored wines, the first glass is very pleasant, but the muscat odor and high sweetness may limit the appeal of subsequent glasses. One disadvantage of the wine is that it is not fermentation-stable and must be kept refrigerated.

II. Wines having no excess carbon dioxide (still wines)

A. Wines having 14% ethanol or less (table wines)

This group of wines is distinguished from all the rest not only by definition but also with respect to legal and tax considerations. Generally the least taxes are paid on these unflavored, still wines having 14% ethanol or less.

1. White—having distinguishable varietal character

The most important requirement of this large group of wines is that they have a recognizable varietal character. Not all wines carrying varietal names meet this requirement, owing to too warm or cool a climate for the grapes, overcropping, harvesting too soon, or excessive blending with neutral-flavored wines. In general, people nowadays prefer the fresher, younger white wines. However, some of the heavier-bodied (more alcoholic) white types, such as Chardonnay, can profit by some wood aging and bottle aging.

The most common infirmities of this group of wines (besides lack of varietal character) are excessive sulfur dioxide, too dark a color, an oxidized odor, and cloudiness (from bacteria, yeast, or excess metal). Some white table wines are too noticeably high in wood (oak) flavor, from being aged in new or old barrels for too long. Our rule is that if you can identify the odor as woody it is excessive. The woody odor should be a subtle, undistinguishable aspect of the complexity of the wine.

Excessive ethanol content (over 14%) is not illegal if one pays the higher tax. However, experience shows that dry white table wines with more than 14% ethanol are usually flat and alcoholic, and often have off odors from overripe or moldy grapes. Sweet table wines made from botrytised grapes can have slightly more than 14% ethanol without deterioration. Even among the sweet types, some of the best are not high in ethanol: many German *Auslese* types have only 8 or 10%, for example.

a. *District named. France:* Chablis, Graves, Mâcon, Meursault, Montrachet, Pouilly-Fuissé, Sancerre, etc.

Germany: Franken, Moselle (Piesport*), Rheingau (Hattenheim*), Rheinhessen, etc.

Some of the district-labeled wines also have varietal labels. Many have both the district and the vineyard given on the label. District labeling is also used in other countries (Spain, Italy, etc.). However, such labels are meaningful only when the varieties and methods of production used in the district in question are standardized.

The distinctiveness of varietal character varies markedly depending on the region and season, the time of harvest, the amount of overcropping, and the amount of blending with neutral-flavored wines.

*Name of village within district. The label may also have the vineyard name.

b. *Varietal named.* Aligoté, Chardonnay, Chenin blanc,* Emerald Riesling, Flora, French Colombard, Gewürztraminer, Sauvignon blanc, Sauvignon vert, Sémillon, Sylvaner,* Walschriesling,* White (Johannisberg) Riesling, etc.

Not all varietal-labeled wines are of high quality. We have yet to taste a fine French Colombard. Walschriesling (with rare exceptions) and Sauvignon vert make only ordinary wines. Some types have very little varietal character: Chasselas doré, Green Hungarian, Thompson Seedless, Trebbiano (Ugni blanc, Saint-Émilion), Veltliner, etc.

2. White—having no distinguishable varietal character

In the United States these wines are usually labeled with semigeneric names, such as chablis and rhine. In Europe many such wines have district or proprietary names—for example, many Portuguese, Spanish, Italian, Russian, and Greek wines, including some with varietal labels. Contrary to the opinions of wine snobs, good and even fine wines can be found in this class. Many blended white table wines that are made from good varieties grown under proper climatic conditions and harvested at optimum maturity, and that are properly processed and aged, are of excellent character.

The main problem with these semigeneric wines is that there are often no recognized standards to insure that the wine has the desired typical character, except for the standards that the producers themselves may impose, more or less regularly. For example, one Napa Valley winery has blended a superior chablis for years. Other wineries produce chablis that taste flat and lack character or quality.

In an attempt to bring some order into this chaos Amerine et al. (1972) recommended that California chablis be dry and California rhine be sweet. There is

*Varietal character is not pronounced except under special conditions.

no evidence to date that this recommendation has been heeded. In fact, both California chablis and California rhine are now more likely to be sweet than dry. Fortunately many semigeneric type names are gradually disappearing in the United States. The names California or American white chianti, dry sauterne, hock, moselle, and the like are now rarely used.

3. Pink (or rosé)

At one time these were all dry pink wines. They have been labeled Grenache rosé or Gamay rosé or simply rosé. Some California Pinot noirs also belong in this group. Occasionally a Cabernet or Zinfandel rosé has been produced. Aside from the attraction of the name, they are seldom of particular merit compared to the corresponding red wines. Rosés are produced in France (Loire, Tavel, and Provence), Italy, and elsewhere. Some Portuguese wines are really rosés, although they are not labeled as such.

The consumer's problem is how to distinguish the dry rosé from the sweet rosé. The best policy (already recommended, page 40) would be for the producer to state the sugar content on the label. Failing that, one can only guess whether the wine will be dry or sweet.

Unfortunately Grenache is not the best variety for producing a rosé in the Central Valley of California. Because of the prestige of the name Grenache, however, a great deal of this variety has been planted there. In the hot climate of the Central Valley the color of the wine is likely to be orange-pink and the flavor distressingly flat. Rosé wines should be pink, not amber, orange, or purple. A fruity character is essential, and that requires a good total acidity in the must and the wine. For this reason we doubt that the wines should be aged for more than a year or two. With few exceptions we prefer rosés with 11 to 12% ethanol rather than 12 to 14%.

4. Red—having distinguishable varietal character

As with the analogous white wines (section 1 above), the most important requirement for this group of wines is recognizable varietal character. And likewise the main problem is the lack of that character due to too warm or cool a climate for the grapes, overcropping, harvesting too soon, or excessive blending with neutral-flavored wines. A Pinot noir with 10 to 11% ethanol cannot have enough Pinot noir aroma to make a fine wine. Growing the grapes in too warm a region or harvesting them too late often results in raisin flavors and an unpalatable dessert-wine or warm-climate character. These practices also yield wines that may never mature. We are not in sympathy with some California red table wines of 15 and 16% ethanol that have appeared on the market, nor with similar, high-ethanol wines produced in Yugoslavia (Dingač wines in Dalmatia) and Spain (Priorato region) when these wines are sold as table wines.

Another, more difficult, problem is deciding how long red table wines should be aged. Too many potentially fine red Bordeaux and California Cabernet Sauvignons have been and are being drunk too soon—long before they have reached their best quality from bottle aging. But who is to store the wines the requisite time? For the producers it entails serious financial problems. Consumers often do not have the space to store the wines, or at least not at a suitable temperature.

a. *District named. France:* Beaujolais, Bordeaux, Burgundy, Châteauneuf-du-Pape, Hermitage, Médoc, Pomerol, Rhône, Saint-Émilion, etc.

Italy: Barolo.

Spain: Rioja.

Of the hundreds of Portuguese, Spanish, Italian, Yugoslavian, and Greek red table wines with district

labels, most do not have a distinguishable varietal character, or at least not consistently.

b. *Varietal named.* Barbera, Cabernet franc, Cabernet Sauvignon,* Gamay,† Grignolino,† Merlot,* Nebbiolo,† Petite Sirah, Pinot noir, Ruby Cabernet, Zinfandel, etc.

Many varietal-labeled red table wines, both in the United States and abroad, have little recognizable aroma of the grape for which they are named. These include some of the direct-producer varieties and many Italian so-called varietals. Even when the grape could have a recognizable varietal character from being grown on trees or arbors or being too lightly pruned, it may be overcropped to the point of extinction of this character. We have known some California producers to boast of their 10- to 12-ton-per-acre yields of Ruby Cabernet. Unfortunately the wines smell and taste like it.

Varieties that rarely yield wines with a recognizable varietal character are Carignane, Early Burgundy, Mataro, Mondeuse, Royalty, Rubired, etc.

5. Red—having no distinguishable varietal character

As with the analogous white wines (section 2 above), not all California red wines with semigeneric names (such as claret and burgundy) are of ordinary character. There is no law that prevents a producer from making a fine Cabernet Sauvignon and labeling it claret. He is most unlikely to do this, however, because the market price for Cabernet Sauvignon is much higher

---

*Although Cabernet Sauvignon and Merlot have some of the same odor characteristics they differ 3 to 1 and even 5 to 1 in the amounts of some components, as determined by gas-liquid chromatography (Ribéreau-Gayon, 1973). Of course, the size of the GLC peak need not be related to the strength of the odor.

†Varietal character is not pronounced except under special conditions.

"It's a naive domestic burgundy without any breeding, but I think you'll be amused by its presumption."

than for California claret. Moreover, a new blend of varieties could very well produce a fine wine that, because no variety amounted to at least 51% of the total, would not be eligible for a varietal label. Yet the wine might be of excellent, even unique, quality. Perhaps vineyard-district labeling, if it produced a consistent flavor, would be more appropriate for such blends.

B. Wines having more than 14% ethanol (dessert wines)

These are almost all fortified wines. However, where tradition rules and price is not a factor, some very sweet, unfortified wines of less than or more than 14% ethanol that are clearly dessert types are produced. The number of types of dessert wines is small enough that each can be discussed here.

1. Sherry—dry

    a. *Baked process.* Some but not all California sherries are made by this process. If the wine is dry when baked, it will not have too much caramel character.

If, in addition, it is aged in reasonably small cooperage for one to five years it acquires flavor complexity. A limit of 1.5% sugar would ensure that the "dry" sherries are indeed dry to most people's palates.

b. *Yeast process.* Whether produced by the film-yeast (flor) or submerged-culture process the wines should have a light color and a noticeable acetaldehyde odor. In the film-yeast process (used primarily in Spain) the acetaldehyde content builds up slowly. The longer the wine is under the film, the more complex the bouquet becomes. As the wine ages, the yeast film sinks to the bottom from time to time and undergoes autolysis (self-digestion by the action of autogenous enzymes), which also contributes to the complexity of the wine. In addition, the fractional blending in the solera system not only equalizes the character of the wine but makes it more complex.

The difference in bouquet between film-yeast sherries and submerged-culture sherries is that the former are much more complex, with less free-acetaldehyde odor. An aging period, such as is used in the solera system, is desirable in both processes. Old flor sherries develop into darker amontillados, which are much appreciated. Partly because of the concentration of the wine during aging, old amontillados may be slightly sweet.

2. Sherry—sweet

a. *Baked process.* A number of California sweet baked sherries are marketed. They have a distinct caramel flavor. Most have 10% sugar or more, and an amber color. We doubt that aging would improve their quality except in small cooperage (less than 500 gallons).

b. *Aged process.* Sweet sherries are also made in Spain and occasionally in California by aging in the warmer

part of the bodega. In Spain the wines may have some flor character because of the complicated final solera blending. Too much caramel or raisin odor is considered a defect.

It is worth noting that the use of the word *solera* on California sherries and ports is increasing—unfortunately. If the average age of the wine were increased to a constant, as in a normal Spanish solera blending, we would not find fault with this. Sometimes, however, the word seems to be used merely as a sales gimmick.

A number of sherries of intermediate degrees of flor and nonflor character and of sweetness are produced.

3. Madeira

This is another baked dessert wine. It may be slightly sweet, medium-sweet, or sweet; in Madeira these variants are named Sercial, Boal (or Bual), and Malmsey, respectively. They are quite amber in color, owing to the use of Jacquez (red) grapes. Some have more of a baked character than others. We find most of them to be sweeter than we like, but the sweetness is obviously needed to mask the bitterness produced by baking. Some Portuguese Madeiras have had an excessive amount of volatile acidity so it is advisable to sample the wine before purchasing any large amount.

We have shown elsewhere (Roessler and Amerine, 1973) that one should take claims of great antiquity for Madeiras—even at prices of $20 to $25 per bottle—with a grain of salt. In fact, we doubt that much commercial Madeira of the advertised ages exists, unless the law of compound interest has been repealed and someone has found a method of preventing the accumulation of fixed acids. We don't know what a California (or American in general) madeira should be. We have had some well-aged Russian *maderas* that tasted much like a respectable, aged, sweet sherry.

4. Málaga

This is a Spanish, raisin-flavored wine that is traditionally made from raisins, or at least semi-raisins. It is sweet and flat. We can't think of when or where it could be served in the United States. Because it is rather low in ethanol (about 15%) for a dessert wine, some of our students have suggested it as the wine to serve your "dry" maiden aunt when she comes to tea.

5. Marsala

This Sicilian, blended, sweet dessert wine owes its primary character to the use of *cotto* (boiled-down grape juice). Whether one likes this bitter-burnt flavor or not, it is a necessary part of Marsala and is what makes it useful in cooking. Marsalas are amber in color and sweet (despite what the label says). To drink them straight is more of a chore than a pleasure for us. In fact, we have never met a Marsala connoisseur except in the production and sales departments of Marsala producers or distributors. We don't know what a California (or American) marsala should be and, from those we have tasted, we don't *want* to know. Fortunately very few have appeared on the market.

6. Muscatel

A large number of dessert wines are produced from various muscat varieties. In California the predominant variety is Muscat of Alexandria. In France, Italy, and the Soviet Union, Muscat blanc (the same as Muscat Frontignan or Muscat Canelli) is commonly used. These and other varieties are also used in Australia, South Africa, and elsewhere. Because of the low acidity of muscat varieties the wines must be rather sweet to mask, at least partially, their flat taste. If the grapes are picked too early they lack muscat flavor. If picked too late they may raisin, and this will be reflected in the wine's caramel-raisin flavor and dark color.

Should the wine be aged? If it is aged it will almost certainly darken in color. If it is not aged the fortification spirits may be obvious and the wine may be "hot" in taste and feel. All things considered, we favor picking the grapes not too late and aging the wine for not more than two or three years—possibly less. Thus we prefer fruity, gold-colored muscatels. Many people, however, prefer older and darker muscatels.

7. Port

This sweet red dessert wine originated in the Douro Valley of Portugal, where it is still produced. There are three types. *Tawny* ports owe their color to long aging or to the use of tawny-colored grapes (and sometimes, no doubt, to vineyard mixtures of red and white grapes). *Ruby* ports are ruby red and are aged for only a few years. The best (darkest) ruby ports are bottled after two years and aged to make *vintage* ports.

Most ports from the Douro Valley have a distinct odor (apparently by design) of higher alcohols from the spirits used for fortification. American consumers, however, prefer lower levels of the higher alcohols in their dessert wines than do the Portuguese. Tawny ports should not be too sweet. Ruby ports must be fruity and not astringent. Vintage ports develop a fine bouquet, but only after ten to twenty years of bottle aging.

Similar, but by no means identical, types of sweet red wines are produced in Australia, California, South Africa, and the Soviet Union. Some are of excellent quality, whereas others appear to be produced from ordinary red varieties that lack flavor and/or acidity, color, and sugar. Such varieties give wines with a neutral, flat flavor and low color. In some wines the color is adjusted with poor-quality varieties, such as Salvador or other hybrids (Royalty, etc.). Heating ruby-colored ports to give them a tawny color is illegal in Portugal

and possibly should be elsewhere. The heated wines usually acquire a caramel odor and have a high hydroxymethylfurfural content.

8. Tokay

In Hungary the Aszu type of Tokay is a sweet, unfortified wine that is more or less oxidized in odor. This is probably due to too much aging in small casks. We have found few such wines that were of exceptional quality, despite their price, but this may be because the finer Tokays are less often produced today than before World War II. California tokay is a blend of angelica or white port (neutral dessert wines), port, and sherry.

Wines with Added Flavors

From earliest times some wines have had flavors added. In such wines one looks for a proper balance of the flavor that is characteristic of the type. Since the flavor is added deliberately one may be quite critical when there is an excess or deficiency. Likewise, since these are wines that improve little with age (in fact, they often deteriorate), one may insist that they be brilliantly clear and of the precise color commercially attributed to the type.

I. Herb-based

A. Vermouth—dry

These wines are nowadays usually light yellow but this is a commercial, not intrinsic, quality factor. "Dry" vermouths are not really dry—they have about 4% sugar. One should not tolerate any more than this. The "occupational disease" of dry vermouths is excessive bitterness, and sometimes noticeable astringency. This is probably the reason for the relatively high sugar content: to mask the bitterness and astringency.

B. Vermouth—sweet

These wines are almost always a full amber color but a reddish hue is commercially acceptable. Since they are very sweet (10 to 14% sugar), bitterness or astringency is seldom a problem. A few producers cannot resist the temptation to use too much vanilla or peppermint in their vermouth formulations. Baked sweet sherries usually have too much caramel odor to be used as base wines for sweet vermouths.

C. Byrrh

Byrrh is a sweet, medium-red, French proprietary wine containing cinchona. The obvious bitterness and astringency are normal. As a rule the wine is not aged, but connoisseurs of Byrrh are reported to favor bottle aging for several years (to reduce the bitterness?). A sediment can be tolerated in aged samples but not in market samples.

D. Dubonnet

Dubonnet is another French proprietary wine. It is less red than Byrrh (there is a white Dubonnet also) and the herb mixture is not bitter, nor is it as pronounced as in vermouth. For some years Dubonnet has also been made in California for the American market. The flavor appears to be very similar but the base wine seems to us less tart than that of the French product.

II. Fruit-based and fruit-flavor-based

Fruit wines have been produced for many years. The chief factors in their sensory quality are the degree of specific fruit flavor and the balance of sugar and acid in the finished wines. Most (all?) fruit wines lose much of their specific fruit character within a year of production. Since the natural fruits (such as blackberries, peaches, and gooseberries) contain too little sugar and too much acid to produce a balanced wine, amelioration with sugar and water is needed. The sugar increases the

final ethanol content and the water reduces the acidity. In order to mask the still high acidity some fruit wines are finished with 5 to 10% sugar. Fruit wine producers also claim, probably with justification, that the fruit character is improved by an increase in sugar content.

Since 1957 many fruit-flavored wines have been produced in the United States. Thunderbird, Silver Satin, and other proprietary wines have citrus flavors added. Wines with both less than and more than 14% ethanol are made, with varying amounts of sugar (from 5 to 14%). Passion fruit and other flavors are used in similar products, such as Bali Hai. For each of these wines the distinctive proprietary character seems to be the first consideration. Is the fruit flavor distinctive but not too much so? In our opinion some are too distinctive and the consumer is likely to lose interest. This is a problem with all flavored wines. Does the wine have a reasonable shelf life? We have found a number of such flavored wines that darkened and lost an appreciable amount of their fruit character in no more than three or four months of aging at room temperature. Others are stable for a year or more. We believe that improvement in quality could be achieved with greater complexity of flavor.

More recently, proprietary wines using grape and apple base wines and having more or less excess carbon dioxide have been produced. Again the shelf life is usually short. Perhaps the producers should call attention to this fact. As an example of what can be done, consider the dairy industry, which now regularly marks many of its products with a date beyond which freshness is not guaranteed. It is also worth noting the short shelf life that some conscientious beer producers permit their products, especially in warm climates. If *vins nouveaux* continue to be produced (we wouldn't bet on it) we would also recommend that a date of three to six months following the vintage be given as the cutoff date for optimum quality.

The strawberry and other flavored wines are pleasant enough with the first taste but they do not often maintain *our* interest. After the wine ages for a year or two the typical

fruit character is usually more or less attenuated. For those who do find such wines interesting we believe the fruity flavor should be typical of the fruit named and not have any foreign character. Moreover, we see nothing inherently wrong with an artificial flavor if its presence is clearly stated. The labels on some of the imported cherry and plum wines do not make it clear whether the fruit flavor is derived entirely from the fruit named.

There are only a few wines with ripe fruits used for flavoring. Originally in Spain, red wine, sugar, and citrus fruits (plus carbonated water or ice, sometimes) were used to produce sangria, especially as a summer drink. Several similar beverages have been produced in the United States and in Spain as bottled wines. We have found some of them to be lacking in freshness, to have an "off" citrus note, and to be disappointing in general. We realize, however, that several have had considerable consumer acceptance. We applaud their success but are unable to understand why such ordinary wines should enjoy it.

Wine is the intellectual part of a meal; meats are merely the material part.
—A. Dumas

Drinking the right wine at the right time is an art.
—H. A. Vachell

II
STATISTICAL
PROCEDURES

No food product has a longer history of quality evaluation than wine. Homer, Pliny, and Horace wrote of wines that were famous long before, or at the beginning of, the Christian era. The fame of these wines was undoubtedly based on subjective comparisons, or perhaps even on some sort of deliberate sensory examinations.

Prior to 1940 many quality evaluations in the wine industry were performed by only one or two professionals. Even today, considerable quantities of wine are purchased by skilled wine brokers who base their selections solely on their own evaluations. However, with increasing consumer demand for better wines, greater competition among wine producers, and the development of appropriate statistical procedures for the analysis of sensory data, many wine professionals have concluded that it is unsound to rely on the quality and standards-of-identity judgments of only one or two individuals.

Today it is standard practice in many wineries and wine-distributing companies (and, indeed, throughout the entire food industry) to have regular panel evaluations, not only for quality control of their own products, but also for comparisons with competing products. The data obtained in such evaluations should be subjected to appropriate statistical analysis. Unfortunately, reported differences among wines often imply significance when there is, in fact, no statistical justification for such a conclusion. It is the purpose of Part II of this book to encourage the use of statistical procedures for the analysis of sensory data.

Fundamentals

In Part I of this book we have referred to the importance of statistical procedures in providing tests of significance. A discussion of significance of experimental data is usually based on a comparison of the actual results with those that would be obtained if chance alone were the determining factor. Since the interpretation of such tests depends upon the probabilities of the events in question, some understanding of the concept of probability is essential.

Probability. Briefly, the probability of an event can be defined as the relative frequency of that event in a large number of trials. From this definition it is clear that probability is a number between 0 and 1. An event with probability $p = 0$ cannot occur, and one with probability $p = 1$ is certain to occur. When we say that the probability of getting heads on the toss of a well-balanced coin is $\frac{1}{2}$, we mean that one of every two tosses, *on the average*, will give heads. In other words, it is probable that in a large number of tosses 50% heads and 50% tails will be obtained. This does not mean that in 10 tosses of a coin we will get *exactly* 5 heads and 5 tails, nor that in 100 tosses we will get exactly 50 heads and 50 tails. However, if we continue tossing the coin indefinitely, the ratio of the number of heads (or tails) to the total number of tosses will approach the value $\frac{1}{2}$ (0.5) ever more closely.

Imagine that a judge is presented with three glasses, two of which contain the same wine and the third a different but very

similar wine. If he cannot detect a difference among the three, chance alone will determine his ability to pick the odd wine. The probability that he will be successful in doing this is $\frac{1}{3}$; the probability that he will fail is $\frac{2}{3}$.

In a sequence of trials in each of which a certain result may or may not occur, the occurrence of the result is called a *success* and its nonoccurrence a *failure*. In a sequence of coin tosses, for example, getting heads might be designated a success; getting tails would therefore constitute a failure. This terminology is purely conventional, and the result called success need not necessarily be the desired one. The sum of the probabilities of success and failure for a given result is always equal to 1. Therefore, if the probability of success is p, the probability of failure is $1 - p$.

Problems requiring a statistical treatment of events (or results) often entail decisions based on a limited number of observations, the conclusions from which are to apply to a much larger category of events, of which those actually observed are only a part. The larger category about which we wish information is called the *population* (or universe) and the actual observations constitute the *sample*. If the sample is selected in such a way that all components of the population have an equal chance of being included, the sample is called a *random sample*. A quantity calculated from a sample, e.g., its standard deviation (see page 130), is called a *sample statistic*, or simply a *statistic*. Using a statistic to draw conclusions concerning a population from a sample of that population is called *statistical inference*. For such conclusions to be valid the sample must be randomly selected.

Null Hypothesis. The statistical method used in any scientific investigation originates with an investigator's idea, which leads to a tentative hypothesis about the population to be studied. This hypothesis, commonly called the *null hypothesis*, must be a specific assumption, made about some statistical measure of the population, with which to compare the experimental results. For example, in the toss of a fair coin the null hypothesis, $p = \frac{1}{2}$, states that in a single toss the chances are one in two (50:50) that a head will show.

In a consideration of a judge's ability to differentiate between two wine samples of differing quality, the null hypothesis, $p = \frac{1}{2}$, states that the chances are 50:50 that the judge will make the correct decision, i.e., it states that he does not have the sensory ability to detect a difference. In the previous example of the judge trying to select the odd wine sample from three, two of which are alike, the null hypothesis, $p = \frac{1}{3}$, states that the chances are one in three that the judge will correctly select the odd sample, i.e., it states that he does not have the sensory ability required for this task. In a comparison of the average quality ratings (scores) of two different wines, the null hypothesis, $\mu_1 - \mu_2 = 0$, states that the difference between the mean scores μ_1 and μ_2 for the two populations is zero, i.e., there are no quality differences between the two wine populations from which the samples were selected.

Statistical methods allow us to predict whether or not a null hypothesis is likely to be true or false. A *statistical test*, which is a decision rule or procedure, is then applied to the observed results to decide whether they agree sufficiently well with the expected values to support the null hypothesis or to suggest its rejection in favor of an *alternative hypothesis*. An alternative to the null hypothesis ($p = \frac{1}{2}$) of no sensory ability to differentiate between two wine samples might be $p > \frac{1}{2}$. This alternative hypothesis states that in a single trial the probability of the judge's making the correct decision is greater than $\frac{1}{2}$, i.e., it states that he does have some sensory ability to perform the task. If this hypothesis is true, the chances of his being successful in detecting a difference are therefore better than 50:50. Analogously, an alternative to the null hypothesis of $p = \frac{1}{3}$ might be $p > \frac{1}{3}$. The null hypothesis is usually designated H_0 and the alternative hypothesis H_1.

An alternative hypothesis is called a *one-sided alternative* and the corresponding test a *one-tailed test* if the hypothesis specifies a value on only one side of the value stated in the null hypothesis. The alternative hypotheses $p > \frac{1}{2}$ and $p > \frac{1}{3}$ are therefore both

one-sided. If, however, an alternative hypothesis specifies values on both sides of the value stated in the null hypothesis, it is called a *two-sided alternative* and the corresponding test is called a *two-tailed test*. One- and two-tailed tests are illustrated in Figures 1 and 2. We will discuss these illustrations in detail shortly.

Types of Errors.   Decision rules are seldom infallible and may lead to rejection of a true hypothesis, which is called an error of the first kind, or a *type I error*. Or, they may lead to acceptance of a false hypothesis, which is called an error of the second kind, or a *type II error*. The probabilities of occurrence of these errors can be minimized but never reduced to zero.

Experimental results rarely lead to obvious conclusions, and the question immediately arises as to the dividing line between acceptance and rejection of the null hypothesis. By a commonly accepted convention the null hypothesis is rejected if, under the

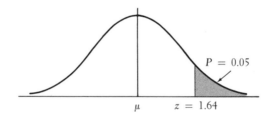

FIGURE 1
One-tailed test, 5% level.

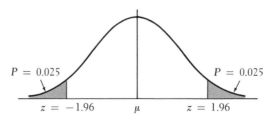

FIGURE 2
Two-tailed test, 5% level.

hypothesis, the result observed in the sample would occur by chance alone *at most* once in 20 trials ($P \leq 0.05$).* Such a result is called *significant.* If, under the null hypothesis and by chance alone, the result would occur at most once in 100 trials ($P \leq 0.01$), it is called *highly significant,* and if it would occur at most once in 1000 trials ($P \leq 0.001$), it is called *very highly significant.* These are known as the 5%, 1%, and 0.1% levels of significance, respectively. It should be understood, however, that, although we accept or reject the null hypothesis on the basis of these levels, we have not proved or disproved it, because there is always the possibility, however remote, that the difference between the observed result and that expected under the null hypothesis could have arisen by chance alone. At the 5% level of significance ($P = 0.05$) we wrongly reject the null hypothesis 5% of the time; at the 1% level ($P = 0.01$) we wrongly reject it 1% of the time; and at the 0.1% level ($P = 0.001$) we wrongly reject it 0.1% of the time, or once every 1000 times, on the average.

Frequency Distributions

For large sets of data comprising many values of a given variable, some form of summarization is needed so that the main features can be readily observed. The simplest method of arranging the data is to divide the whole range of values into a number of equal intervals called class intervals and to count the number of values falling within each such interval. The number of values within a class interval is called the class frequency, or simply the *frequency.* This set of frequencies is called a *frequency distribution.* If the actual frequencies are expressed as fractions of the total frequency, the resulting distribution is called a *probability distribution.* Before considering specific testing procedures we will briefly discuss the usefulness of two frequency distributions—the normal

*The small p introduced earlier is used to denote the probability of a simple event, such as getting heads in a single toss of a coin. The capital P is used to denote the probability of a composite of simple events, such as getting 3 heads in 5 tosses of a coin.

and chi-square (χ^2) distributions—in problems concerning sensory evaluation.

Normal Distribution. The normal distribution can be used to estimate the probabilities of chance results in a judge's performance, but *only* in a task in which there are only *two* possible events, such as picking the odd sample correctly (success) or picking it incorrectly (failure). Probabilities in the distribution are represented by areas under the *normal probability curve*, which is bell-shaped and symmetrical about the mean, μ, of the distribution. Because the value of any normally distributed variable *must* fall somewhere, i.e., because the probability of its falling *anywhere* is 1, the total area (probability) under the curve is equal to 1. Tables for the normal probability curve list the values of the areas (probabilities) corresponding to various values of z, the *normal deviate*, which is defined as the deviation $X - \mu$ measured in terms of the standard deviation, σ:

$$z = \frac{X - \mu}{\sigma} \tag{1}$$

Here X is the value of any normally distributed variable with mean μ, and σ, the standard deviation, is a measure of the dispersion (scatter) in the distribution of X-values about the mean. The smaller the value of σ, the more tightly the X-values cluster about the mean; approximately $\frac{2}{3}$ of them fall between $\mu - \sigma$ and $\mu + \sigma$. The probability of a chance result is a maximum (midpoint on the curve) when $z = 0$, i.e., when $X = \mu$.

In sensory evaluations in which the null hypothesis, H_0, specifies the probability p of success (correct choice) in a single trial, the mean μ (expected number of successes) in n trials is equal to np, and the standard deviation σ can be shown to be $\sqrt{np(1 - p)}$. The *observed* number X of successes is obtained by counting and is therefore always a whole number (integer). When it is used in finding areas under the normal probability curve—which is continuous and therefore permits fractional as well as integral values—X, if it is greater than μ, must be reduced by the number 0.5. This is called a *correction for continuity*. For

Table 1. Values of z and χ^2 at three levels of significance.

LEVEL OF SIGNIFICANCE	DIFFERENCE (ONE-TAILED)		PREFERENCE (TWO-TAILED)	
	$\pm z$	χ^2	z	χ^2
5% (significant)	± 1.64	2.71	1.96	3.84
1% (highly significant)	± 2.33	5.41	2.58	6.64
0.1% (very highly significant)	± 3.09	9.55	3.30	10.82

example, 5 or more on a counting scale is recorded as 4.5 or more on a continuous scale. Then the normal deviate becomes

$$z = \frac{(X - 0.5) - \mu}{\sigma} = \frac{(X - 0.5) - np}{\sqrt{np(1 - p)}} \tag{2}$$

Appendix A gives areas under the normal probability curve to the right of positive values of z or to the left of the corresponding negative values of z. Because the curve is symmetrical the two areas are the same, so only the area to the right of a positive value of z is shown in the graph there and only positive values of z are listed. For a one-tailed test the notation $+z_{.05}$ is used to denote that value of z to the right of which 5% of the total area lies, as shown in Figure 1. Analogously, $-z_{.05}$ would be the value to the left of which 5% of the area lies. From Table 1 we see that, in a one-tailed test, $+z_{.05} = +1.64$ and $-z_{.01} = -2.33$. In a two-tailed test the notation $z_{.05}$ denotes that value of z that defines two tail areas, each of which contains 2.5% of the total area, as shown in Figure 2. From Table 1 we see that, in a two-tailed test, $z_{.05} = 1.96$ and $z_{.01} = 2.58$.

Example 1. A judge is presented with three glasses of wine. Two glasses contain the same wine and the third glass a different but similar wine. He is asked to pick the odd sample. What is the probability that, by chance alone, he will be successful 9 or more times in 18 trials?

The formulation of the question ($9 \leq X \leq 18$) implies that we need to find the area under the normal probability curve between the z values corresponding to $X = 9$ and $X = 18$. Be-

cause the probability of the judge's being successful in all 18 trials is vanishingly small, however, the area under the curve to the right of the z value corresponding to $X = 18$ is so small that we can include it without introducing any significant error. We can therefore simply let $X = 9$ and find the entire area (to within the accuracy of 4 significant figures, as given in Appendix A) to the right of the corresponding z value.

The probability p of a correct choice in a single trial is $\frac{1}{3}$ and the number of trials n is 18. Therefore $\mu = np = 6$, $\sigma = \sqrt{np(1 - p)} = \sqrt{18(\frac{1}{3})(\frac{2}{3})} = \sqrt{4} = 2$, and, since $X = 9$,

$$z = \frac{(X - 0.5) - \mu}{\sigma} = \frac{(9 - 0.5) - 6}{2} = \frac{2.5}{2} = 1.25$$

From Appendix A we see that, for $z = 1.25$, $P = 0.1056$. This is the probability (i.e., the chance is about 10 to 11%) that, by chance alone, the judge will correctly identify the odd sample 9 or more times in 18 trials.

Chi-Square (χ^2) ***Distribution.***   The chi-square distribution is useful in comparing a set of k observed frequencies (o) with a corresponding set of k expected or hypothesized frequencies (e), particularly when k is greater than 2. The appropriate statistic, which is called *chi-square*, is defined as

$$\chi^2 = \sum \frac{(o - e)^2}{e} \tag{3}$$

where the Greek letter Σ denotes the sum of the k terms $(o_1 - e_1)^2/e_1 + (o_2 - e_2)^2/e_2 + \cdots + (o_k - e_k)^2/e_k$. If the events in question are those of success and failure, as in the examples we have been considering, then $k = 2$, so there are two observed frequencies and two expected frequencies. Chi-square is never negative because in each term the numerator is squared and the denominator is positive. If the observed and expected frequencies agree exactly in every one of the k terms, then $\chi^2 = 0$. It has a positive value if there is any difference between an observed and expected frequency, and it increases as the difference becomes greater.

The distribution of χ^2 depends upon the number of independent differences, called *degrees of freedom* (*df*). Since the sum of all the expected frequencies, $\sum e$, must agree with the sum of all the observed frequencies, $\sum o$, the sum of all the differences is $\sum(o - e) = 0$. Therefore only $k - 1$ of the expected values are independent, and the remaining one can be calculated from the relation $\sum(o - e) = 0$. The number of degrees of freedom is therefore, $k - 1$. Values of χ^2 for various combinations of probabilities and numbers of degrees of freedom are given in Appendix B.

Imagine a series of n trials, with X observed successes and $n - X$ failures. If the null hypothesis specifies the probability of success in a single trial as p, and therefore that of failure as $1 - p$, χ^2 takes the form

$$\chi^2 = \frac{(|X - np| - 0.5)^2}{np} + \frac{[|(n - X) - n(1 - p)| - 0.5]^2}{n(1 - p)}$$

$$= (|X - np| - 0.5)^2[1/np + 1/n(1 - p)]$$

$$= \frac{(|X - np| - 0.5)^2}{np(1 - p)} \tag{4}$$

where $|X - np|$ is the *absolute value* of the expression $X - np$, i.e., it is the value without regard to algebraic sign (it can therefore be interpreted as a positive quantity). As in the normal distribution, the number -0.5 is a correction for continuity because the χ^2 curve is also continuous, whereas the observed frequencies can only be integers. This correction is applicable only for 1 *df*, which holds for the examples we have been considering, because $k = 2$ (success and failure). In this case the one-tailed probability associated with a value of χ^2 equals the two-tailed probability associated with the corresponding value of z, the normal deviate.

Example 2. Use χ^2 to estimate the probability in Example 1.

$$\chi^2 = \frac{(|X - np| - 0.5)^2}{np(1 - p)} = \frac{(|9 - 6| - 0.5)^2}{18(\frac{1}{3})(\frac{2}{3})} = \frac{(2.5)^2}{4}$$

$$= 1.56$$

From Appendix B we see that, for 1 *df*, $\chi^2 = 1.56$ is very close to the value 1.64, which corresponds to a probability of 0.20.

Since this equals the total probability for both tails of the normal distribution, the one-tailed probability is close to 0.10, which agrees with the result obtained in Example 1.

The applications and appropriateness of the statistical terms and reasoning outlined above will be evident in the discussions and examples that follow.

Difference Tests

Difference tests are used in the comparison of two wines to evaluate objectively the differences between them, to test the ability of judges to make comparisons of chemical constituents or sensory characteristics, and, on the basis of preference ratings, to establish quality differences.

Sensory evaluations are usually conducted by a small laboratory panel of judges or by members of the consuming public. The number of panelists in laboratory testing varies with conditions, such as the number of qualified persons available. Many investigators recommend panels of 5 to 10 members; we agree. Large panels are customary in preference tests in which the only criterion for the selection of members is representativeness of some consumer population. Laboratory panels can suggest probable consumer reactions but any resulting conclusions relating to the consuming public should be very carefully evaluated. We view such conclusions with considerable skepticism because the relation of the laboratory panel to the consuming public is generally not clear.

The results of a sensory evaluation have little meaning unless the panelists have demonstrated the ability to detect differences that *can* be detected, and to do so consistently. These differences are often very subtle and difficult to detect. Obviously the panel should consist of individuals with the greatest sensitivity and experience. *When no difference can be established, the question of preference is obviously irrelevant.*

Although in the usual statistical analysis the assumptions and test procedures used for one judge making n comparisons are the same as those used for n judges making a single comparison each,

these two experiments are not the same. In all difference tests it is customary to assume an unchanging fundamental probability. Tests based on this assumption are more reliable when performed by one "competent" judge, but even then their validity is doubtful owing to the possibility of fatigue and the effects of various psychological factors (see page 50). The problems encountered in panel or consumer tests are even more complicated because of varying thresholds and differing directions of preference. To conform to basic assumptions in detecting possible differences it is clearly important to use the best judge or judges available.

It has already been pointed out (page 62) that in all trials in wine evaluations the samples should be presented as uniformly as possible—at the same temperature, in identical glasses, but in different orders. Three testing procedures in common use are the paired-sample, duo-trio, and triangle tests.

Paired-Sample Test.   In this test the judge is presented with two samples and asked to identify the one with the greater intensity of a specific constituent or well-defined characteristic (see Figure 3). Or, he may be asked to express a preference. This procedure may be carried out by one judge several times or by a panel of judges one or more times. Based on the null hypothesis of no difference, about one-half of the responses should be correct by chance alone, i.e., $H_0: p = \frac{1}{2}$.

Type of test
(e.g., sweetness of wine)

Taste both samples. Circle the sweeter of the two.

Test	Samples
1	_____ _____
2	_____ _____
3	_____ _____

Name _____ Date _____

FIGURE 3
Record form for paired-sample test.

The paired-sample test is useful not only in quality control and preference evaluation but also in the selection of judges. The presence of more or less of some constituent in one of the samples may already be known to the experimenter, or it can be determined by a specific chemical test. If, in several trials, the judge makes the differentiation correctly significantly more often than would be expected by chance ($p = \frac{1}{2}$), the experimenter can infer that the judge does possess some ability to detect that particular constituent. In this case a one-tailed test is applicable and the alternative hypothesis is H_1: $p > \frac{1}{2}$ because the judge shows ability only if he can make the correct choice more often than he could by guessing. The one-tailed *region of significance* in the normal distribution is shown in Figure 4 for the 5% level. Calculated values of z that exceed $+1.64$, the value at the 5% level ($+z_{.05}$), indicate a significant differentiation ability.

In preference testing the judge is asked to express a preference between two wines. A statistically significant preponderance of selections of one wine over the other then indicates a significant preference difference and, therefore (assuming the judge's tastes are conventional), a significant, objective quality difference. Since either wine may be the preferred one (i.e., since the selection of a given wine very infrequently is just as meaningful as its selection very frequently), the alternative hypothesis here is H_1: $p \neq \frac{1}{2}$ and the two-tailed test is applicable. The two-tailed region of significance in the normal distribution is shown in Figure 5 for the 5%

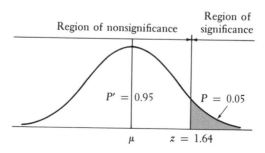

FIGURE 4

One-tailed test, 5% level. H_0: $p = \frac{1}{2}$. H_1: $p > \frac{1}{2}$.

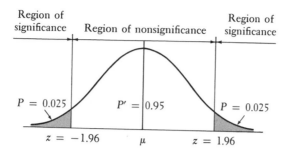

FIGURE 5

Two-tailed test, 5% level. H_0: $p = \frac{1}{2}$. H_1: $p \neq \frac{1}{2}$.

level. Calculated values of z that numerically exceed 1.96, the value at the 5% level ($z_{.05}$), indicate a significant preference or quality difference.

Duo-Trio Test. This test is a modified paired-sample test, in which a reference sample is identified and presented first, followed by two coded samples, one of which is identical to the reference sample. The judge is asked to decide which of the two coded samples is the same as the reference sample (see Figure 6). As in the paired-sample test, the null hypothesis is $H_0: p = \frac{1}{2}$ because, by chance alone, the judge will pick the correct sample about one-

Type of test
(e.g., comparison of old and new blends)

Taste or smell (or both) the reference sample and the two coded samples. Decide which of the latter is the same as the reference sample.

Test	Coded samples		Sample same as reference sample
1	____	____	____
2	____	____	____
3	____	____	____

Name _____ Date _____

FIGURE 6

Record form for duo-trio test.

half of the time. Since this is a difference test, it is one-tailed. It is especially applicable in quality control, in which a sample is to be compared with a reference standard.

Triangle Test. In the triangle test the judge is presented with three samples, two of which are identical. He is asked to select the odd sample (see Figure 7). The probability of a correct choice by chance alone is one-third, i.e., the null hypothesis is $H_0: p = \frac{1}{3}$. The test is easy to administer and is also useful in quality control.

The duo-trio and triangle procedures should be used only for difference (one-tailed) testing, as described above, because it has been shown that having two samples of one wine and one sample of the other tends to cause bias in preference judgments.

For various numbers of trials in the paired-sample and duo-trio tests, Appendix C gives the minimum numbers of correct judgments required to establish a significant difference (one-tailed test) at the 5%, 1%, and 0.1% levels. Also given, for the paired-sample test, are the minimum numbers of agreeing judgments required to establish a significant preference (two-tailed test). Appendix D gives analogous information for establishing a significant difference in the triangle test. Values for $X > \mu$ that are not in the tables can be found by solving the following equations:

Type of test
(e.g., difference in wine flavored by two agents)

Taste or smell (or both) all three samples. Decide which of the three is unlike the other two.

Test	Samples			Sample unlike the other two
1	_____	_____	_____	_____
2	_____	_____	_____	_____
3	_____	_____	_____	_____

Name _____ Date _____

FIGURE 7
Record form for triangle test.

$$X = \frac{n + z\sqrt{n} + 1}{2} \quad \text{or} \quad X = \frac{n + \sqrt{n\chi^2} + 1}{2}$$

for $p = \frac{1}{2}$ (one- or two-tailed) (5)

and

$$X = \frac{2n + 2.83z\sqrt{n} + 3}{6} \quad \text{or} \quad X = \frac{2n + 2.83\sqrt{n\chi^2} + 3}{6}$$

for $p = \frac{1}{3}$ (one-tailed only) (6)

In n trials (number of judges or judgments) the minimum number of correct or agreeing judgments required for significance is the next greater integer above the value of X obtained from the appropriate equation above, for the value of z or χ^2 found in Table 1. Values of z for other levels of significance can be found in Appendix A, and values of χ^2 in Appendix B.

Example 3. In a paired-sample test a judge is given two glasses containing a dry white table wine, to one of which a small amount of ethyl acetate has been added. Fourteen times in 20 trials he correctly identifies the adulterated sample. From Appendix C we see that in 20 trials at least 15 correct judgments are required for significance at the 5% level. On the basis of this test, therefore, the judge is not able to detect the ethyl acetate that has been added.

Example 4. In a paired-sample test 50 judges are asked to express their preference for one of two wines. Thirty-six preferences are expressed for wine S_1 and 14 for wine S_2. From Appendix C we see that the minimum number of agreeing judgments required for significance at the 5% level in a two-tailed test is 33, and at the 1% level, 35. On the basis of this test, wine S_1 is judged better than wine S_2 at both the 5% (significant) and 1% (highly significant) levels. Therefore the chances of being wrong in rejecting the null hypothesis (H_0: $p = \frac{1}{2}$) of there being no difference between the wines are less than one in 100.

Example 5. In a duo-trio test of 24 trials, how many correct identifications of the identical samples are required for significance at the 5% and 1% levels? From Appendix C we see that, for a one-tailed test, at least 17 and 19 correct identifications are required for significance at the 5% and 1% levels, respectively.

Example 6. In a triangle test a judge correctly identifies the odd sample in 13 of 23 trials. He therefore indicates ability at the 5% level of significance because, from Appendix D, at least 13 correct identifications are required at this level.

Example 7. In a paired-sample preference test with 64 trials, how many agreeing judgments are required for significance at the 5% level? Since $n = 64$ does not appear in Appendix C, we use Equation 5 to determine X, the number of agreeing judgments required.

$$X = \frac{64 + 1.96\sqrt{64} + 1}{2} = \frac{64 + 1.96(8) + 1}{2} = 40.3$$

Therefore at least 41 agreeing judgments are required at the 5% level of significance.

In testing procedures entailing two or more wines, differences among wine samples can be established by quantitative measures obtained from score cards or other means of scoring, by ranking, or by hedonic rating. We will discuss each of these procedures, but first we must examine in more detail the procedures for selecting judges.

Sequential Procedure for Selection of Judges

When paired-sample, duo-trio, and triangle tests are used in the selection of judges, a predetermined number of trials is employed and those candidates showing the greatest ability are selected. Questions have been raised regarding the number of trials needed and the quality of the judges thus obtained. Often too

little testing is done because of limitations of time and suitable experimental material.

Sequential procedures can provide considerable improvement over other selection procedures and can save valuable time and materials. In a sequential testing plan the number of trials is not predetermined, and the decision to terminate the experiment at any time depends upon the previous results. The sequential procedure described here is a modification of that developed by Wald (1947) and adapted by Bradley (1953).

Let p be the true proportion of correct decisions that would be obtained in paired-sample, duo-trio, or triangle tests if the potential judge were to continue testing indefinitely. This is a measure of his inherent ability in the test in question. Values of p_0 and p_1 are specified such that individuals having abilities equal to or greater than p_1 will be accepted as judges, and those with abilities equal to or less than p_0 will be rejected. The testing plan depends upon the values assigned to p_0 and p_1 and also upon the values of α and β, the probabilities of committing errors of the first and second kind, respectively (α is the probability of rejecting a qualified judge and β is the probability of accepting an unqualified one). Potential judges are accepted or rejected on the basis of their performance with respect to a chart of two parallel straight lines L_0 and L_1, which are uniquely determined by the assigned values of p_0, p_1, α, and β. These lines divide the plane into three regions: one of acceptance, one of rejection, and one of indecision, as shown in Figure 8.

The equations of the lines are

$$L_0: d_0 = a_0 + bn \quad \text{and} \quad L_1: d_1 = a_1 + bn \qquad (7)$$

where n is the total number of trials, d (either one) is the accumulated number of correct decisions, b is the common slope of the two lines, and a_0 and a_1 are the intercepts on the vertical axis. The common slope b of L_0 and L_1 is

$$b = k_2/(k_1 + k_2) \qquad (8)$$

and the intercepts a_0 and a_1 are

$$a_0 = -e_1/(k_1 + k_2) \quad \text{and} \quad a_1 = e_2/(k_1 + k_2) \qquad (9)$$

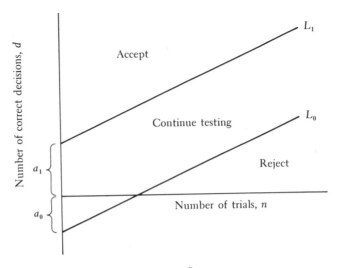

Sequential test chart.

where

$$k_1 = \log(p_1/p_0) = \log p_1 - \log p_0$$
$$k_2 = \log[(1 - p_0)/(1 - p_1)] = \log(1 - p_0) - \log(1 - p_1)$$
$$e_1 = \log[(1 - \beta)/\alpha] = \log(1 - \beta) - \log \alpha$$
$$e_2 = \log[(1 - \alpha)/\beta] = \log(1 - \alpha) - \log \beta$$

After each trial the experimenter plots the point (d, n), representing the accumulated number of correct decisions (vertical scale) versus the total number of trials (horizontal scale). Each plotted point is therefore one n unit to the right of the preceding point, and is either one d unit above the preceding point or on the same horizontal level, depending on whether the decision was correct or incorrect, respectively. Testing continues until a plotted point falls on or above the upper line, resulting in acceptance of the candidate as a judge, or on or below the lower line, resulting in his rejection.

The number of trials required depends upon the ability of the potential judge and on the assigned values of p_0, p_1, α, and β, which are determined by the experimenter. Before committing himself to a given set of values the experimenter may wish to know the average number of trials that can be expected for that set of values. The number of trials required can be decreased by increasing the difference between p_0 and p_1 or by increasing α or β, or both. If competent judges are in good supply the experimenter may wish to increase α and accept a greater risk of rejecting a competent judge.

The average number of trials to be expected, $\bar{n}$, can be obtained from among four calculated values corresponding to special values of p, as shown below.

$p = 0$ (no ability)

$$\bar{n}_0 = e_1/k_2$$

$p = p_0$ (maximum unacceptable ability)

$$\bar{n}_{p_0} = \frac{(1 - \beta)e_1 - \beta e_2}{(1 - p_0)k_2 - p_0 k_1}$$

$p = p_1$ (minimum acceptable ability)

$$\bar{n}_{p_1} = \frac{(1 - \alpha)e_2 - \alpha e_1}{p_1 k_1 - (1 - p_1)k_2}$$

$p = 1$ (infallible ability)

$$\bar{n}_1 = e_2/k_1$$

The average number of trials to be expected is the largest of these four values.

Example 8. Suppose that a triangle test is used as a basis for selecting judges in a sequential procedure. For the assigned values $p_0 = 0.45$, $p_1 = 0.70$, $\alpha = 0.10$, and $\beta = 0.05$, find the average number of trials to be expected. (Competent judges are in good supply, so α is being taken as 0.10.)

We begin by finding the values of k and e:

$$k_1 = \log(0.70/0.45) = 0.1919$$
$$k_2 = \log(0.55/0.30) = 0.2632$$
$$e_1 = \log(0.95/0.10) = 0.9777$$
$$e_2 = \log(0.90/0.05) = 1.2553$$

We then use these values in the four equations for $\bar{n}$:

$$\bar{n}_0 = 0.9777/0.2632 = 3.7$$

$$\bar{n}_{p_0} = \frac{(0.95)\,(0.9777) - (0.05)\,(1.2553)}{(0.55)\,(0.2632) - (0.45)\,(0.1919)} = \frac{0.866}{0.058} = 14.9$$

$$\bar{n}_{p_1} = \frac{(0.90)\,(1.2553) - (0.10)\,(0.9777)}{(0.70)\,(0.1919) - (0.30)\,(0.2632)} = \frac{1.032}{0.055} = 18.8$$

$$\bar{n}_1 = 1.2553/0.1919 = 6.5$$

We see that the test will require an average of 19 trials. The number required for each candidate will, of course, depend upon his inherent ability, p.

Example 9. Using the values of k and e calculated in Example 8, find the equations of the lines L_0 and L_1.

From Equations 8 and 9 we obtain

$$b = 0.2632/0.4551 = 0.578$$

$$a_0 = -0.9777/0.4551 = -2.15$$

$$a_1 = 1.2553/0.4551 = 2.76$$

The equations of the lines are therefore

$$L_0: \quad d_0 = -2.15 + 0.578n$$

$$L_1: \quad d_1 = 2.76 + 0.578n$$

Example 10. The performances of two candidates for wine judge, A and B, are shown in the table below, where a 1 indicates a correct decision and a 0 an incorrect decision. Evaluate their performances with respect to the lines L_0 and L_1 and determine the number of trials after which each candidate is either accepted or rejected.

No. of trials	n:	1	2	3	4	5	6	7	8	9	10	11	12	13	14	15	16	17	18	19
Decisions	A:	1	0	1	0	0	0	1	0	1	1	0	0	0						
	B:	1	1	1	0	1	0	0	1	1	1	0	1	1	1	0	1	1	1	1
No. of correct	A:	1	1	2	2	2	2	3	3	4	5	5	5	5						
decisions, d	B:	1	2	3	3	4	4	4	5	6	7	7	8	9	10	10	11	12	13	14

The performances of A and B are shown in Figure 9, in which the number of correct decisions is plotted against the

121

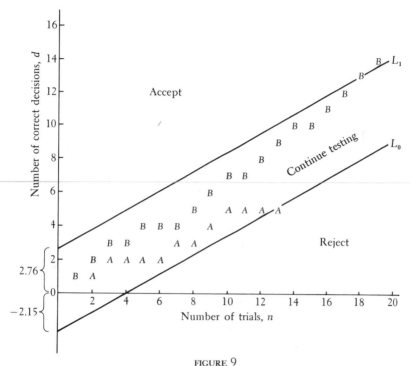

FIGURE 9
Performances of candidates A and B in a sequential test procedure.

total number of trials. By the criteria specified for the sequential procedure, we see that A is rejected as a judge after 13 trials and B is accepted after 19 trials.

Scoring

With experienced judges scoring is usually the most acceptable procedure for establishing differences among wine samples because it measures the magnitudes of the differences. The scoring scale to be used must be clearly defined and understood by all the judges. A 9-point quality scale (see Figure 10) has been widely used. It is an example of an ordinal scale (Stone et al., 1974). The judge

Wine sample ————————

Check the appropriate quality.

———————— Excellent

———————— Very good

———————— Good

———————— Below good, above fair

———————— Fair

———————— Below fair, above poor

———————— Poor

———————— Very poor

———————— Extremely poor

Name ———————————————————————— Date ————————————

FIGURE 10

A 9-point quality scale.

checks the appropriate quality, which is converted to a numerical score: 1 for extremely poor to 9 for excellent.

In the evaluation of overall wine quality, score cards usually provide for 10-point or 20-point rating scales. On the basis of a 20-point scale the following groupings are suggested: (a) *superior* (17–20 points)—wines of fine quality, well-balanced, no pronounced defects, and free of excess "young" character; (b) *standard* (13–16 points)—the wines of commerce (including ordinary bottled wines), not deficient in any important characteristic, but lacking proper age or the balance required for fine quality; (c) *below standard* (9–12 points)—wines lacking some required characteristic or suffering from some malady (wines with off odors or off taste or high volatile acidity); (d) *unacceptable*, or *spoiled* (1–8 points)—wines so spoiled that they must be discarded. See pages 130–161 for methods of analyzing the results.

Davis Score Card. The original, so-called Davis score card (see Figure 11) was developed by the staff of the Department of Viticulture and Enology at the University of California, Davis, as a method of rating the large number of experimental wines that were produced there. Later it was used as a training device for students who were beginning their education in the sensory evaluation of wines. This score card overemphasized some factors

Wine sample _____

Characteristic	Weight
Appearance	2
Color	2
Aroma and bouquet	4
Volatile acidity	2
Total acidity	2
Sweetness	1
Body	1
Flavor	2
Bitterness	2
General quality	2

Ratings: *superior* (17–20); *standard* (13–16); *below standard* (9–12); *unacceptable,* or *spoiled* (1–8).

Name _____ Date _____

FIGURE 11

The Davis score card. (The meanings specified for the total scores serve to assure relative uniformity of the judges' interpretations of these terms.)

(acescence, for example) and underemphasized others (aroma and bouquet being the worst examples). Among its other defects was that it did not differentiate between bitterness and astringency (page 42). The concepts of flavor (now generally regarded as odor perceived via the mouth) and general quality were not clearly defined. It also became apparent that the definitions of superior (17–20 points), standard (13–16 points), below standard (9–12 points), and unacceptable, or spoiled (1–8 points) varied from judge to judge, depending on the judge's experience and the severity of his judgment.

Despite these deficiencies the Davis score card has been successfully used by highly skilled judges at Davis without serious difficulty. In fact, the staff has learned to use it with remarkable precision of the results and their interpretation. As a pedagogical tool it has proved useful for both regularly enrolled students and those taking adult wine-appreciation courses. The above-mentioned problems are always explained to the students. A modified Davis score card is shown in Figure 12.

Wine sample _____

Characteristic	Weight
Appearance	2
Color	2
Aroma and bouquet	6
Total acidity	2
Sweetness	1
Body	1
Flavor	2
Bitterness	1
Astringency	1
General quality	2

Ratings: *superior* (17–20); *standard* (13–16); *below standard* (9–12); *unacceptable*, or *spoiled* (1–8).

Name _____ Date _____

FIGURE 12

A modified Davis score card.

In recent years the Davis score card has been used (or misused) by professional and amateur groups with less success. Most of the difficulty arises from varying interpretations of the score card. Some amateurs assign high scores to all the wines, whereas professionals usually spread their scores over a larger range. Disaster occurs when amateurs and professionals judge together and the average scores for the individual wines are used to rank the wines. This cannot be done safely without appropriate statistical analysis of the data, and the latter is hardly ever done.

One solution to this problem would be to hold one or more practice sessions of the group and discuss the meaning of the scores. Another possible solution would be to use the shorter, 10-point score card devised by Ough and Baker (1961). However, bunching of the scores in the 8-to-10-point range would then be even more acute than bunching in the 17-to-20-point range of the 20-point scale.

We recommend using only professional judges if the objective is to rank a group of wines in order of merit *by their scores.* The judges, though experienced, will still require one or more practice

sessions in which their scores are compared. Although it may embarrass a judge to be found scoring too high or too low, it is essential that this be revealed if the average scores are to be meaningful. Also, judges may have very different standards of excellence for different types of wines. With samples before them the judges should discuss the various types of wines to be evaluated. Questions such as the following must be discussed: What range of color will be tolerated in a given type of wine? What is the typical varietal aroma? How much fermentation bouquet can be allowed (especially in young white wines)? Are dry and sweet wines to be judged together? How much credit should be given for bottle bouquet (as in a well-aged red wine)? With respect to these and similar questions the differences between superior and standard wines must be clear to all the judges.

Other Score Cards.   A 20-point score card that avoids the detailed evaluation required for the Davis score card is shown in Figure 13 and appears very useful. Two noteworthy features of this score card are the provision for listing specific defects and the specification of the minimum acceptable number of points for each of the three categories. One disadvantage is the heavy weight given to taste in evaluating the wine.

Klenk (1972) has used the following, very similar 20-point score card: color, 2; appearance, 2; odor, 4; taste, 12. Again the taste contribution to quality seems to us to be greatly overemphasized. In competitions in which this scale was used, the gold medal was given to wines that scored 19.6 to 20, the silver medal to wines scoring 18.6 to 19.5, and the bronze medal to wines scoring 17.6 to 18.5. For example, Klenk gives data for 8 wines, each of which was judged by 4 judges. The averages were 20 and 19.9 (gold medal), 19.0, 19.0, and 18.8 (silver medal), and 18.5, 18.5, and 17.8 (bronze medal). Statistical analysis of Klenk's data shows that differences of less than 0.51 between average scores were not significant. Therefore the silver-medal wines and the first two bronze-medal wines were not significantly different from one another.

Klenk has also used a 40-point score card scaled as follows: color, 3; appearance, 3; odor, 10; taste, 24. We believe that this is too

Wine Evaluation
Seagram Wine Quality Laboratory

To: _____   Date: _____ Sample no.: _____

From: _____   Location: _____

Brand: _____   Type: _____

Producer: _____   Country: _____

Age: _____ % Ethanol: _____   No. of bottles: _____

Samples recd. from: _____   Date evaluated: _____

Identification of case, bottle, date, etc.: _____

Appearance	*Points*
Ordinary sound wine _____	3
Outstanding color and clarity (+1) _____	
Defects (−1 to −3) _____	
Total appearance points	
(Maximum 4; minimum acceptable 2)	

Odor	*Points*
Ordinary sound wine _____	2
Positive attributes (+1 to +2) _____	
Defects (−1 to −2) _____	
Total odor points	
(Maximum 4; minimum acceptable 1)	

Taste	*Points*
Ordinary sound wine _____	7
Positive attributes (+1 to +5) _____	
Defects (−1 to −7) _____	
Total taste points	
(Maximum 12; minimum acceptable 5)	
Total wine rating	
(Maximum 20; minimum acceptable 9)	

Ratings: *great* (18–20); *fine* (15–17); *good* (12–14); *fair* (9–11); *poor*, or *unacceptable* (below 9). Wine is also unacceptable if it does not meet the minimum in all three categories. Unless it also *exceeds* the minimum in at least one category, it cannot meet the overall minimum of 9 points.

FIGURE 13

A 20-point score card.
(Courtesy of Joseph E. Seagram & Sons, Inc.)

great a range for normal use because judges cannot differentiate 40 levels of quality.

The typical 20-point score card is well suited for the evaluation of still table wines, but it requires modification for other types of wines. For example, the persistence of the sparkle in sparkling wines must be taken into account; either flavor or general quality may be invoked as a means of subtracting points for lack of persistence. In dessert wines (except muscatels) aroma is not a prominent characteristic; greater emphasis must be given to bouquet.

Another score card that has been used in international judgings is that of the *Office International de la Vigne et du Vin*, in Paris (see Figure 14). The perfect score is 0. Defects are marked on an increasing scale for each category as a multiplying factor ($\times 0$, $\times 1$, $\times 4$, $\times 9$, $\times 16$). As with all score cards, some degree of familiarity with the terms is necessary. Odor intensity and odor quality seem clear enough. The difference between taste intensity and taste quality is by no means so clear. Taste intensity would *seem* to pertain to the positive aspects of sweetness, sourness, and bitterness, i.e., the ideal intensity of each. Taste quality would then pertain to the balance (or lack of it) in the overall taste character.

Characteristic	Weight	Multiplying factor for increasing defects				
		$\times 0$	$\times 1$	$\times 4$	$\times 9$	$\times 16$
Appearance	1	___	___	___	___	___
Color	1	___	___	___	___	___
Odor intensity	1	___	___	___	___	___
Odor quality	2	___	___	___	___	___
Taste intensity	2	___	___	___	___	___
Taste quality	3	___	___	___	___	___
Harmony or balance	2	___	___	___	___	___

Multiplying factors: *outstanding* (0); *very good* (1); *good* (4); *acceptable* (9); *unacceptable* (16).

Name _____ Date _____

FIGURE 14

Score card of the Office International de la Vigne et du Vin, *Paris.*

The *Associazione Enotecnici Italiani* (1975), in Milan, has proposed a 100-point score card (see Figure 15). This system will probably work as well as most others, although it has several disadvantages: a 100-point scale is too large, the words *finesse* and *harmony* are difficult to define in sensory terms, and old red wines and most dessert wines would score low in freshness. It does have the advantage, however, of forcing the judge to quantify his judgments, from *bad* to *excellent*, on several wine attributes.

When other evaluation methods are used, such as ranking or hedonic rating, it is still necessary that the judges understand the problems discussed above and that they agree as closely as possible on the definitions and interpretations of the terms to be used in describing the wines.

	Weight	Excellent 4	Good 3	Average 2	Mediocre 1	Bad 0
Visual						
Appearance	2	____	____	____	____	____
Color	2	____	____	____	____	____
Olfactory						
Finesse	2	____	____	____	____	____
Intensity	2	____	____	____	____	____
Freshness	2	____	____	____	____	____
Taste						
Body	2	____	____	____	____	____
Harmony	2	____	____	____	____	____
Intensity	2	____	____	____	____	____
Final taste-odor sensation	3	____	____	____	____	____
Typicalness	3	____	____	____	____	____
General impression	3	____	____	____	____	____

Name _____ Date _____

FIGURE 15

Score card adapted from that published by the
Associazione Enotecnici Italiani *(1975), Milan.*

Rank the 6 samples in order of increasing ethanol content.

Highest _____

_____

_____

_____

_____

Lowest _____

Name _____ Date _____

FIGURE 16

Ranking wines in order of percent ethanol.

Ranking

In the ranking procedure the judges are asked to arrange a series of two or more samples in increasing or decreasing order with respect either to the intensity of a particular characteristic or to their own preference (see Figure 16). The test is simple to administer, may not require highly skilled judges, and makes possible a distribution-free analysis. It does, however, disregard degrees of difference among the wines and is therefore usually less sensitive to the effects of such differences than tests based on scoring. See pages 161–167 for methods of analyzing the results.

Hedonic Rating

Hedonic rating is what the name implies: quality evaluation based on the pleasure that the judge finds in the wine. The evaluations are usually made on 5- to 9-point balanced scales ranging from extreme disapproval to extreme approval, such as the one shown in Figure 10. The results are converted to numerical scores, which are then treated by rank analysis or the analysis of variance (these topics are discussed later). The procedure is used by both experts and untrained consumers, but is more appropriate for the latter group.

What do the results of hedonic rating mean? Are they merely a subjective preference opinion? If so, averaging the scores is not very meaningful. However, if they denote a degree of quality relative to some theoretical, agreed-upon standard of perfection, then the average score may have objective value. In fact, if tested by appropriate statistical procedures, the differences among the average scores of the various wines may reveal significant differences among the wines, or they may indicate no significant differences. See pages 145–147 for methods of analyzing the results.

Tests of Significance of Scores

Regardless of the type of evaluation procedure used, the overall results for each wine in the test are usually expressed in terms of a single numerical score. These scores can be analyzed statistically to determine if significant differences exist. Although the usual statistical procedures presuppose a normal distribution of scores, moderate deviations from such a distribution do not invalidate the results. Studies have shown that the distribution of scores in most tests is only moderately asymmetrical, and the usual test procedures are valid. Sometimes the scores fit a *bimodal distribution* (one with two peaks in its graph), which means that we may be dealing with two types of judges who differ significantly in their quality standards or preferences. It may then be desirable to separate and compare the scores for the two groups making up the bimodal distribution.

Variability. Tests of significance entailing means (averages) of scores are based on estimates of the variability of that population of which the scores constitute a random sample (see page 102). The customarily used estimates of the variability are the variance, v, of a sample distribution of scores and its square root, $s = \sqrt{v}$. The latter represents what is called the best estimate of the standard deviation of the population, as determined from a sample of that population.* The variance is thus a measure of the dispersion of the observed values of a variable (here, the score) about the mean value. If $X_1, X_2, X_3, \cdots, X_n$ represent n sample scores, their mean value is

$$\overline{X} = \frac{X_1 + X_2 + X_3 + \cdots + X_n}{n} = \frac{\sum X}{n} \qquad (10)$$

where, in analogy with our previous usage, the Greek letter Σ denotes the sum of the n values of X.

The best estimate of the variance of the population of which the n scores are a random sample is defined as

$$v = s^2 = \frac{\sum(X - \overline{X})^2}{n - 1} = \frac{\sum X^2 - (\sum X)^2/n}{n - 1} = \frac{\sum X^2 - C}{n - 1} \qquad (11)$$

where $C = (\sum X)^2/n$ is a correction term that converts the sum of the squares of the deviations of the scores from 0, $\sum(X - 0)^2 = \sum X^2$, into the sum of the squares of the deviations of the scores from their mean value, $\overline{X}$, $\sum(X - \overline{X})^2$. It is customary to refer to the numerator of the expression for v as the *sum of squares* (SS) and to the denominator as the corresponding number of *degrees of freedom* (df). The latter is $n - 1$ because $\sum(X - \overline{X}) = 0$ and therefore only $n - 1$ of the differences $X - \overline{X}$ are independent. A sum of squares divided by the number of degrees of freedom gives an unbiased estimate of the variance of the population.

Example 11. From the 8 sample scores $X = 8, 7, 6, 5, 5, 6, 8$, and 7, verify numerically that $\sum(X - \overline{X}) = 0$ and that $\sum(X - \overline{X})^2 = \sum X^2 - C$. Find the value of s, the best estimate of the standard deviation of the population from which the sample was selected.

Partial calculations are shown in Table 2, from which we see immediately that $\sum(X - \overline{X}) = 0$. Using the other sums shown there, we obtain $C = (52)^2/8 = 338$, so

*Note that the standard deviation of the population is denoted by σ (see page 106) but the best estimate of it, based on the actual sample, is denoted by s.

Table 2. Partial calculations for the scores
given in Example 11.

X	X − X̄	(X − X̄)²	X²
8	1.5	2.25	64
7	0.5	0.25	49
6	−0.5	0.25	36
5	−1.5	2.25	25
5	−1.5	2.25	25
6	−0.5	0.25	36
8	1.5	2.25	64
7	0.5	0.25	49
Total 52	0	10.00	348
Mean 6.5			

$$\sum X^2 - C = 348 - 338 = 10 = \sum (X - \overline{X})^2$$

From Equation 11 we obtain $v = 10/7 = 1.43$, so

$$s = \sqrt{v} = \sqrt{1.43} = 1.20$$

We will encounter calculations of this kind again (see page 137) in the discussion of analysis of variance.

The *t*-Distribution

When the standard deviation σ of the population is known, the normal distribution is applicable in "either-or" decision problems, such as: is there a significant difference between these two mean scores or not? If σ is unknown and must be estimated from a sample by calculating s, the sampling distribution of the resulting statistic (see page 130) is no longer a normal one. The appropriate test statistic in this case is denoted by t. Like χ^2, t has a different distribution for each value of the number of degrees of freedom. When the population is normal, the *t*-curve is symmetrical and bell-shaped, but non-normal. As the size of the sample from which

s is calculated increases, the t-curve approaches the normal curve as a limiting form.

Values of t for various combinations of probabilities and numbers of degrees of freedom are given in Appendix E. The probabilities shown at the top of the table pertain to a two-tailed test, and those shown at the bottom of the table are the corresponding values for a one-tailed test.

Two Sets of Scores (Unpaired). Statistical tests for significant difference are based on the null hypothesis that no difference exists. This assumption applies both to population mean scores and standard deviations. The statistic t is useful in determining significance in such tests. If, for two sets of scores, no score from one set corresponds to any particular score from the other set (as, e.g., in the sets of scores obtained for one wine by two different panels of judges), the scores are independent, or *unpaired*, and the t-distribution furnishes the appropriate test of significance for comparing the mean scores of the two sets. Suppose there are n_1 X-scores and n_2 Y-scores (n_1 may or may not equal n_2); t is then defined as

$$t = \frac{\overline{X} - \overline{Y}}{\sqrt{\left(\dfrac{n_1 + n_2}{n_1 n_2}\right)\left[\dfrac{\sum X^2 + \sum Y^2 - (\sum X)^2/n_1 - (\sum Y)^2/n_2}{n_1 + n_2 - 2}\right]}}$$

$$(df = n_1 + n_2 - 2) \qquad (12)$$

The significance of the result is determined by comparing the calculated value of t with the two-tailed values given in Appendix E, for the appropriate number of degrees of freedom. Calculated values of t that exceed those in the table indicate significant differences between the mean scores $\overline{X}$ and $\overline{Y}$, at the level of significance in question. In other words, such values of t lead to rejection of the null hypothesis of no difference.

Example 12. A panel of 6 judges scores a wine on a 10-point scale (see X-scores in Table 3) and a second panel of 8 judges scores the same wine, using the same scale (see Y-scores in

Table 3. A wine scored by two panels of judges (see Example 12).

	PANEL		
X	Y	X²	Y²
9	8	81	64
8	7	64	49
7	6	49	36
9	5	81	25
7	5	49	25
8	6	64	36
	8		64
	7		49
Total 48	52	388	348
Mean 8.0	6.5		

Table 3). Is there a significant difference at the 5% level between the mean scores for the two panels?

Using the total and mean values obtained in Table 3, we solve Equation 12:

$$t = \frac{8.0 - 6.5}{\sqrt{\left[\dfrac{6+8}{6(8)}\right]\left[\dfrac{388 + 348 - (48)^2/6 - (52)^2/8}{6 + 8 - 2}\right]}}$$

$$= \frac{1.5}{\sqrt{0.340}} = \frac{1.5}{0.583} = 2.57$$

From Appendix E we see that $t_{.05}(12\ df) = 2.179$. Since the calculated value $t = 2.57$ is greater than the tabular value 2.179, the null hypothesis of no difference must be rejected, and the analysis indicates that the mean scores for the two panels are significantly different. The two panels are therefore not using the same standards of judgment in evaluating the wine.

Two Sets of Scores (Paired). If one judge compares the same two wines on several different occassions, or if each member of a panel

of judges compares the same two wines, a set of *paired* scores results. For the *n* paired scores X and Y, the differences $D = X - Y$ are then computed, and the mean difference $\overline{D} = \sum D/n$ between the mean scores $\overline{X}$ and $\overline{Y}$ is tested with the *t*-distribution. The expression for t in this case is

$$t = \frac{\overline{D}}{\left(\dfrac{1}{n}\right)\sqrt{\dfrac{n\sum D^2 - (\sum D)^2}{n-1}}} = \frac{\sum D}{\sqrt{\dfrac{n\sum D^2 - (\sum D)^2}{n-1}}}$$

$$(df = n - 1) \qquad (13)$$

Again the calculated value of t is compared with the two-tailed values given in Appendix E to determine the significance of the result.

Example 13. A panel of 7 judges scores two wines on a 20-point scale, as shown in Table 4. Is there a significant difference at the 5% level between the mean scores of the wines?

Using the total values for D and D^2 obtained in Table 4, we solve Equation 13:

Table 4. Two wines scored by 7 judges (see Example 13).

	WINE			
JUDGE	X	Y	D	D²
A	15	14	1	1
B	12	14	−2	4
C	14	15	−1	1
D	17	14	3	9
E	11	11	0	0
F	16	14	2	4
G	15	13	2	4
Total	100	95	5	23
Mean	14.3	13.6	0.714	

$$t = \frac{5}{\sqrt{\dfrac{7(23) - (5)^2}{7 - 1}}} = \frac{5}{\sqrt{22.7}} = \frac{5}{4.76} = 1.05$$

From Appendix E we see that $t_{.05}$ (6 df) = 2.447. Since the calculated value $t = 1.05$ is less than the tabular value 2.447, there is no reason to reject the null hypothesis. Therefore the mean scores of the wines are not significantly different, i.e., this panel of judges cannot distinguish between the two wines.

Analysis of Variance

Scores for Several Wines.   In comparing the mean scores of more than two wines, the t-distribution is no longer appropriate. Instead, the statistical technique called *analysis of variance* is used to determine whether there are significant differences in the mean scores of the wines. The analysis of variance is essentially an arithmetic process for partitioning a total sum of squares (page 131) into components associated with various sources of variation.

To analyze a number, say k, of wines, for each of which n scores are available, a so-called *one-way*, or single-classification, analysis of variance is appropriate. Such a classification is shown in Table 5,

Table 5. One-way analysis of variance.

	WINE					
	1	2	3	$\cdots$	k	
	X_{11}	X_{21}	X_{31}	$\cdots$	X_{k1}	
	X_{12}	X_{22}	X_{32}	$\cdots$	X_{k2}	
	X_{13}	X_{23}	X_{33}	$\cdots$	X_{k3}	
	$\vdots$	$\vdots$	$\vdots$	X_{ij}	$\vdots$	
	X_{1n}	X_{2n}	X_{3n}	$\cdots$	X_{kn}	
Total	W_1	W_2	W_3	$\cdots$	W_k	Grand total $G = \Sigma W_i$
Mean	$\overline{X}_1$	$\overline{X}_2$	$\overline{X}_3$	$\cdots$	$\overline{X}_k$	Total no. of scores = kn

where X_{ij} represents the j-th score of the i-th wine sample (i can have any value from 1 to k, and j can have any value from 1 to n). The variance of this classification of scores can be estimated in three ways, from three sums of squares (two of which include a relevant correction term, C) and their corresponding numbers of degrees of freedom. The three sums of squares in question are the *total* sum of squares, the *sample* sum of squares (i.e., the sum of squares between means of wine samples), and the *error* sum of squares (i.e., the sum of squares within samples). The correction term and the three sums of squares are defined as follows:

$$C = (\text{Grand total})^2/kn = G^2/kn \qquad (14)$$

$$\text{Total } SS = \sum_{ij}X_{ij}^2 - C \qquad (df = kn - 1) \qquad (15)$$

$$\text{Sample } SS = n(\sum_i \overline{X}_i^2 - G^2/kn^2)$$

$$= (W_1^2 + W_2^2 + \cdots + W_k^2)/n - C$$

$$= \sum_i W_i^2/n - C \qquad (df = k - 1) \qquad (16)$$

$$\text{Error } SS = (\sum_j X_{1j}^2 - W_1^2/n) + (\sum_j X_{2j}^2 - W_2^2/n) + \cdots$$

$$+ (\sum_j X_{kj}^2 - W_k^2/n)$$

$$= \sum_{ij} X_{ij}^2 - \sum_i W_i^2/n \qquad [df = k(n - 1)] \qquad (17)$$

From these relations it follows that

$$\text{Total } SS = \text{Sample } SS + \text{Error } SS \qquad (18)$$

and

$$\text{Total } df = \text{Sample } df + \text{Error } df \qquad (19)$$

The within-sample sum of squares (Error SS) is usually calculated by subtracting the between-sample sum of squares (Sample SS) from the total sum of squares (Total SS). The value of the *error mean square* (the error variance) is given by $v = \text{Error } SS/\text{Error } df$. It is often referred to as a *generalized error term* because it is a measure of the error variation contributed by all the samples.

It is independent of any differences that might exist among the sample means. The value of the *sample mean square* (Sample SS/Sample *df*), on the other hand, is a measure of the differences among the sample means; the larger the differences, the larger the sample mean square. The null hypothesis is that the samples come from *k* populations, all having the same means μ and the same variances v. This implies equality among the sample means.

The sample mean square and the error mean square provide two independent estimates of the common population variance. They are compared by calculating their ratio, which is a statistic called *F*:

$$F = \frac{\text{Sample mean square}}{\text{Error mean square}} \qquad (20)$$

This calculated *F*-value is compared with the tabular values given in Appendixes F-1, F-2, or F-3. The *F*-distribution is represented by double-entry tables with respect to the degrees of freedom. The degrees of freedom for the numerator are shown in the top rows of the tables, and the degrees of freedom for the denominator are shown in the left-hand columns. Calculated *F*-values that exceed the tabular values for the appropriate values of *df* indicate rejection of the null hypothesis of no differences among the sample means, i.e., there are significant differences. (If the sample mean square is less than the error mean square, $F < 1$ and the result is nonsignificant by definition. The null hypothesis is then accepted without the need to refer to the table.) A significant *F*-value implies that the evidence is sufficiently strong to indicate differences among the sample means, but it does not reveal *which* of the various differences among the sample means may be statistically significant. To determine these differences is the next step in the analysis.

Least Significant Difference.   One procedure for determining which wine-sample means are significantly different, following the demonstration of a significant *F*-value, is to calculate the *least significant difference* (LSD), which is the smallest difference that could exist between two significantly different sample means:

 139

$$LSD = t_\alpha \sqrt{2v/n} \qquad [df = k(n - 1)] \qquad (21)$$

where t_α is the t-value, with $k(n - 1)$ degrees of freedom, at the significance level α, v is the error variance, and n is the number of scores on which each mean is based. For the difference between two means to be significant at the level of significance selected, the observed difference must exceed the LSD-value.

Example 14. Given 5 scores for each of 4 wines, as shown in Table 6, analyze the results for significance.

$$C = (142)^2/20 = 1008.2$$

$$\text{Total } SS = (10)^2 + (8)^2 + \cdots + (6)^2 - C$$

$$= 1066 - 1008.2 = 57.8 \qquad (19 \, df)$$

$$\text{Wine } SS = \frac{(42)^2 + (43)^2 + (31)^2 + (26)^2}{5} - C$$

$$= 5250/5 - 1008.2 = 41.8 \qquad (3 \, df)$$

$$\text{Error } SS = 57.8 - 41.8 = 16.0 \qquad (16 \, df)$$

It is customary to combine these results into a so-called *analysis of variance table,* as shown in Table 7, where $ms = SS/df$ is the mean square (the error ms is also denoted by v, as we have seen above).

Table 6. Five scores for each of 4 wines
(see Example 14).

	WINE				
	S_1	S_2	S_3	S_4	
	10	9	7	6	
	8	9	5	5	
	7	8	6	4	
	9	10	7	5	
	8	7	6	6	
Total	42	43	31	26	$G = 142$
Mean	8.4	8.6	6.2	5.2	

Table 7. Analysis of variance table for the data in Example 14.

Source	SS	df	ms	F	$F_{.05}$	$F_{.01}$	$F_{.001}$
Total	57.8	19					
Wines	41.8	3	13.9	13.9***	3.24	5.29	9.00
Error	16.0	16	1.0				

Since the calculated F-value is larger than any of the three tabular values from Appendixes F, significant differences among the means of the wine scores are indicated at all three levels. The level of significance of a calculated F-value is often denoted by one or more asterisks: one for the 5% level, two for the 1% level, and three for the 0.1% level. In this example the significance of the calculated F-value is denoted by 13.9***. Significance at any given level obviously implies significance at all lower levels.

For the 1% level we use the t-value from Appendix E to calculate the LSD by Equation 21:

$$LSD = t_{.01}(16\ df)\sqrt{2(1.0)/5} = 2.921\sqrt{0.40} = 1.85$$

Significance is usually shown by ranking the mean scores and underlining those that are *not* significantly different. The difference between any two scores that are not connected by an underline is therefore significant. For the mean scores in the present example we would write

	WINE			
	S_2	S_1	S_3	S_4
Mean	8.6	8.4	6.2	5.2

Thus there is no significant difference between wines S_1 and S_2 because the difference between their mean scores, 0.2, is less than 1.85, the calculated LSD. However, each of these wines is significantly better than wines S_3 and S_4. Wines S_3 and S_4 are not significantly different from each other.

Duncan's New Multiple-Range Test. Some experimenters prefer one of the newer tests for establishing significance among the sample means. These tests do not require the preliminary F-test but are applied directly to the mean scores. One such test is *Duncan's new multiple-range test,* in which, after ranking, each sample mean is compared with every other sample mean, using a set of significant differences that depend upon, and increase with, the increase in the range between the ranked means. The smallest value is obtained for adjacent means, and the largest value for the extremes. In Duncan's test the shortest significant range R_p for comparing the largest and smallest of p mean scores, after they have been ranked, is given by

$$R_p = Q_p \sqrt{v/n} \qquad [df = k(n-1)] \qquad (22)$$

where the number of degrees of freedom is that for the error variance v. The appropriate value of Q_p can be obtained from Appendixes G-1, G-2, or G-3.

Example 15. Use Duncan's new multiple-range test to establish significance for the data in Example 14.

For the 1% level, $\sqrt{v/n} = \sqrt{1.0/5} = \sqrt{0.2} = 0.447$, and the values of Q_p for $p = 2, 3$, and 4 are obtained from Appendix G-2. The results are summarized in Table 8. We see that the R_p-values are appropriate for making the following comparisons:

$R_2 = 1.85$ S_2 with S_1, S_1 with S_3, and S_3 with S_4
$R_3 = 1.93$ S_2 with S_3, and S_1 with S_4
$R_4 = 1.98$ S_2 with S_4

Table 8. Duncan's new multiple-range test (1% level) for the data in Example 14 (see Example 15).

SHORTEST SIGNIFICANT RANGE			COMPARISON				
p 2	3	4					
Q_p 4.13	4.31	4.42	Wine	S_2	S_1	S_3	S_4
R_p 1.85	1.93	1.98	Mean	8.6	8.4	6.2	5.2

The results are the same as those obtained in Example 14. There is no significant difference between wines S_1 and S_2, but each of these wines is significantly better than wines S_3 and S_4. Wines S_3 and S_4 are not significantly different from each other.

If the mean scores of the wines are based on different numbers of individual scores, that is, n_1 scores for the first wine, n_2 scores for the second wine, ... , n_k scores for the k-th wine, the analysis is very similar but the following modifications must be made:

1. Sample $SS = W_1^2/n_1 + W_2^2/n_2 + \cdots + W_k^2/n_k - C$

2. Effective number of replications n_{eff} replaces n:

$$n_{eff} = \left(\frac{1}{k-1}\right)\left(\frac{\sum n_j - \sum n_j^2}{\sum n_j}\right)$$

where $\sum n_j$ is the total number of wine samples in the experiment.

3. $LSD = t_\alpha \sqrt{2v/n_{eff}}$ and $R_p = Q_p \sqrt{v/n_{eff}}$
where t_α and Q_p are based on $\sum n_j - k$ degrees of freedom.

Table 9. Two-way analysis of variance
(randomized complete-block design).

Judge	Wine 1	2	3	$\cdots$	k	Total
1	X_{11}	X_{21}	X_{31}	$\cdots$	X_{k1}	T_1
2	X_{12}	X_{22}	X_{32}	$\cdots$	X_{k2}	T_2
3	X_{13}	X_{23}	X_{33}	$\cdots$	X_{k3}	T_3
$\vdots$	$\vdots$	$\vdots$	$\vdots$	X_{ij}	$\vdots$	$\vdots$
n	X_{1n}	X_{2n}	X_{3n}	$\cdots$	X_{kn}	T_n
Total	W_1	W_2	W_3	$\cdots$	W_k	$G = \Sigma T_j = \Sigma W_i$
Mean	$\overline{X}_1$	$\overline{X}_2$	$\overline{X}_3$	$\cdots$	$\overline{X}_k$	Total no. of scores $= kn$

Scoring of Several Wines by Several Judges. In the customary sensory evaluation in which a panel of n judges scores each of k wines, the so-called *two-way*, or double-classification, analysis of variance is appropriate in testing for significance. In this classification the total sum of squares, calculated as the variation among all scores, is subdivided into three parts: a sum of squares based on the variation among wines, a sum of squares based on the variation among judges, and a remainder sum of squares. The latter is not the result of variation among wines or judges but is a measure of the unexplained variation, or error variation. The degrees of freedom are subdivided in the same way. This is known as a *randomized complete-block design*; its pattern is shown in Table 9. The definitions are as follows (compare them with Equations 14–19):

		df
(a)	$C = G^2/kn$	
(b)	Total $SS = \sum X_{ij}^2 - C$	$kn - 1$
(c)	Wine $SS = \sum W_i^2/n - C$	$k - 1$
(d)	Judge $SS = \sum T_j^2/k - C$	$n - 1$
(e)	Error $SS = $ (b) $-$ (c) $-$ (d)	$(kn - 1) - (k - 1) - (n - 1)$ $= (k - 1)(n - 1)$

From these sums of squares and the corresponding numbers of degrees of freedom, three independent estimates of the population variance are computed. On the assumption that the groups making up the total set of measurements (scores) are random samples from populations with the same means, the three estimates of the population variance can be expected to differ only within the limits of chance fluctuation. There are two null hypotheses here, namely, that the population means for the wines are all the same and that those for the judges are all the same. These hypotheses are tested by comparing the among-wine variance and the among-judge variance, respectively, with the error variance. The comparisons consist of calculating the variance ratios

$$F = \frac{\text{variance for wines}}{\text{error variance}} \quad \text{and} \quad F = \frac{\text{variance for judges}}{\text{error variance}} \quad (23)$$

To establish significance, as before, the calculated values of F are compared with the tabular values at the three levels of significance.

Example 16. Five judges score 4 wines on a 20-point scale, as shown in Table 10. Are there significant differences among the sample means at the 1% level?

Substituting the data into the equations given above, we obtain

$$C = (267)^2/20 = 3564.45$$

$$\text{Total } SS = (13)^2 + \cdots + (12)^2 - C = 142.55 \qquad (19\ df)$$

$$\text{Wine } SS = \frac{(67)^2 + \cdots + (52)^2}{5} - C = 112.95 \qquad (4\ df)$$

$$\text{Judge } SS = \frac{(56)^2 + \cdots + (56)^2}{4} - C = 8.80 \qquad (3\ df)$$

$$\text{Error } SS = 142.55 - 112.95 - 8.80 = 20.80$$

$$(19 - 4 - 3 = 12\ df)$$

These results and the remaining calculations are shown in Table 11.

Since the calculated F-value for wines is greater than the tabular value, significant differences among the means of the

Table 10. Five judges score 4 wines on a 20-point scale (see Example 16).

| | WINE | | | | |
JUDGE	S_1	S_2	S_3	S_4	TOTAL
1	13	18	15	10	56
2	15	16	12	11	54
3	14	15	11	9	49
4	12	17	13	10	52
5	13	19	12	12	56
Total	67	85	63	52	267 = G
Mean	13.4	17.0	12.6	10.4	

Table 11. Analysis of variance table for the data in Example 16.

Source	SS	df	ms	F	$F_{.01}$	$F_{.001}$
Total	142.55	19				
Wines	112.95	4	28.24	16.32***	5.41	9.63
Judges	8.80	3	2.93	1.69	5.95	
Error	20.80	12	1.73			

wine scores do exist at the 1% level. (In fact, they exist at the 0.1% level, as implied by the three asterisks on the calculated F-value.) The calculated F-value for judges is less than the tabular value, so there are no significant differences among the judges, i.e., they have been consistent in their scoring.

Specific differences among the wines can be tested by calculating the least significant difference:

$$LSD = t_\alpha \sqrt{2v/n} = t_{.01}(12\ df)\sqrt{2(1.73)/5} = 3.055\sqrt{0.692}$$
$$= 2.54$$

Therefore 2.54 is the smallest difference that can exist between two significantly different sample means. Again using the method of underlining mean scores that are not significantly different, we write

WINE

	S_2	S_1	S_3	S_4
Mean	17.0	13.4	12.6	10.4

We see that wine S_2 is significantly better than wines S_1, S_3, and S_4. Wine S_1 is significantly better than wine S_4. Wines S_1 and S_3 are not significantly different, and wines S_3 and S_4 are not significantly different.

Hedonic Rating.   Hedonic rating of wines is usually done with a scale of 5, 7, or 9 points. The usual 9-point scale comprises the following categories: *like extremely* (4); *like very much* (3); *like*

moderately (2); *like slightly* (1); *neither like nor dislike* (0); *dislike slightly* (−1); *dislike moderately* (−2); *dislike very much* (−3); *dislike extremely* (−4). (See also Figure 10.) To analyze the results the numerical values shown in parentheses are used and the analysis of variance is applied. Any set of consecutive integers could be used instead of these numbers, but those used here result in the smallest intermediate values.

Example 17. Fifty judges rate 4 wines on a 7-point hedonic scale, as shown in Table 12. Are there significant differences in the judges' preference among the wines?

$$C = (227)^2/200 = 257.64$$

$$\text{Total } SS = 729 - 257.64 = 471.36 \qquad (199 \; df)$$

$$\text{Wine } SS = \frac{(109)^2 + (89)^2 + (28)^2 + (1)^2}{50} - C$$

$$= 411.74 - 257.64 = 154.10 \qquad (3 \; df)$$

$$\text{Error } SS = 471.36 - 154.10 = 317.26 \qquad (196 \; df)$$

Table 12. Fifty judges assign hedonic ratings to 4 wines (see Example 17).

| | | | | FREQUENCY OF RESPONSE, f | | | | |
| | | | | WINE | | | | |
RATING	X	S_1	S_2	S_3	S_4	Σf	$(\Sigma f)X$	$(\Sigma f)X^2$
Like very much	3	22	8	2	5	37	111	333
Like moderately	2	17	25	13	8	63	126	252
Like slightly	1	10	15	18	3	46	46	46
Neither like nor dislike	0	0	2	5	10	17	0	0
Dislike slightly	−1	1	0	4	15	20	−20	20
Dislike moderately	−2	0	0	6	9	15	−30	60
Dislike very much	−3	0	0	2	0	2	−6	18
Total Σf		50	50	50	50	200		
ΣfX		109	89	28	1		227 = G	
ΣfX^2								729
Mean $\Sigma fX/\Sigma f$		2.18	1.78	0.56	0.02			

Table 13. Analysis of variance table for the data in Example 17.

SOURCE	SS	df	ms	F	$F_{.05}$	$F_{.01}$	$F_{.001}$
Total	471.36	199					
Wines	154.10	3	51.4	31.7***	2.60	3.78	5.42
Error	317.26	196	1.62				

Table 14. Duncan's new multiple-range test (0.1% level) for the data in Example 17.

SHORTEST SIGNIFICANT RANGE			COMPARISON			
p 2	3	4	Wine S_1	S_2	S_3	S_4
Q_p 4.65	4.80	4.90	Mean 2.18	1.78	0.56	0.02
R_p 0.837	0.864	0.882				

These results and the remaining calculations are shown in Table 13. [Since F-values for 196 degrees of freedom (denominator) are not given in Appendixes F, the values for $df = \infty$ are used.]

Since $F = 31.7$ (calculated) exceeds $F_{.001} = 5.42$ (tabular), very highly significant differences among the mean scores of the wines are indicated. If Duncan's new multiple-range test is applied, we have

$$R_p = Q_p\sqrt{v/n} = Q_p\sqrt{1.62/50} = Q_p(0.18)$$

The results are summarized in Table 14. (Again the numbers for $df = \infty$ are used.)

In this example we see that wines S_1 and S_2 are significantly better than wines S_3 and S_4. Wine S_1 is not significantly different from wine S_2, and wine S_3 is not significantly different from wine S_4.

Interaction. The term *interaction* is used in statistics to describe a differential response to two variables, usually referred to as *factors*, which may or may not act independently of each other. In

the analysis of variance, interaction is expressed by a so-called residual term, which provides another estimate of variance. It reflects the relations between experimental factors or the failure of one factor to vary in accord with variations in the second factor. For example, judges differ in their susceptibility to physical and mental fatigue and in their reactions to the foods they consume. Such differences can lead to interaction effects when the same judges evaluate the same wines at two different times. (Time is always one of the factors in interaction effects in wine evaluation.)

Some possible situations are shown in Figure 17, which relates the scoring of two wines by two judges to the time of day. If the lines joining the morning and afternoon scores for each judge are parallel, there is no interaction. The greater the departure from parallelism, the greater the interaction, owing to the differential

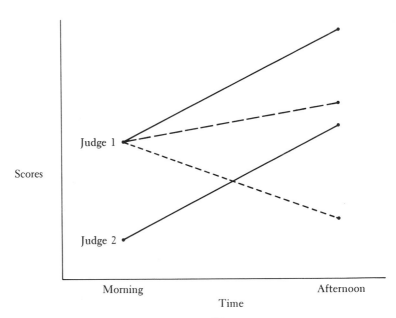

FIGURE 17
Changes in scores with time. The two solid lines show no interaction between the judges' scores and time. The lower solid line and the two dashed lines show different degrees of interaction.

response of the judges to the factors time and, say, fatigue. Small departures from parallelism may be caused by variation in, or treatment of, wine samples or as a result of random sampling errors. The problem is to test statistically whether an observed departure from parallelism is greater than could reasonably be expected to occur by chance alone.

The significance of an interaction is determined by comparing its estimate of variance with that of experimental error. A significant interaction is one that is too large to be explained on the basis of chance alone, under the null hypothesis of no interaction. A nonsignificant interaction leads to the conclusion that the factors in question act independently of each other. The existence or nonexistence of interactions can only be determined when scores are replicated.

Example 18. Five judges score 4 wines on two successive days, called time I and time II. The results are shown in Table 15. Analyze the results for significance, to determine whether there is interaction.

For the 40 individual scores we have

$$C = (310)^2/40 = 2402.5$$
$$\text{Total SS} = (10)^2 + (9)^2 + \cdots + (5)^2 - C$$
$$= 2504 - 2402.5 = 101.5 \qquad (39 \, df)$$

Table 15. Five judges score 4 wines on two successive days (see Example 18).

JUDGE	TIME I WINE S_1	S_2	S_3	S_4	TOTAL	JUDGE	TIME II WINE S_1	S_2	S_3	S_4	TOTAL
1	10	10	8	6	34	1	8	9	6	7	30
2	9	9	6	8	32	2	7	8	6	6	27
3	10	10	9	8	37	3	9	8	7	9	33
4	8	8	8	5	29	4	10	9	8	5	32
5	8	7	6	4	25	5	9	10	7	5	31
Total	45	44	37	31	157	Total	43	44	34	32	153

If the individual scores for the two times are added, as shown in Table 16, the result is a classification of wines and judges called a *two-way pattern*. Since the entries in the table are the totals of two scores, the denominators of the equations for the sums of squares are twice as great as in the usual analysis, and the means are obtained by dividing the totals by 10 (5 judges × 2 times). The correction term remains the same because it always pertains to the same totals. The total sum of squares for this pattern is called a *subtotal sum of squares* to distinguish it from the total sum of squares for the independent scores. The calculations follow.

$$\text{Subtotal } SS = \frac{(18)^2 + (16)^2 + \cdots + (9)^2}{2} - C$$

$$= 2481 - 2402.5 = 78.5 \qquad (19 \, df)$$

$$\text{Wine } SS = \frac{(88)^2 + (88)^2 + (71)^2 + (63)^2}{10} - C$$

$$= 2449.8 - 2402.5 = 47.3 \qquad (3 \, df)$$

$$\text{Judge } SS = \frac{(64)^2 + (59)^2 + \cdots + (56)^2}{8} - C$$

$$= 2416.75 - 2402.5 = 14.25 \qquad (4 \, df)$$

Table 16. Combined (two-way) scores for times
for the data in Table 15.

	WINES × JUDGES (DISREGARD TIMES)				
		WINE			
JUDGE	S_1	S_2	S_3	S_4	TOTAL
1	18	19	14	13	64
2	16	17	12	14	59
3	19	18	16	17	70
4	18	17	16	10	61
5	17	17	13	9	56
Total	88	88	71	63	310 = G
Mean	8.80	8.80	7.10	6.30	

Interaction $SS = 78.5 - 47.3 - 14.25 = 16.95$
(Wine × Judge) $(19 - 3 - 4 = 12\ df)$

The next step in the analysis is to combine the total scores for the 5 judges, which results in a two-way pattern of wines and times, as shown in Table 17. Since the entries in the table are the totals of 5 individual scores, the denominators of the equations are 5 times as great as in the usual analysis. The calculations follow.

$$\text{Subtotal } SS = \frac{(45)^2 + (43)^2 + \cdots + (32)^2}{5} - C$$

$$= 2451.2 - 2402.5 = 48.7 \qquad (7\ df)$$

$$\text{Wine } SS = 47.3 \quad \text{(from preceding pattern)} \qquad (3\ df)$$

$$\text{Time } SS = \frac{(157)^2 + (153)^2}{20} - C$$

$$= 2402.9 - 2402.5 = 0.4 \qquad (1\ df)$$

Interaction $SS = 48.7 - 47.3 - 0.4 = 1.0$
(Wine × Time) $(7 - 3 - 1 = 3\ df)$

Next the total scores for the 4 wines are combined to give a two-way pattern of judges and times, as shown in Table 18. Since the entries in the table are the totals of 4 individual scores, the denominators of the equations are 4 times as great as in the usual analysis. The calculations follow.

Table 17. Combined (two-way) scores for judges
for the data in Table 15.

	WINES × TIMES (DISREGARD JUDGES)				
		WINE			
TIME	S_1	S_2	S_3	S_4	TOTAL
I	45	44	37	31	157
II	43	44	34	32	153
Total	88	88	71	63	$310 = G$
Mean	8.80	8.80	7.10	6.30	

Table 18. Combined (two-way) scores for wines for the data in Table 15.

JUDGES × TIMES (DISREGARD WINES)						
	JUDGE					
TIME	1	2	3	4	5	TOTAL
I	34	32	37	29	25	157
II	30	27	33	32	31	153
Total	64	59	70	61	56	$310 = G$
Mean	8.00	7.38	8.75	7.62	7.00	

$$\text{Subtotal } SS = \frac{(34)^2 + (30)^2 + \cdots + (31)^2}{4} - C$$

$$= 2429.5 - 2402.5 = 27.0 \qquad (9\ df)$$

$$\text{Judge } SS = 14.25 \qquad (4\ df)$$

$$\text{Time } SS = 0.4 \qquad (1\ df)$$

$$\text{Interaction } SS = 27.0 - 14.25 - 0.4 = 12.35$$
$$\text{(Judge} \times \text{Time)} \qquad (9 - 4 - 1 = 4\ df)$$

These results and the remaining calculations are shown in Table 19. (Recall the meaning of the asterisks on the calculated F-values, mentioned in Example 14.)

Table 19. Analysis of variance table for the data in Example 18.

SOURCE	SS	df	ms	F	$F_{.05}$	$F_{.01}$	$F_{.001}$
Total	101.50	39					
Wines	47.30	3	15.77	20.48***	3.49	5.95	10.80
Judges	14.25	4	3.56	4.62*	3.26	5.41	
Times	0.40	1	0.40				
Interactions							
W × J	16.95	12	1.41	1.83	2.69		
W × T	1.00	3	0.33				
J × T	12.35	4	3.09	4.01*	3.26	5.41	
Error	9.25	12	0.77				

We see that the wines are significantly different at all three levels, and that the values for the judges and the judge $\times$ time interaction are significant at the 5% level. The significant interaction indicates that the judges have reacted differently at the two times, as can be seen from their total scores at the two times. The total scores for the first three judges are less at time II than at time I, but the last two judges have total scores greater at time II than at time I. This might mean that we are dealing with two different types of judges. It could be the result of different foods consumed on the two days, varying mental or physical conditions, temperature differences, or other causes.

The least significant differences can now be used to make specific comparisons of the mean scores for the wines and for the judges.

Wines: $LSD = t_{.001}(12\ df)\sqrt{2(0.77)/10} = 4.318\sqrt{0.154}$
$= 1.69$

	WINE			
	S_1	S_2	S_3	S_4
Mean	8.80	8.80	7.10	6.30

Judges: $LSD = t_{.05}(12\ df)\sqrt{2(0.77)/8} = 2.179\sqrt{0.192}$
$= 0.96$

	JUDGE				
	3	1	4	2	5
Mean	8.75	8.00	7.62	7.38	7.00

Some experimenters combine the sum of squares and number of degrees of freedom for nonsignificant interactions with the sum of squares and number of degrees of freedom, respectively, for the error, and use the resulting value as a revised error term. This increases the number of degrees of freedom upon which the error is based. The results of these calculations for the data in Example 18 are shown in Table 20. The corresponding LSD values are shown below.

Table 20. Analysis of variance table for the data in Example 18, with nonsignificant interactions combined with error.

SOURCE	SS	df	ms	F	$F_{.05}$	$F_{.01}$	$F_{.001}$
Total	101.50	39					
Wines	47.30	3	15.77	15.46***	2.96	4.60	7.27
Judges	14.25	4	3.56	3.49*	2.73	4.11	
Times	0.40	1	0.40				
J × T	12.35	4	3.09	3.06*	2.73	4.11	
Error	27.20	27	1.01				

Wines: $LSD = t_{.001}(27\ df)\sqrt{2(1.01)/10} = 3.690\sqrt{0.202} = 1.66$

Judges: $LSD = t_{.05}(27\ df)\sqrt{2(1.01)/8} = 2.052\sqrt{0.252} = 1.03$

This procedure results in slight changes in the significance patterns when the F-values are close to the borderline between significance and nonsignificance. It often yields a smaller value for the error variance, although in Example 18 it yields a larger value.

Incomplete Blocks

In wine judging, if each judge scores all the samples at the same session, the randomized complete-block design discussed previously (page 142) is appropriate. However, the judge finds it increasingly difficult to make satisfactory ratings as the number of wines presented to him at one time becomes larger. The number of samples that can be reliably scored at any one session depends upon several factors, including the type of wine being evaluated. If the judge at any one session scores only some of the wines under study, the result is an *incomplete-block design*, and the scores in question constitute an incomplete block. Sometimes the judge rates only one incomplete block and sometimes several, with intervening rest periods. Incomplete-block designs reduce the need for the judge to have long-term memory because he need be consistent in his level of judgment only within the incomplete-block limit.

An incomplete-block design in which each block contains the same number of samples, k, and in which each pair of samples appears together in the same block the same number of times, λ, is called a balanced incomplete-block design. In such designs all pairs of samples are compared with approximately the same precision.

Since only some of the wines are judged at the same time, and since each wine is compared with every other wine, only certain arrangements of blocks, samples within blocks, and replications are possible. The relevant procedures and possible incomplete-block designs for specific numbers of samples and judges can be found in Fisher and Yates (1974) and Cochran and Cox (1957).

The customary notation and method of analysis is outlined below.

t = number of samples (wines)

r = number of replications

b = number of blocks (judges)

k = number of samples per block

N = total number of scores in the design = $tr = bk$

λ = number of times each pair of samples appears in the same block = $r(k - 1)/(t - 1)$

W_i = total score for sample i

B_i = sum of totals for blocks in which sample i appears

$A_i = kW_i - B_i$ represents, for sample i, the sample effect adjusted for and free of the effects of the blocks in which it appears ($\sum A_i = 0$)

The calculations and the analysis of variance follow the usual patterns except for the sample sum of squares adjusted for blocks, which is defined as

$$\text{Wine SS (adj.)} = \frac{\sum A_i^2}{kt\lambda} \qquad (24)$$

Since each A_i is free of block effects, it represents, for sample i, an estimated sample effect w_i that provides an adjustment to the

general mean score, namely, an adjusted mean score for the sample. The adjusted mean for each sample is $\mu + w_i$, where $w_i = A_i/t\lambda$; $(\sum w_i = 0)$. In using the *LSD* or Duncan's new multiple-range test to compare adjusted mean scores for samples, the value of the effective error variance to be used instead of v is

$$v_{\text{eff}} = v\left[\frac{k(t-1)}{t(k-1)}\right] \qquad (25)$$

Example 19. Six wines are scored on a 10-point scale by judges in 10 blocks of 3 samples each. There are 5 scores for each wine sample, each of which is compared twice with every other sample in the same block. The pattern is shown in Table 21. Analyze the data for significance.

In this design $t = 6$, $b = 10$, $k = 3$, $r = 5$, and $\lambda = 2$. The calculations are shown below.

Table 21. Six wines scored on a 10-point scale by judges in 10 blocks of 3 samples each (incomplete-block design; see Example 19).

BLOCK (JUDGE)	S_1	S_2	S_3	S_4	S_5	S_6	TOTAL
1	4	5			5		14
2	6	7				6	19
3	6		7	5			18
4	7	5				7	19
5	4			6	4		14
6			6		4	10	20
7		8	7	5			20
8		10	4		6		20
9		6		4		9	19
10				4	5	8	17
Total W_i	27	36	29	24	24	40	$180 = G$
kW_i	81	108	87	72	72	120	$\mu = 180/30$
B_i	84	92	97	88	85	94	$= 6.00$
A_i	-3	16	-10	-16	-13	26	
w_i	-0.25	1.33	-0.83	-1.33	-1.08	2.17	
$\mu + w_i$	5.75	7.33	5.17	4.67	4.92	8.17	

$$C = (180)^2/30 = 1080$$

$$\text{Total } SS = (4)^2 + (5)^2 + \cdots + (8)^2 - C$$

$$= 1168 - 1080 = 88 \qquad (29 \, df)$$

$$\text{Block } SS = \frac{(14)^2 + (19)^2 + \cdots + (17)^2}{3} - C$$

$$= 1096 - 1080 = 16 \qquad (9 \, df)$$

$$\text{Wine } SS \text{ (adj.)} = \frac{\sum A_i^2}{kt\lambda} = \frac{(-3)^2 + (16)^2 + \cdots + (26)^2}{3(6)(2)}$$

$$= 1466/36 = 40.72 \qquad (5 \, df)$$

$$\text{Error } SS = 88 - 16 - 40.72$$

$$= 31.28 \quad \text{(intra-block error)} \qquad (15 \, df)$$

These results and the remaining calculations are shown in Table 22.

The analysis indicates significant differences among the sample means at the 5% level because the calculated value $F = 3.89$ exceeds the tabular value $F_{.05} = 2.90$. If the LSD is used to test for specific differences among the wines, we have

$$LSD = t_{.05}(15 \, df) \sqrt{\frac{2v}{r}\left[\frac{k(t-1)}{t(k-1)}\right]}$$

$$= 2.131 \sqrt{\left[\frac{2(2.09)}{5}\right]\left[\frac{3(5)}{6(2)}\right]} = 2.131 \sqrt{(0.836)(1.25)}$$

$$= 2.131 \sqrt{1.04} = 2.17$$

WINE

	S_6	S_2	S_1	S_3	S_5	S_4
Mean	8.17	7.33	5.75	5.17	4.92	4.67

We see that there is no significant difference between wines S_6 and S_2. Wine S_6 is significantly better than wines S_1, S_3, S_5, and S_4. Wine S_2 is not significantly different from wines S_1 and S_3 but is significantly better than wines S_5 and S_4. There are no significant differences among wines S_1, S_3, S_5, and S_4.

Table 22. Analysis of variance table for the data in Example 19.

SOURCE	SS	df	ms	F	$F_{.05}$	$F_{.01}$
Total	88.00	29				
Blocks	16.00	9	1.78			
Wines (adj.)	40.72	5	8.14	3.89*	2.90	4.56
Error	31.28	15	2.09			

Sometimes it is possible to have the judges score each of the wines in an incomplete-block design, scoring a part of the total number at different times. For each judge the incomplete blocks are grouped to form a replication. This design permits the removal of variations in replications from the block sum of squares. *Balanced lattices* are of this type of design. They are useful and the calculations are simple. The number of such designs is limited because the number of samples must be a perfect square, k^2, grouped in blocks of k samples with $k + 1$ replications.

Example 20. Nine wines are scored on a 10-point scale by 4 judges, each judge scoring all 9 samples in 3 incomplete blocks of 3 samples each, as shown in Table 23. Test the wine scores for significance.

In this design $k = 3, t = k^2 = 9, r = k + 1 = 4,$ and $\lambda = 1$. The calculations are shown below.

$$C = (211)^2/36 = 1236.69$$

$$\text{Total } SS = (9)^2 + (3)^2 + \cdots + (3)^2 - C$$

$$= 1399 - 1236.69 = 162.31 \qquad (35\ df)$$

$$\text{Block } SS = \frac{(19)^2 + (16)^2 + \cdots + (14)^2}{3} - C$$

$$= 1255 - 1236.69 = 18.31 \qquad (11\ df)$$

$$\text{Replication } SS = \frac{(53)^2 + (50)^2 + (55)^2 + (53)^2}{9} - C$$

$$= 1238.11 - 1236.69 = 1.42 \qquad (3\ df)$$

$$\text{Block (in repl.) } SS = 18.31 - 1.42 = 16.89 \qquad (8\ df)$$

Table 23. Nine wines scored on a 10-point scale by 4 judges in blocks of 3 samples each (balanced lattice; see Example 20).

Replication (judge)	Block	S_1	S_2	S_3	S_4	S_5	S_6	S_7	S_8	S_9	Total
I	1	9	3	7							19
	2				5	4	7				16
	3							9	7	2	18 — 53
II	4	8			4			8			20
	5		5			3			7		15
	6			8			4			3	15 — 50
III	7	9				4				3	16
	8			7	4				8		19
	9		5				6	9			20 — 55
IV	10			7		3		9			19
	11	7					7		6		20
	12		5		6					3	14 — 53
Total	W_i	33	18	29	19	14	24	35	28	11	211 = G
	kW_i	99	54	87	57	42	72	105	84	33	633
	B_i	75	68	72	69	66	71	77	72	63	633
	A_i	24	−14	15	−12	−24	1	28	12	−30	0
	w_i	2.67	−1.56	1.67	−1.33	−2.67	0.11	3.11	1.33	−3.33	0
	$\mu + w_i$	8.53	4.30	7.53	4.53	3.19	5.97	8.97	7.19	2.53	$\mu = 211/36$ = 5.86

$$\text{Wine } SS \text{ (adj.)} = \frac{\sum A_i^2}{kt\lambda}$$

$$= \frac{(24)^2 + (-14)^2 + \cdots + (-30)^2}{3(9)(1)}$$

$$= 131.33 \qquad\qquad (8\ df)$$

$$\text{Error } SS = 162.31 - 18.31 - 131.33$$

$$= 12.67 \quad \text{(intra-block error)} \qquad (16\ df)$$

These results and the remaining calculations are shown in Table 24.

We will use Duncan's new multiple-range test to compare the adjusted mean scores of the wines. The standard error of an adjusted mean score is

$$\frac{R_p}{Q_p} = \sqrt{\frac{v}{r}\left[\frac{k(t-1)}{t(k-1)}\right]} = \sqrt{\frac{0.79}{4}\left[\frac{3(8)}{9(2)}\right]} = \sqrt{0.26} = 0.51$$

The results are summarized in Table 25.

The incomplete-block designs that we have described involve only what is known as the *intra-block error* and are based on the assumption that the blocks are fixed. If the block effects are assumed to be random, however, more efficient estimates of the treatment means can sometimes be obtained by a procedure called *recovery of inter-block information*. This procedure is described in Cochran and Cox (1957). It is recommended only for large experiments in which the numbers of degrees of freedom for blocks and error exceed 25.

Table 24. Analysis of variance table for the data in Example 20.

SOURCE	SS	df	ms	F	$F_{.001}$
Total	162.31	35			
Blocks	18.31	11			
Replications	1.42	3			
Blocks (in repl.)	16.89	8	2.11	2.67	
Wines (adj.)	131.33	8	16.42	20.78***	6.19
Error	12.67	16	0.79		

Table 25. Duncan's new multiple-range test (1% level)
for the data in Example 20.

	SHORTEST SIGNIFICANT RANGE							
p	2	3	4	5	6	7	8	9
Q_p	4.13	4.31	4.42	4.51	4.57	4.62	4.66	4.70
R_p	2.11	2.20	2.25	2.30	2.33	2.36	2.38	2.40

	COMPARISON							
Wine	S_7	S_1	S_3	S_8	S_6	S_4	S_2	S_5	S_9
Mean	8.97	8.53	7.53	7.19	5.97	4.53	4.30	3.19	2.53

Ranking Procedures

In evaluating wines, judges may find it difficult to express preferences in terms of a quantitative measure. They usually find it much easier to rank the wines. Since ranking gives no indication of the magnitudes of the differences among the wines under study, it does not supply as much information as scoring. On the other hand, it not only simplifies the procedure for the judging panel, but also often represents as satisfactory a method of detecting the differences as is required.

Pairs of Ranks. When only two wines are being compared, pairs of ranks are obtained. One test that is then used is based on the signs of the differences between the paired values. The procedure is identical to that used in preference testing of paired samples. The null hypothesis of equal numbers of positive and negative differences ($H_0: p = 0.5$) is tested approximately by calculating

$$\chi^2 = \frac{(|n_1 - n_2| - 1)^2}{n_1 + n_2} \tag{26}$$

where n_1 and n_2 are the numbers of positive and negative differences, respectively, $|n_1 - n_2|$ represents the numerical (non-negative) value of the difference between them, and χ^2 is based on one degree of freedom.

Example 21. Two wines, S_1 and S_2, are ranked 15 times, as shown below. Is there a significant difference between them?

S_1	1	1	2	1	2	1	1	2	1	1	1	2	1	1	1
S_2	2	2	1	2	1	1	1	1	2	2	2	1	2	2	2
Sign	+	+	−	+	−	0	0	−	+	+	+	−	+	+	+

The + sign means that wine S_1 was ranked above wine S_2 and the − sign means that wine S_2 was ranked above wine S_1. Ties (denoted by 0) are disregarded in the analysis. The + sign appears 9 times and the − sign 4 times. Therefore

$$\chi^2 = \frac{(|9 - 4| - 1)^2}{13} = 16/13 = 1.23$$

Appendix B shows that $\chi^2_{.05}(1\ df) = 3.84$, which is larger than the calculated value. There is therefore no reason to reject the null hypothesis, and no significant difference between the two wines is indicated.

The advantages of this test are simplicity, no requirement of equal variances, and relative insensitivity to recording errors. The disadvantage, however, is that it disregards the magnitude of the difference, if any, between the wines. This problem is inherent in ranking procedures.

Ranking of Several Wines by Two Judges.   To determine whether two judges are significantly different in their rankings of several wines, *Spearman's rank correlation coefficient* can be used to test the agreement between the rankings. This correlation coefficient is defined as

$$R = 1 - \frac{6\sum d^2}{k(k^2 - 1)} \tag{27}$$

where $\sum d^2$ is the sum of the squares of the differences between the rank values given by the two judges to each of k wine samples. (If any wines in one ranking are tied, each is assigned the mean of the rank values they would otherwise have had.) The value of R can vary from -1 (totally opposite rankings by the two judges) to $+1$ (perfect agreement between the judges). The intermediate value $R = 0$ indicates that the two rankings are totally unrelated, i.e., they are the result of chance alone. This, in fact, is the null hypothesis, which can be written $H_0 : \rho = 0$, where ρ is the *population rank correlation*.

Little reliability can be placed on a value of R obtained from the rankings of fewer than 10 samples. The significance of a calculated value of R can be determined by comparing the value of

$$t = R\sqrt{\frac{k - 2}{1 - R^2}} \qquad (28)$$

with the appropriate t-value, based on $k - 2$ degrees of freedom, in Appendix E. For significance the calculated t-value must exceed the tabular value. A significant positive t-value indicates that the judges agree in their rankings. The significance of calculated R-values can also be determined by the use of Appendix H. Calculated values that exceed those in the table are significantly different from zero and indicate agreement in the rankings.

Example 22. Two judges rank 10 wines, as shown below. Is there a significant difference in their rankings?

	WINE									
JUDGE	1	2	3	4	5	6	7	8	9	10
J_1	2	1	10	7	8	6	3	4	5	9
J_2	3	1	8	9	10	7	4	2	5	6
DIFFERENCE										
d	−1	0	2	−2	−2	−1	−1	2	0	3
d^2	1	0	4	4	4	1	1	4	0	9

$$\sum d^2 = 28$$

The null hypothesis ($H_0 : \rho = 0$) is that there is no correlation between the rankings. Solving Equations 27 and 28, we obtain

$$R = 1 - \frac{6(28)}{10(99)} = 0.830$$

$$t = 0.830\sqrt{\frac{8}{1 - 0.689}} = 4.21$$

From Appendix E we see that $t_{.01}(8\ df) = 3.355$. Since the calculated value $t = 4.21$ exceeds the tabular value, we reject (at the 1% level) the null hypothesis and conclude that the value $R = 0.830$ is highly significantly different from 0. The agreement between the rankings of the two judges is therefore highly significant. If we use Appendix H (recalling that $df = 10 - 2 = 8$) we see that any value of R greater than 0.7646 is significant at the 1% level. Therefore $R = 0.830$ is highly significant. Using Appendix H eliminates the need to calculate t.

This procedure can also be applied in the evaluation of judging ability. Adding increasing amounts of some constituent to a wine provides a set of samples of known order. If a panelist is asked to rank the set for increasing amounts of the constituent, we have an accurate standard with which to compare his ranking, and Spearman's rank correlation coefficient is appropriate for rating his competence.

Ranking of Several Wines by Two or More Judges.   The ranking of k wines by n judges is a very common procedure. Two methods of analyzing the data are presented here.

Method 1. A quick appraisal of possible significant differences among a set of rankings can be made by the use of Appendixes I-1 and I-2. These tables list ranges of *rank totals*, which are the sums of the n individual rank values for a given wine. Rank totals that lie *outside* the ranges shown in the tables indicate results significantly different from those that would be obtained by chance alone.

Example 23. Twelve judges rank 5 wines, yielding the following rank totals: S_1 (34), S_2 (20), S_3 (52), S_4 (26), S_5 (48). Use Appendixes I to determine whether there are significant differences among these rankings.

Appendix I-1 shows that for 12 rankings of 5 samples there are significant differences at the 5% level for rank totals not within the range 25–47. Thus we see that wine S_2 is ranked significantly low, and wines S_3 and S_5 are ranked significantly high. At the 1% level the range is 22–50, so at this level wine S_2 is ranked significantly low and wine S_3 is ranked significantly high.

For small values of k and n, there may be more significance than is indicated by the tables of rank totals. In such situations the following method of analyzing the data is more effective.

Method 2. Rankings can be replaced by a set of quantities called *normal scores*, which are listed in Appendix J. Then the usual procedures for analyzing normally distributed data are appropriate. For example, Appendix J shows that for 6 ranked wines the normal scores that replace the rank values 1, 2, 3, 4, 5, and 6 are 1.267, 0.642, 0.202, −0.202, −0.642, and −1.267, respectively. This transformation converts the ranking into a normal population, and the usual analysis of variance procedure is applied. Since the positive and negative values of the normal scores are distributed symmetrically about their mean value, 0, the total for each judge is zero and therefore the grand total, G, is also zero. This greatly simplifies the computations.

Example 24. Five judges rank 6 wines, as shown in Table 26. Use Appendix J to analyze the results for significance.

The rankings are converted to normal scores as shown in Table 27. The calculations follow.

Table 26. Six wines ranked by 5 judges (see Example 24).

JUDGE	S_1	S_2	S_3	S_4	S_5	S_6
1	6	4	2	3	5	1
2	3	6	4	1	5	2
3	1	2	5	3	6	4
4	5	6	3	1	4	2
5	6	5	4	2	3	1
Rank total	21	23	18	10	23	10

Table 27. Normal scores for the rankings in Table 26.

JUDGE	S_1	S_2	S_3	S_4	S_5	S_6	TOTAL
				WINE			
1	−1.267	−0.202	0.642	0.202	−0.642	1.267	0
2	0.202	−1.267	−0.202	1.267	−0.642	0.642	0
3	1.267	0.642	−0.642	0.202	−1.267	−0.202	0
4	−0.642	−1.267	0.202	1.267	−0.202	0.642	0
5	−1.267	−0.642	−0.202	0.642	0.202	1.267	0
Total	−1.707	−2.736	−0.202	3.580	−2.551	3.616	0 = G
Mean	−0.341	−0.547	−0.040	0.716	−0.510	0.723	

$$C = 0$$
$$\text{Total } SS = 10[(1.267)^2 + (0.642)^2 + (0.202)^2]$$
$$= 20.583 \qquad\qquad (29\ df)$$
$$\text{Wine } SS = [(-1.707)^2 + (-2.736)^2 + \cdots + (3.606)^2]/5$$
$$= 8.568 \qquad\qquad (5\ df)$$
$$\text{Error } SS = 20.583 - 8.568 = 12.015 \qquad\qquad (24\ df)$$

These results and the remaining calculations are shown in Table 28.

Since the calculated F-value of 3.41 exceeds the tabular value of 2.62, significant differences at the 5% level are indicated, and the LSD can be used to determine which wines are significantly different from each other.

$$LSD = t_{.05}(24\ df)\sqrt{2(0.501)/5} = 2.064\sqrt{0.200} = 0.923$$

Table 28. Analysis of variance table for
the data in Example 24.

SOURCE	SS	df	ms	F	$F_{.05}$	$F_{.01}$
Total	20.583	29				
Wines	8.568	5	1.71	3.41*	2.62	3.90
Error	12.015	24	0.501			

Using the mean normal scores, the differences can be summarized as follows:

WINE

	S_6	S_4	S_3	S_1	S_5	S_2
Mean	0.723	0.716	−0.040	−0.341	−0.510	−0.547

We see that at the 5% level there are no significant differences among wines S_3, S_4, and S_6, but wines S_4 and S_6 are significantly better than wines S_1, S_2, and S_5. There are no significant differences among wines S_1, S_2, S_3, and S_5. (As in all such analyses Duncan's new multiple-range test, which does not require the calculation of F, could be used instead of the LSD procedure.)

The two methods that have been presented here for analyzing ranked data have the advantage over other methods that they provide ways of establishing significant differences among individual wines. Other methods merely indicate whether significant differences do or do not exist among the wines taken as a group.

Descriptive Sensory Analysis

The best-known method of descriptive sensory analysis is the *flavor profile* developed by the Arthur D. Little Company, Cambridge, Massachusetts. It has been used in product development, quality control, and laboratory research by numerous food and drug companies (Amerine et al., 1965a). In this method a panel of highly trained judges is used to identify the individual and overall odor and flavor characteristics of a food, in terms of the sensory impressions they create. Properly trained panels achieve considerable agreement, after group discussion, on overall sensory impressions and the intensities and order of detection of the various sensory factors. Disadvantages of the flavor profile method are the expense of training the judges, the possible bias introduced by a dominant (assertive) member of the panel during the group discussion, and the difficulty of statistical analysis of the results.

For an example of a record form for the descriptive sensory analysis of wines, see Figure 18. As in the flavor profile method, many winery staff members and private groups make their decisions on the quality of a wine after group discussion of the results obtained in the individual sensory examinations. Is group discussion beneficial or does it entail too great a risk of prejudicial influences? Meyers and Lamm (1975) have studied this problem; the answer is by no means as unequivocal as one would wish. There is first of all the danger of a dominant individual's imposing his judgment on the group, by either his reputation or force of personality. If this occurs, group discussion is useless except as an ego-cultivating exercise for the dominant individual (e.g., the winery owner). Jones (1958) and Foster et al. (1955) have noted that a group judgment is not the same as a group of judgments, because an individual can sway the group judgment. (The obvious analogy with trial juries here is inescapable.)

Even if there is no dominant individual, the group influence itself may be detrimental. As Meyers and Lamm say, "What people learn from discussion is mostly in the direction supporting the majority's initial preference." The problem is that, probably subconsciously, members of the group usually show a disproportionate interest in facts and opinions that support their initial preferences and tend to ignore those facts and opinions that do not. This appears to be true for both verbal and written opinions. If knowledge of the positions of other members of the panel has a polarizing effect (and how can it help but do so if the owner or winemaker is present?), we recommend that all the panelists withhold information on their initial preferences.

Stone et al. (1974) have introduced a quantitative method of descriptive sensory analysis. The various sensory attributes of the product are evaluated separately. For each attribute a scale of 6 inches is provided, with two labeled anchor points $\frac{1}{2}$ inch from the ends of the scale and one at the center. For example, the scale for sweetness would look like this:

Weak   Moderate   Strong

	Identification	Intensity 0 to 10	Quality −5 to +5
Prior to Tasting			
1. *Visual*			
Appearance: cloudy, dull (hazy), clear, brilliant			
Color: straw yellow, greenish yellow, yellow, gold, amber; pink, violet-pink, eye-of-the-partridge (light brownish red), ruby red, violet-red, brownish red (tawny)			
Intensity: light, strong			
Gas release: none, fine bubbles, medium bubbles, large bubbles			
2. *Olfactory**			
Complex: vinous, distinct, varietal, flowery, musty(?), oxidized			
Specific: ethyl acetate, fusel oils, hydrogen sulfide, mercaptan, sulfur dioxide			
In-Mouth			
3. *Gustatory*			
Balanced: thin, full-bodied			
Specific: sweet, sour, bitter, salty			
4. *Olfactory (flavor)**			
Complex: earthy, fruity, herbaceous, woody			
Specific (identify)			
5. *Texture*: astringent, burning, prickly, foreign*			

*The chemical origin of the sensory impression should be specified if possible.

Name ———————————————— Date ——————————

FIGURE 18

Record form for descriptive sensory analysis of wines.
(Adapted from J. Puisais et al., 1974.)

After tasting the product the judge marks a cross at the point representing the magnitude of the sensation in question. The distance from the end of the scale to the cross is a measure of this magnitude. Stone et al. believe that the scale is linear, i.e., that with several data points a straight-line plot of measured distance versus true sweetness (or other sensory attribute) is obtained.

The procedure requires extensive training with the product (about 20 hours) and individual testing. The individual and panel data are evaluated by analysis of variance. Correlation coefficients are calculated to determine the degree of correlation between the scales. Primary sensory values are measured by principal component analysis, factor analysis, etc. Finally, a multidimensional model can be developed and its relation to consumer response or other external factors can be established.

From the data one should be able to identify inconsistent responses (indicating the need for more training) and the adequacy of the judge's discrimination between different levels of a given sensory attribute. One can also determine whether individual scales are producing consistent results and whether the scales are adequately discriminating between products. Finally, the extent to which products differ in the specific attributes can be measured, and the most accurate and consistent judges can be identified.

Computer programs for one-way and two-way analyses of variance are used to measure the agreement between a judge and the panel as a whole. The interaction sum of squares is estimated for each judge and the F-value is calculated. A high F-value for an individual judge indicates his disagreement with the panel, i.e., there is interaction between the product and the judge.

Our conclusion is that descriptive sensory analysis, in the hands of highly trained personnel, should prove useful in solving certain industrial and research sensory evaluation problems.

Some Suggested Exercises

The serious amateur wine judge usually wishes to improve his judging ability, but how does he go about it? Obviously he prac-

tices. His main problem is finding a fixed frame of reference for each of the major odor and taste components of wines. What, for example, is low or high sourness? How does a low concentration of acetaldehyde smell compared with a high concentration? Can one distinguish low, moderate, and high concentrations of sulfur dioxide in wines?

The following exercises are intended to help answer these and similar questions. They should also prove useful in selecting the best judges for many sensory evaluation panels. However, there is certainly no direct relation between one's inherent taste or odor sensitivity and one's ability to evaluate wine quality. For each specific sensory characteristic, one must also know the level of intensity that is appropriate in the wine in question, and one must be able to recognize the proper balance among the various sensory characteristics. Experience is what really counts.

Obviously most people do not have a supply of citric acid or glycerol or ethyl acetate, nor do they have the equipment for measuring or weighing such chemicals. We suggest that you solicit the interest and help of an enologically-inclined chemist or pharmacist. They do have the necessary chemicals and equipment, or can get them without difficulty. (See also Marcus, 1974.)

Thresholds. A suggested series of concentrations for testing sensitivity to sucrose (sweetness) in aqueous solution is 0.1, 0.3, 0.7, and 1.2% by weight. The "A-not-A" type of test may be used, although other methods work equally well. In this test a water blank (the standard) is tasted first. Then one of the sucrose solutions (in a random order) or another blank is tasted. The judge decides whether the sample presented is the same as or different from the standard. (For a record form see Figure 19.) The test is repeated 6 times for each concentration, including the blank (30 times in all). Typical results for such a test might be the following:

	SAMPLE				
	BLANK	0.1%	0.3%	0.7%	1.2%
Correct decision	3	3	4	5	6
% Correct	50	50	66.7	83.3	100

Nature of difference: _____

Taste (or smell) the standard (S) and the sample. Decide whether the sample is the same as or different from the standard.

Sample no.	Same as S	Different from S
_____	_____	_____
_____	_____	_____
_____	_____	_____
_____	_____	_____

Name _____ Date _____

FIGURE 19

Record form for an A-not-A test.

What is this judge's threshold for sucrose in water? Obviously 50% of his decisions should be correct by chance alone. The percentage of correct decisions *above* chance is defined as $P_c = 2 \times (P_o - 50)$, where P_o is the percentage of correct decisions observed. In practice the threshold is usually taken to be that concentration at which the judge makes 50% correct decisions above chance ($P_c = 50$), i.e., 75% correct decisions observed ($P_o = 75$), since $2(75 - 50) = 50$. In the present example the sucrose threshold is therefore somewhere between 0.3 and 0.7%. A more exact threshold could be established by repeating the test with solutions between 0.3 and 0.7% sucrose, e.g., 0.3, 0.35, 0.43, 0.53, and 0.68%.

The results can be plotted on log-probability paper, with P_c on the probability axis (ordinate) and concentration on the log axis (abscissa). Draw a straight line as close to the data points as possible. The intersection of this line with a horizontal line drawn from $P_c = 50$ defines the concentration threshold. For a still more accurate value the line can be plotted by the method of least squares, either manually or with an electronic calculator or computer. For purposes of demonstration we suggest that the group results be pooled and the average threshold calculated. However, it is instructive to compare the thresholds of various members of the group. For this purpose the test should probably be repeated until there are at least 15 correct decisions for each individual.

This type of test can also be used to determine the thresholds for many other substances, in either wine or water. For example, the following amounts of various chemicals could be added to the base wine or water (the standards), which constitutes the first of five samples in the series: acetaldehyde (40, 80, 140, and 200 mg per liter); acetic acid (3, 5, 9, and 14 grams per liter); biacetyl (4, 8, 12, and 20 mg per liter); citric acid (0.2, 0.4, 0.8, and 1.6 grams per liter); ethyl acetate (30, 60, 100, and 150 mg per liter); sorbic acid (50, 100, 175, and 275 mg per liter); sulfur dioxide (40, 90, 150, and 250 mg per liter); tartaric acid (0.03, 0.07, 0.10, and 0.15 gram per liter). The sulfur dioxide test should be the last one attempted, and should be made no more than once per day.

When water is used as the standard rather than a base wine, these tests establish the absolute thresholds of the judges (see page 73). When wines are used the thresholds should be interpreted as difference thresholds (except for sorbic acid), because the concentration of the component in the base wine may already exceed that corresponding to the absolute threshold. Care should be exercised in selecting a fairly neutral wine of normal composition as the base wine. If testing time is limited one may use four concentrations instead of five (omitting the lowest).

Thresholds can also be determined by the methods of just noticeable difference (*jnd*) and just not noticeable difference (*jnnd*). In the former test the samples are presented in order of increasing concentration, from below threshold to well above threshold. The judge indicates the first sample that he finds just noticeably different (sweeter, sourer, etc.) from the preceding sample. (For a record form see Figure 20.) This test can be used for determining absolute as well as difference thresholds. Because the errors of expectation and habituation may occur, the test should be done in both directions, i.e., *jnd* and *jnnd*. In the latter test the samples are presented in order of *decreasing* concentration; the judge indicates the first sample that he finds just *not* noticeably different from the preceding sample.

For example, the test for a *jnd* is done 5 times with a series of wines containing citric acid. The base wine (nothing added) contains 0.50 gram per 100 ml; the amounts of citric acid added to

Nature of difference: _____

Sample order: C H J K N R T

Taste (or smell) the samples, from the lowest concentration (left) to the highest (right). Indicate the first sample that is just noticeably different in taste (or smell) from the preceding sample.

Difference first noticed in sample _____

Name _____ Date _____

FIGURE 20
Record form for a just-noticeable-difference test.

make the remaining four samples are 0.02, 0.05, 0.10, and 0.25 gram per 100 ml, giving samples with 0.52, 0.55, 0.60, and 0.75 gram per 100 ml, respectively. In the *jnd* series the actual *jnd* is 0.55 three times and 0.60 twice; in the corresponding *jnnd* series (also done 5 times) the actual *jnnd* is 0.55 three times and 0.52 twice. The weighted means of these two sets of data are given by

$$\frac{0.55(3) + 0.60(2)}{5} = 0.57 \qquad (jnd)$$

$$\frac{0.55(3) + 0.52(2)}{5} = 0.54 \qquad (jnnd)$$

and the overall mean value is therefore 0.55. Thus this judge's difference threshold for citric acid in wine is $0.55 - 0.50 = 0.05$ gram per 100 ml. The usual measures of central tendency, significance, probable error, etc., can be applied.

Off Odors. The threshold tests for acetaldehyde, biacetyl, ethyl acetate, sorbic acid, and sulfur dioxide (listed above) can also be used for familiarizing the student with common off odors. Other off odors can be produced by adding a small amount of the substance in question to a neutral wine. For example, about 5 to 10 parts per billion of hydrogen sulfide will be detectable. For the higher alcohols, 400 mg per liter of 3-methyl-1-butanol (isoamyl alcohol) will be adequate to give a fusel oil odor to the wine. Securing wines with typical and easily detectable off odors of corkiness, moldiness, or woodiness may be difficult. One should inquire of  wine merchants or wineries for help in locating such wines.

Other Exercises. Most of the procedures discussed previously can also be used in the training and selection of judges. For detecting differences of a nonspecific character (an unidentified off odor, for example), the duo-trio test (page 113) and triangle test (page 114) are most useful. Judges who cannot distinguish the off odor can be screened out. When potential judges are being trained, those who fail to detect the odor will know that they must practice to reach the requisite proficiency, or be disqualified. The duo-trio and triangle tests can also be used in blending wines to match a standard—an important winery operation. They are useful not only in winery operations but also in the training and selection of blenders.

Paired-sample tests (page 111) can be used for establishing quality differences. However, ranking (page 129) and scoring (page 121) are often the preferred procedures. Can an individual correctly rank a series of wines in increasing order of Cabernet aroma, sweetness, sourness, ethanol content, etc.? Those who are deficient in one or more such skills need further training and practice, or should simply not be used on a sensory evaluation panel for which the skill in question is a requirement.

Because individuals differ in their understanding of the tests, some preliminary training is desirable so that all the potential judges start the test series on an approximately equal basis. In all training tests, the statistical significance of the results must be calculated unless it is obvious from inspection of the data that the results are insignificant.

Quality. For judging the quality of wines we recommend the scoring of groups of 5 to 7 wines of a closely related type, e.g., wines of the same variety but from different wineries or of different vintages, wines of a given region or district, etc. Should the wines be served "blind" or with the labels showing? For beginning students we favor the latter method because it gives the student the best chance to associate the label with the odor, taste, and flavor

of the wine. However, this assumes that the students, and especially the instructor, are completely unprejudiced—a very big assumption. For more advanced students, "blind" judgings are much to be preferred. At home the wines should be served with the labels showing unless some consensus opinion is desired. In this case the wines should be served "blind." Ranking procedures are then usually preferred, but if the group has had experience in using a particular score card, scoring can be employed. (See also pages 59–62.)

When you can measure what you are speaking about, and express it in numbers, you know something about it; but when you cannot measure it, when you cannot express it in numbers, your knowledge is of a meager and unsatisfactory kind: it may be the beginning of knowledge, but you have scarcely, in your thoughts, advanced to the stage of science.

                                        —Lord Kelvin

PLATE 1
Wine glass painted black on the outside to prevent observation of appearance or color.

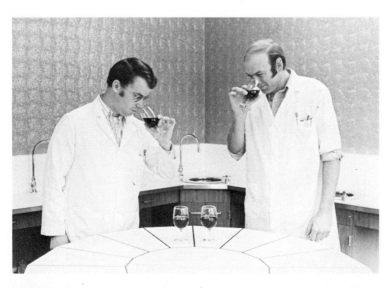

PLATE 2
Lazy susan serving table. Note sections for separating samples. (Courtesy of E. and J. Gallo, Modesto, Cal.)

PLATE 3
Panelist in booth. Note opening for serving.

PLATE 4
Assistant serving samples. (Courtesv of E. and J. Gallo, Modesto, Cal.)

PLATE 5
Glasses being served and awaiting service.

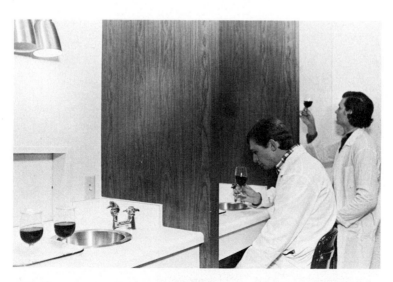

PLATE 6
*Two panelists in booths. Note spittoon basins and special lights.
(Courtesy of E. and J. Gallo, Modesto, Cal.)*

PLATE 7
Tulip-shaped, all-purpose wine glass.

PLATE 8
Tulip-shaped glass for red table wines.

PLATE 9
Tulip-shaped glass for white table wines.

PLATE 10
Hollow-stem glass for sparkling wines.

PLATE 12
Corkscrews and other openers. Left to right: screw type, lever principle,
U-shaped puller, and hollow-needle pump opener.

PLATE 13
*Tears of a 12% solution
of ethanol in water.*

PLATE 14
*Tears of an 18% solution
of ethanol in water.*

PLATE 15
Herman Wente, one of the best of the post-
Prohibition judges of California wines,
examining the appearance and color of a
white wine. (Courtesy of Wines & Vines.)

PLATE 16
Two judges (M.A.A. and E.B.R.) evaluating wines. Note buckets used
as spittoons.

Appendixes

Appendix A   Normal Distribution

The entries in this table are the areas under the normal probability curve to the right of the marginal value of the normal deviate z (or to the left of $-z$), i.e., they are the probabilities that a random value of z will equal or exceed the marginal value.

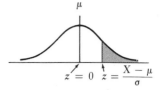

$$z = 0 \qquad z = \frac{X - \mu}{\sigma}$$

z	.00	.01	.02	.03	.04	.05	.06	.07	.08	.09
0.0	.5000	.4960	.4920	.4880	.4840	.4801	.4761	.4721	.4681	.4641
0.1	.4602	.4562	.4522	.4483	.4443	.4404	.4364	.4325	.4286	.4247
0.2	.4207	.4168	.4129	.4090	.4052	.4013	.3974	.3936	.3897	.3859
0.3	.3821	.3783	.3745	.3707	.3669	.3632	.3594	.3557	.3520	.3483
0.4	.3446	.3409	.3372	.3336	.3300	.3264	.3228	.3192	.3156	.3121
0.5	.3085	.3050	.3015	.2981	.2946	.2912	.2877	.2843	.2810	.2776
0.6	.2743	.2709	.2676	.2643	.2611	.2578	.2546	.2514	.2483	.2451
0.7	.2420	.2389	.2358	.2327	.2296	.2266	.2236	.2206	.2177	.2148
0.8	.2119	.2090	.2061	.2033	.2005	.1977	.1949	.1922	.1894	.1867
0.9	.1841	.1814	.1788	.1762	.1736	.1711	.1685	.1660	.1635	.1611
1.0	.1587	.1562	.1539	.1515	.1492	.1469	.1446	.1423	.1401	.1379
1.1	.1357	.1335	.1314	.1292	.1271	.1251	.1230	.1210	.1190	.1170
1.2	.1151	.1131	.1112	.1093	.1075	.1056	.1038	.1020	.1003	.0985
1.3	.0968	.0951	.0934	.0918	.0901	.0885	.0869	.0853	.0838	.0823
1.4	.0808	.0793	.0778	.0764	.0749	.0735	.0721	.0708	.0694	.0681
1.5	.0668	.0655	.0643	.0630	.0618	.0606	.0594	.0582	.0571	.0559
1.6	.0548	.0537	.0526	.0516	.0505	.0495	.0485	.0475	.0465	.0455
1.7	.0446	.0436	.0427	.0418	.0409	.0401	.0392	.0384	.0375	.0367
1.8	.0359	.0351	.0344	.0336	.0329	.0322	.0314	.0307	.0301	.0294
1.9	.0287	.0281	.0274	.0268	.0262	.0256	.0250	.0244	.0239	.0233
2.0	.0228	.0222	.0217	.0212	.0207	.0202	.0197	.0192	.0188	.0183
2.1	.0179	.0174	.0170	.0166	.0162	.0158	.0154	.0150	.0146	.0143
2.2	.0139	.0136	.0132	.0129	.0125	.0122	.0119	.0116	.0113	.0110
2.3	.0107	.0104	.0102	.0099	.0096	.0094	.0091	.0089	.0087	.0084
2.4	.0082	.0080	.0059	.0075	.0073	.0071	.0069	.0068	.0066	.0064
2.5	.0062	.0060	.0059	.0057	.0055	.0054	.0052	.0051	.0049	.0048
2.6	.0047	.0045	.0044	.0043	.0041	.0040	.0039	.0038	.0037	.0036
2.7	.0035	.0034	.0033	.0032	.0031	.0030	.0029	.0028	.0027	.0026
2.8	.0026	.0025	.0024	.0023	.0023	.0022	.0021	.0021	.0020	.0019
2.9	.0019	.0018	.0018	.0017	.0016	.0016	.0015	.0015	.0014	.0014
3.0	.0013	.0013	.0013	.0012	.0012	.0011	.0011	.0011	.0010	.0010
3.1	.0010	.0009	.0009	.0009	.0008	.0008	.0008	.0008	.0007	.0007
3.2	.0007	.0007	.0006	.0006	.0006	.0006	.0006	.0005	.0005	.0005
3.3	.0005	.0005	.0005	.0004	.0004	.0004	.0004	.0004	.0004	.0003
3.4	.0003	.0003	.0003	.0003	.0003	.0003	.0003	.0003	.0003	.0002
3.6	.0002	.0002	.0001	.0001	.0001	.0001	.0001	.0001	.0001	.0001
3.9	.0000									

Appendix B Chi-Square Distribution

The entries in this table are the χ^2-values for distributions with from 1 to 30 degrees of freedom, at 10 values of the probability.

	PROBABILITY OF A LARGER VALUE OF χ^2									
df	0.99	0.95	0.50	0.30	0.20	0.10	0.05	0.02	0.01	0.001
1	0.0002	0.004	0.46	1.07	1.64	2.71	3.84	5.41	6.64	10.83
2	0.020	0.103	1.39	2.41	3.22	4.60	5.99	7.82	9.21	13.82
3	0.115	0.35	2.37	3.66	4.64	6.25	7.82	9.84	11.34	16.27
4	0.30	0.71	3.36	4.88	5.99	7.78	9.49	11.67	13.28	18.46
5	0.55	1.14	4.35	6.06	7.29	9.24	11.07	13.39	15.09	20.52
6	0.87	1.64	5.35	7.23	8.56	10.64	12.59	15.03	16.81	22.46
7	1.24	2.17	6.35	8.38	9.80	12.02	14.07	16.62	18.48	24.32
8	1.65	2.73	7.34	9.52	11.03	13.36	15.51	18.17	20.09	26.12
9	2.09	3.32	8.34	10.66	12.24	14.68	16.92	19.68	21.67	27.88
10	2.56	3.94	9.34	11.78	13.44	15.99	18.31	21.16	23.21	29.59
11	3.05	4.58	10.34	12.90	14.63	17.28	19.68	22.62	24.72	31.26
12	3.57	5.23	11.34	14.01	15.81	18.55	21.03	24.05	26.22	32.91
13	4.11	5.89	12.34	15.12	16.98	19.81	22.36	25.47	27.69	34.53
14	4.66	6.57	13.34	16.22	18.15	21.06	23.68	26.87	29.14	36.12
15	5.23	7.26	14.34	17.32	19.31	22.31	25.00	28.26	30.58	37.70
16	5.81	7.96	15.34	18.42	20.46	23.54	26.30	29.63	32.00	39.25
17	6.41	8.67	16.34	19.51	21.62	24.77	27.59	31.00	33.41	40.79
18	7.02	9.39	17.34	20.60	22.76	25.99	28.87	32.35	34.80	42.31
19	7.63	10.12	18.34	21.69	23.90	27.20	30.14	33.69	36.19	43.82
20	8.26	10.85	19.34	22.78	25.04	28.41	31.41	35.02	37.57	45.32
21	8.90	11.59	20.34	23.86	26.17	29.62	32.67	36.34	38.93	46.80
22	9.54	12.34	21.34	24.94	27.30	30.81	33.92	37.66	40.29	48.27
23	10.20	13.09	22.34	26.02	28.43	32.01	35.17	38.97	41.64	49.73
24	10.86	13.85	23.34	27.10	29.55	33.20	36.42	40.27	42.98	51.18
25	11.52	14.61	24.34	28.17	30.68	34.38	37.65	41.57	44.31	52.62
26	12.20	15.38	25.34	29.25	31.80	35.56	38.88	42.86	45.64	54.05
27	12.88	16.15	26.34	30.32	32.91	36.74	40.11	44.14	46.96	55.48
28	13.56	16.93	27.34	31.39	34.03	37.92	41.34	45.42	48.28	56.89
29	14.26	17.71	28.34	32.46	35.14	39.09	42.56	46.69	49.59	58.30
30	14.95	18.49	29.34	33.53	36.25	40.26	43.77	47.96	50.89	59.70

SOURCE: Abridged from Table IV of R. A. Fisher and F. Yates, *Statistical Tables for Biological, Agricultural, and Medical Research*, 6th ed., 1974. Longman Group Ltd., London (previously published by Oliver and Boyd Ltd., Edinburgh). By permission of the authors and publisher.

APPENDIXES

Appendix C   Significance in Paired-Sample and Duo-Trio Tests. H_0: $p = \frac{1}{2}$.

The number n is the number of trials, i.e., the number of judges or judgments in the test.

n	MINIMUM CORRECT JUDGMENTS TO ESTABLISH SIGNIFICANT DIFFERENCE (ONE-TAILED TEST)			MINIMUM AGREEING JUDGMENTS NECESSARY TO ESTABLISH SIGNIFICANT PREFERENCE (TWO-TAILED TEST)		
	$p = 0.05$	$p = 0.01$	$p = 0.001$	$p = 0.05$	$p = 0.01$	$p = 0.001$
7	7	7	—	7	—	—
8	7	8	—	8	8	—
9	8	9	—	8	9	—
10	9	10	10	9	10	—
11	9	10	11	10	11	11
12	10	11	12	10	11	12
13	10	12	13	11	12	13
14	11	12	13	12	13	14
15	12	13	14	12	13	14
16	12	14	15	13	14	15
17	13	14	16	13	15	16
18	13	15	16	14	15	17
19	14	15	17	15	16	17
20	15	16	18	15	17	18
21	15	17	18	16	17	19
22	16	17	19	17	18	19
23	16	18	20	17	19	20
24	17	19	20	18	19	21
25	18	19	21	18	20	21
30	20	22	24	21	23	25
35	23	25	27	24	26	28
40	26	28	31	27	29	31
45	29	31	34	30	32	34
50	32	34	37	33	35	37
60	37	40	43	39	41	44
70	43	46	49	44	47	50
80	48	51	55	50	52	56
90	54	57	61	55	58	61
100	59	63	66	61	64	67

SOURCE: Adapted from a table by E. B. Roessler, G. A. Baker, and M. A. Amerine, *Food Research* 21, 117–121 (1956).

Appendix D   Significance in Triangle Tests. H_0: $p = \frac{1}{3}$.

The number n is the number of trials, i.e., the number of judges or judgments in the test.

n	MINIMUM CORRECT JUDGMENTS TO ESTABLISH SIGNIFICANT DIFFERENCE			n	MINIMUM CORRECT JUDGMENTS TO ESTABLISH SIGNIFICANT DIFFERENCE		
	$p = 0.05$	$p = 0.01$	$p = 0.001$		$p = 0.05$	$p = 0.01$	$p = 0.001$
5	4	5	5	56	26	28	31
6	5	6	6	57	27	29	31
7	5	6	7	58	27	29	32
8	6	7	8	59	27	30	32
9	6	7	8	60	28	30	33
10	7	8	9	61	28	30	33
11	7	8	9	62	28	31	33
12	8	9	10	63	29	31	34
13	8	9	10	64	29	32	34
14	9	10	11	65	30	32	35
15	9	10	12	66	30	32	35
16	10	11	12	67	30	33	36
17	10	11	13	68	31	33	36
18	10	12	13	69	31	34	36
19	11	12	14	70	32	34	37
20	11	13	14	71	32	34	37
21	12	13	15	72	32	35	38
22	12	14	15	73	33	35	38
23	13	14	16	74	33	36	39
24	13	14	16	75	34	36	39
25	13	15	17	76	34	36	39
26	14	15	17	77	34	37	40
27	14	16	18	78	35	37	40
28	15	16	18	79	35	38	41
29	15	17	19	80	35	38	41
30	16	17	19	81	36	38	41
31	16	18	19	82	36	39	42
32	16	18	20	83	37	39	42
33	17	19	20	84	37	40	43
34	17	19	21	85	37	40	43
35	18	19	21	86	38	40	44
36	18	20	22	87	38	41	44
37	18	20	22	88	39	41	44
38	19	21	23	89	39	42	45
39	19	21	23	90	39	42	45
40	20	22	24	91	40	42	46
41	20	22	24	92	40	43	46
42	21	22	25	93	40	43	46
43	21	23	25	94	41	44	47
44	21	23	25	95	41	44	47
45	22	24	26	96	42	44	48
46	22	24	26	97	42	45	48
47	23	25	27	98	42	45	49
48	23	25	27	99	43	46	49
49	23	25	28	100	43	46	49
50	24	26	28	200	80	84	89
51	24	26	29	300	117	122	127
52	25	27	29	400	152	158	165
53	25	27	29	500	188	194	202
54	25	27	30	1000	363	372	383
55	26	28	30	2000	709	722	737

SOURCE: Adapted from a table by E. B. Roessler, J. Warren, and J. F. Guymon, *Food Research* 13, 503–505 (1948).

182 APPENDIXES

Appendix E t-Distribution

The entries in this table are the t-values for distributions with from 1 to ∞ degrees of freedom, at 10 values of the two-tailed probability (sum of the two tail areas) and the 10 corresponding values of the one-tailed probability (one tail area).

df	PROBABILITY OF A LARGER VALUE OF t, SIGN IGNORED (TWO-TAILED TEST)									
	0.5	0.4	0.3	0.2	0.1	0.05	0.02	0.01	0.002	0.001
1	1.000	1.376	1.963	3.078	6.314	12.706	31.821	63.657	318.31	636.619
2	0.816	1.061	1.386	1.886	2.920	4.303	6.965	9.925	22.327	31.598
3	0.765	0.978	1.250	1.638	2.353	3.182	4.541	5.841	10.214	12.941
4	0.741	0.941	1.190	1.533	2.132	2.776	3.747	4.604	7.173	8.610
5	0.727	0.920	1.156	1.476	2.015	2.571	3.365	4.032	5.893	6.859
6	0.718	0.906	1.134	1.440	1.943	2.447	3.143	3.707	5.208	5.959
7	0.711	0.896	1.119	1.415	1.895	2.365	2.998	3.499	4.785	5.405
8	0.706	0.889	1.108	1.397	1.860	2.306	2.896	3.355	4.501	5.041
9	0.703	0.883	1.100	1.383	1.833	2.262	2.821	3.250	4.297	4.781
10	0.700	0.879	1.093	1.372	1.812	2.228	2.764	3.169	4.144	4.587
11	0.697	0.876	1.088	1.363	1.796	2.201	2.718	3.106	4.025	4.437
12	0.695	0.873	1.083	1.356	1.782	2.179	2.681	3.055	3.930	4.318
13	0.694	0.870	1.079	1.350	1.771	2.160	2.650	3.012	3.852	4.221
14	0.692	0.868	1.076	1.345	1.761	2.145	2.624	2.977	3.787	4.140
15	0.691	0.866	1.074	1.341	1.753	2.131	2.602	2.947	3.733	4.073
16	0.690	0.865	1.071	1.337	1.746	2.120	2.583	2.921	3.686	4.015
17	0.689	0.863	1.069	1.333	1.740	2.110	2.567	2.898	3.646	3.965
18	0.688	0.862	1.067	1.330	1.734	2.101	2.552	2.878	3.610	3.922
19	0.688	0.861	1.066	1.328	1.729	2.093	2.539	2.861	3.579	3.883
20	0.687	0.860	1.064	1.325	1.725	2.086	2.528	2.845	3.552	3.850
21	0.686	0.859	1.063	1.323	1.721	2.080	2.518	2.831	3.527	3.819
22	0.686	0.858	1.061	1.321	1.717	2.074	2.508	2.819	3.505	3.792
23	0.685	0.858	1.060	1.319	1.714	2.069	2.500	2.807	3.485	3.767
24	0.685	0.857	1.059	1.318	1.711	2.064	2.492	2.797	3.467	3.745
25	0.684	0.856	1.058	1.316	1.708	2.060	2.485	2.787	3.450	3.725
26	0.684	0.856	1.058	1.315	1.706	2.056	2.479	2.779	3.435	3.707
27	0.684	0.855	1.057	1.314	1.703	2.052	2.473	2.771	3.421	3.690
28	0.683	0.855	1.056	1.313	1.701	2.048	2.467	2.763	3.408	3.674
29	0.683	0.854	1.055	1.311	1.699	2.045	2.462	2.756	3.396	3.659
30	0.683	0.854	1.055	1.310	1.697	2.042	2.457	2.750	3.385	3.646
40	0.681	0.851	1.050	1.303	1.684	2.021	2.423	2.704	3.307	3.551
60	0.679	0.848	1.046	1.296	1.671	2.000	2.390	2.660	3.232	3.460
120	0.677	0.845	1.041	1.289	1.658	1.980	2.358	2.617	3.160	3.373
∞	0.674	0.842	1.036	1.282	1.645	1.960	2.326	2.576	3.090	3.291
df	0.25	0.2	0.15	0.1	0.05	0.025	0.01	0.005	0.001	0.0005

PROBABILITY OF A LARGER VALUE OF t, SIGN CONSIDERED (ONE-TAILED TEST)

SOURCE: Abridged from Table III of R. A. Fisher and F. Yates, *Statistical Tables for Biological, Agricultural, and Medical Research*, 6th ed., 1974. Longman Group Ltd., London (previously published by Oliver and Boyd Ltd., Edinburgh). By permission of the authors and publisher.

Appendix F-1   F-Distribution, 5% Level

The entries in this table are the F-values for which the tail area equals 0.05.

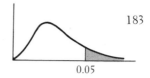

0.05

df FOR DENOMINATOR	df FOR NUMERATOR									
	1	2	3	4	5	6	8	12	24	∞
1	161.4	199.5	215.7	224.6	230.2	234.0	238.9	243.9	249.0	254.3
2	18.51	19.00	19.16	19.25	19.30	19.33	19.37	19.41	19.45	19.50
3	10.13	9.55	9.28	9.12	9.01	8.94	8.84	8.74	8.64	8.53
4	7.71	6.94	6.59	6.39	6.26	6.16	6.04	5.91	5.77	5.63
5	6.61	5.79	5.41	5.19	5.05	4.95	4.82	4.68	4.53	4.36
6	5.99	5.14	4.76	4.53	4.39	4.28	4.15	4.00	3.84	3.67
7	5.59	4.74	4.35	4.12	3.97	3.87	3.73	3.57	3.41	3.23
8	5.32	4.46	4.07	3.84	3.69	3.58	3.44	3.28	3.12	2.93
9	5.12	4.26	3.86	3.63	3.48	3.37	3.23	3.07	2.90	2.71
10	4.96	4.10	3.71	3.48	3.33	3.22	3.07	2.91	2.74	2.54
11	4.84	3.98	3.59	3.36	3.20	3.09	2.95	2.79	2.61	2.40
12	4.75	3.88	3.49	3.26	3.11	3.00	2.85	2.69	2.50	2.30
13	4.67	3.80	3.41	3.18	3.02	2.92	2.77	2.60	2.42	2.21
14	4.60	3.74	3.34	3.11	2.96	2.85	2.70	2.53	2.35	2.13
15	4.54	3.68	3.29	3.06	2.90	2.79	2.64	2.48	2.29	2.07
16	4.49	3.63	3.24	3.01	2.85	2.74	2.59	2.42	2.24	2.01
17	4.45	3.59	3.20	2.96	2.81	2.70	2.55	2.38	2.19	1.96
18	4.41	3.55	3.16	2.93	2.77	2.66	2.51	2.34	2.15	1.92
19	4.38	3.52	3.13	2.90	2.74	2.63	2.48	2.31	2.11	1.88
20	4.35	3.49	3.10	2.87	2.71	2.60	2.45	2.28	2.08	1.84
21	4.32	3.47	3.07	2.84	2.68	2.57	2.42	2.25	2.05	1.81
22	4.30	3.44	3.05	2.82	2.66	2.55	2.40	2.23	2.03	1.78
23	4.28	3.42	3.03	2.80	2.64	2.53	2.38	2.20	2.00	1.76
24	4.26	3.40	3.01	2.78	2.62	2.51	2.36	2.18	1.98	1.73
25	4.24	3.38	2.99	2.76	2.60	2.49	2.34	2.16	1.96	1.71
26	4.22	3.37	2.98	2.74	2.59	2.47	2.32	2.15	1.95	1.69
27	4.21	3.35	2.96	2.73	2.57	2.46	2.30	2.13	1.93	1.67
28	4.20	3.34	2.95	2.71	2.56	2.44	2.29	2.12	1.91	1.65
29	4.18	3.33	2.93	2.70	2.54	2.43	2.28	2.10	1.90	1.64
30	4.17	3.32	2.92	2.69	2.53	2.42	2.27	2.09	1.89	1.62
40	4.08	3.23	2.84	2.61	2.45	2.34	2.18	2.00	1.79	1.51
60	4.00	3.15	2.76	2.52	2.37	2.25	2.10	1.92	1.70	1.39
120	3.92	3.07	2.68	2.45	2.29	2.17	2.02	1.83	1.61	1.25
∞	3.84	2.99	2.60	2.37	2.21	2.10	1.94	1.75	1.52	1.00

Appendix F-2 *F*-Distribution, 1% Level

The entries in this table are the *F*-values for which the tail area equals 0.01.

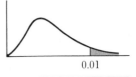

0.01

df FOR DENOMINATOR	df FOR NUMERATOR									
	1	2	3	4	5	6	8	12	24	∞
1	4052	4999	5403	5625	5764	5859	5982	6106	6234	6366
2	98.50	99.00	99.17	99.25	99.30	99.33	99.37	99.42	99.46	99.50
3	34.12	30.82	29.46	28.71	28.24	27.91	27.49	27.05	26.60	26.12
4	21.20	18.00	16.69	15.98	15.52	15.21	14.80	14.37	13.93	13.46
5	16.26	13.27	12.06	11.39	10.97	10.67	10.29	9.89	9.47	9.02
6	13.74	10.92	9.78	9.15	8.75	8.47	8.10	7.72	7.31	6.88
7	12.25	9.55	8.45	7.85	7.46	7.19	6.84	6.47	6.07	5.65
8	11.26	8.65	7.59	7.01	6.63	6.37	6.03	5.67	5.28	4.86
9	10.56	8.02	6.99	6.42	6.06	5.80	5.47	5.11	4.73	4.31
10	10.04	7.56	6.55	5.99	5.64	5.39	5.06	4.71	4.33	3.91
11	9.65	7.20	6.22	5.67	5.32	5.07	4.74	4.40	4.02	3.60
12	9.33	6.93	5.95	5.41	5.06	4.82	4.50	4.16	3.78	3.36
13	9.07	6.70	5.74	5.20	4.86	4.62	4.30	3.96	3.59	3.16
14	8.86	6.51	5.56	5.03	4.69	4.46	4.14	3.80	3.43	3.00
15	8.68	6.36	5.42	4.89	4.56	4.32	4.00	3.67	3.29	2.87
16	8.53	6.23	5.29	4.77	4.44	4.20	3.89	3.55	3.18	2.75
17	8.40	6.11	5.18	4.67	4.34	4.10	3.79	3.45	3.08	2.65
18	8.28	6.01	5.09	4.58	4.25	4.01	3.71	3.37	3.00	2.57
19	8.18	5.93	5.01	4.50	4.17	3.94	3.63	3.30	2.92	2.49
20	8.10	5.85	4.94	4.43	4.10	3.87	3.56	3.23	2.86	2.42
21	8.02	5.78	4.87	4.37	4.04	3.81	3.51	3.17	2.80	2.36
22	7.94	5.72	4.82	4.31	3.99	3.76	3.45	3.12	2.75	2.31
23	7.88	5.66	4.76	4.26	3.94	3.71	3.41	3.07	2.70	2.26
24	7.82	5.61	4.72	4.22	3.90	3.67	3.36	3.03	2.66	2.21
25	7.77	5.57	4.68	4.18	3.86	3.63	3.32	2.99	2.62	2.17
26	7.72	5.53	4.46	4.14	3.82	3.59	3.29	2.96	2.58	2.13
27	7.68	5.49	4.60	4.11	3.78	3.56	3.26	2.93	2.55	2.10
28	7.64	5.45	4.57	4.07	3.75	3.53	3.23	2.90	2.52	2.06
29	7.60	5.42	4.54	4.04	3.73	3.50	3.20	2.87	2.49	2.03
30	7.56	5.39	4.51	4.02	3.70	3.47	3.17	2.84	2.47	2.01
40	7.31	5.18	4.31	3.83	3.51	3.29	2.99	2.66	2.29	1.80
60	7.08	4.98	4.13	3.65	3.34	3.12	2.82	2.50	2.12	1.60
120	6.85	4.79	3.95	3.48	3.17	2.96	2.66	2.34	1.95	1.38
∞	6.64	4.60	3.78	3.32	3.02	2.80	2.51	2.18	1.79	1.00

Appendix F-3   F-Distribution, 0.1% Level

The entries in this table are the F-values for which the tail area equals 0.001.

0.001

df FOR DENOMINATOR	df FOR NUMERATOR									
	1	2	3	4	5	6	8	12	24	∞
1	405284	500000	540379	562500	576405	585937	598144	610667	623497	636619
2	998.5	999.0	999.2	999.2	999.3	999.3	999.4	999.4	999.5	999.5
3	167.0	148.5	141.1	137.1	134.6	132.8	130.6	128.3	125.9	123.5
4	74.14	61.25	56.18	53.44	51.71	50.53	49.00	47.41	45.77	44.05
5	47.18	37.12	33.20	31.09	29.75	28.84	27.64	26.42	25.14	23.78
6	35.51	27.00	23.70	21.92	20.81	20.03	19.03	17.99	16.89	15.75
7	29.25	21.69	18.77	17.19	16.21	15.52	14.63	13.71	12.73	11.69
8	25.42	18.49	15.83	14.39	13.49	12.86	12.04	11.19	10.30	9.34
9	22.86	16.39	13.90	12.56	11.71	11.13	10.37	9.57	8.72	7.81
10	21.04	14.91	12.55	11.28	10.48	9.92	9.20	8.45	7.64	6.76
11	19.69	13.81	11.56	10.35	9.58	9.05	8.35	7.63	6.85	6.00
12	18.64	12.97	10.80	9.63	8.89	8.38	7.71	7.00	6.25	5.42
13	17.81	12.31	10.21	9.07	8.35	7.86	7.21	6.52	5.78	4.97
14	17.14	11.78	9.73	8.62	7.92	7.43	6.80	6.13	5.41	4.60
15	16.59	11.34	9.34	8.25	7.57	7.09	6.47	5.81	5.10	4.31
16	16.12	10.97	9.00	7.94	7.27	6.81	6.19	5.55	4.85	4.06
17	15.72	10.66	8.73	7.68	7.02	6.56	5.96	5.32	4.63	3.85
18	15.38	10.39	8.49	7.46	6.81	6.35	5.76	5.13	4.45	3.67
19	15.08	10.16	8.28	7.26	6.62	6.18	5.59	4.97	4.29	3.52
20	14.82	9.95	8.10	7.10	6.46	6.02	5.44	4.82	4.15	3.38
21	14.59	9.77	7.94	6.95	6.32	5.88	5.31	4.70	4.03	3.26
22	14.38	9.61	7.80	6.81	6.19	5.76	5.19	4.58	3.92	3.15
23	14.19	9.47	7.67	6.69	6.08	5.65	5.09	4.48	3.82	3.05
24	14.03	9.34	7.55	6.59	5.98	5.55	4.99	4.39	3.74	2.97
25	13.88	9.22	7.45	6.49	5.88	5.46	4.91	4.31	3.66	2.89
26	13.74	9.12	7.36	6.41	5.80	5.38	4.83	4.24	3.59	2.82
27	13.61	9.02	7.27	6.33	5.73	5.31	4.76	4.17	3.52	2.75
28	13.50	8.93	7.19	6.25	5.66	5.24	4.69	4.11	3.46	2.70
29	13.39	8.85	7.12	6.19	5.59	5.18	4.64	4.05	3.41	2.64
30	13.29	8.77	7.05	6.12	5.53	5.12	4.58	4.00	3.36	2.59
40	12.61	8.25	6.60	5.70	5.13	4.73	4.21	3.64	3.01	2.23
60	11.97	7.76	6.17	5.31	4.76	4.37	3.87	3.31	2.69	1.90
120	11.38	7.32	5.79	4.95	4.42	4.04	3.55	3.02	2.40	1.54
∞	10.83	6.91	5.42	4.62	4.10	3.74	3.27	2.74	2.13	1.00

SOURCE: Abridged from Table V of R. A. Fisher and F. Yates, *Statistical Tables for Biological, Agricultural, and Medical Research*, 6th ed., 1974. Longman Group Ltd., London (previously published by Oliver and Boyd Ltd., Edinburgh). By permission of the authors and publisher.

Appendix G-1 Duncan's New Multiple Ranges, 5% Level

The entries in this table are the Q_p-values used to find R_p, the shortest significant range, at the 5% level.

(The last entry in each row remains the same for all succeeding values of p.)

df	— NUMBER OF MEANS p WITHIN RANGE BEING TESTED																	
	2	3	4	5	6	7	8	9	10	11	12	13	14	15	16	17	18	19
2	6.085																	
3	4.501	4.516																
4	3.927	4.013	4.033															
5	3.635	3.749	3.797	3.814														
6	3.461	3.587	3.649	3.680	3.694													
7	3.344	3.477	3.548	3.588	3.611	3.622												
8	3.261	3.399	3.475	3.521	3.549	3.566	3.575											
9	3.199	3.339	3.420	3.470	3.502	3.523	3.536	3.544										
10	3.151	3.293	3.376	3.430	3.465	3.489	3.505	3.516	3.522									
11	3.113	3.256	3.342	3.397	3.435	3.462	3.480	3.493	3.501	3.506								
12	3.082	3.225	3.313	3.370	3.410	3.439	3.459	3.474	3.484	3.491	3.496							
13	3.055	3.200	3.289	3.348	3.389	3.419	3.442	3.458	3.470	3.478	3.484	3.488						
14	3.033	3.178	3.268	3.329	3.372	3.403	3.426	3.444	3.457	3.467	3.474	3.479	3.482					
15	3.014	3.160	3.250	3.312	3.356	3.389	3.413	3.432	3.446	3.457	3.465	3.471	3.476	3.478				
16	2.998	3.144	3.235	3.298	3.343	3.376	3.402	3.422	3.437	3.449	3.458	3.465	3.470	3.473	3.477			
17	2.984	3.130	3.222	3.285	3.331	3.366	3.392	3.412	3.429	3.441	3.451	3.459	3.465	3.469	3.473	3.475		
18	2.971	3.118	3.210	3.274	3.321	3.356	3.383	3.405	3.421	3.435	3.445	3.454	3.460	3.465	3.470	3.472	3.474	
19	2.960	3.107	3.199	3.264	3.311	3.347	3.375	3.397	3.415	3.429	3.440	3.449	3.456	3.462	3.467	3.470	3.472	3.473
20	2.950	3.097	3.190	3.255	3.303	3.339	3.368	3.391	3.409	3.424	3.436	3.445	3.453	3.459	3.464	3.467	3.470	3.472
24	2.919	3.066	3.160	3.226	3.276	3.315	3.345	3.370	3.390	3.406	3.420	3.432	3.441	3.449	3.456	3.461	3.465	3.469
30	2.888	3.035	3.131	3.199	3.250	3.290	3.322	3.349	3.371	3.389	3.405	3.418	3.430	3.439	3.447	3.454	3.460	3.466
40	2.858	3.006	3.102	3.171	3.224	3.266	3.300	3.328	3.352	3.373	3.390	3.405	3.418	3.429	3.439	3.448	3.456	3.463
60	2.829	2.976	3.073	3.143	3.198	3.241	3.277	3.307	3.333	3.355	3.374	3.391	3.406	3.419	3.431	3.442	3.451	3.460
120	2.800	2.947	3.045	3.116	3.172	3.217	3.254	3.287	3.314	3.337	3.359	3.377	3.394	3.409	3.423	3.435	3.446	3.457
∞	2.772	2.918	3.017	3.089	3.146	3.193	3.232	3.265	3.294	3.320	3.343	3.363	3.382	3.399	3.414	3.428	3.442	3.454

Appendix G-2 Duncan's New Multiple Ranges, 1% Level

The entries in this table are the Q_p-values used to find R_p, the shortest significant range, at the 1% level.

(The last entry in each row remains the same for all succeeding values of p.)

NUMBER OF MEANS p WITHIN RANGE BEING TESTED

df	2	3	4	5	6	7	8	9	10	11	12	13	14	15	16	17	18	19
2	14.04																	
3	8.261	8.321																
4	6.512	6.677	6.740															
5	5.702	5.893	5.989	6.040														
6	5.243	5.439	5.549	5.614	5.655													
7	4.949	5.145	5.260	5.334	5.383	5.416												
8	4.746	4.939	5.057	5.135	5.189	5.227	5.256											
9	4.596	4.787	4.906	4.986	5.043	5.086	5.118	5.142										
10	4.482	4.671	4.790	4.871	4.931	4.975	5.010	5.037	5.058									
11	4.392	4.579	4.697	4.780	4.841	4.887	4.924	4.952	4.975	4.994								
12	4.320	4.504	4.622	4.706	4.767	4.815	4.852	4.883	4.907	4.927	4.944							
13	4.260	4.442	4.560	4.644	4.706	4.755	4.793	4.824	4.850	4.872	4.889	4.904						
14	4.210	4.391	4.508	4.591	4.654	4.704	4.743	4.775	4.802	4.824	4.843	4.859	4.872					
15	4.168	4.347	4.463	4.547	4.610	4.660	4.700	4.733	4.760	4.783	4.803	4.820	4.834	4.846				
16	4.131	4.309	4.425	4.509	4.572	4.622	4.663	4.696	4.724	4.748	4.768	4.786	4.800	4.813	4.825			
17	4.099	4.275	4.391	4.475	4.539	4.589	4.630	4.664	4.693	4.717	4.738	4.756	4.771	4.785	4.797	4.807		
18	4.071	4.246	4.362	4.445	4.509	4.560	4.601	4.635	4.664	4.689	4.711	4.729	4.745	4.759	4.772	4.783	4.792	
19	4.046	4.220	4.335	4.419	4.483	4.534	4.575	4.610	4.639	4.665	4.686	4.705	4.722	4.736	4.749	4.761	4.771	4.780
20	4.024	4.197	4.312	4.395	4.459	4.510	4.552	4.587	4.617	4.642	4.664	4.684	4.701	4.716	4.729	4.741	4.751	4.761
24	3.956	4.126	4.239	4.322	4.386	4.437	4.480	4.516	4.546	4.573	4.596	4.616	4.634	4.651	4.665	4.678	4.690	4.700
30	3.889	4.056	4.168	4.250	4.314	4.366	4.409	4.445	4.477	4.504	4.528	4.550	4.569	4.586	4.601	4.615	4.628	4.640
40	3.825	3.988	4.098	4.180	4.244	4.296	4.339	4.376	4.408	4.436	4.461	4.483	4.503	4.521	4.537	4.553	4.566	4.579
60	3.762	3.922	4.031	4.111	4.174	4.226	4.270	4.307	4.340	4.368	4.394	4.417	4.438	4.456	4.474	4.490	4.504	4.518
120	3.702	3.858	3.965	4.044	4.107	4.158	4.202	4.239	4.272	4.301	4.327	4.351	4.372	4.392	4.410	4.426	4.442	4.456
∞	3.643	3.796	3.900	3.978	4.040	4.091	4.135	4.172	4.205	4.235	4.261	4.285	4.307	4.327	4.345	4.363	4.379	4.394

Appendix G-3 Duncan's New Multiple Ranges, 0.1% Level

The entries in this table are the Q_p-values used to find R_p, the shortest significant range, at the 0.1% level.

(The last entry in each row remains the same for all succeeding values of p.)

NUMBER OF MEANS p WITHIN RANGE BEING TESTED

df	2	3	4	5	6	7	8	9	10	11	12	13	14	15	16	17	18	19
2	44.69																	
3	18.28	18.45																
4	12.18	12.52	12.67															
5	9.714	10.05	10.24	10.35														
6	8.427	8.743	8.932	9.055	9.139													
7	7.648	7.943	8.127	8.252	8.342	8.409												
8	7.130	7.407	7.584	7.708	7.799	7.869	7.924											
9	6.762	7.024	7.195	7.316	7.407	7.478	7.535	7.582										
10	6.487	6.738	6.902	7.021	7.111	7.182	7.240	7.287	7.327									
11	6.275	6.516	6.676	6.791	6.880	6.950	7.008	7.056	7.097	7.132								
12	6.106	6.340	6.494	6.607	6.695	6.765	6.822	6.870	6.911	6.947	6.978							
13	5.970	6.195	6.346	6.457	6.543	6.612	6.670	6.718	6.759	6.795	6.826	6.854						
14	5.856	6.075	6.223	6.332	6.416	6.485	6.542	6.590	6.631	6.667	6.699	6.727	6.752					
15	5.760	5.974	6.119	6.225	6.309	6.377	6.433	6.481	6.522	6.558	6.590	6.619	6.644	6.666				
16	5.678	5.888	6.030	6.135	6.217	6.284	6.340	6.388	6.429	6.465	6.497	6.525	6.551	6.574	6.595			
17	5.608	5.813	5.953	6.056	6.138	6.204	6.260	6.307	6.348	6.384	6.416	6.444	6.470	6.493	6.514	6.533		
18	5.546	5.748	5.886	5.988	6.068	6.134	6.189	6.236	6.277	6.313	6.345	6.373	6.399	6.422	6.443	6.462	6.480	
19	5.492	5.691	5.826	5.927	6.007	6.072	6.127	6.174	6.214	6.250	6.281	6.310	6.336	6.359	6.380	6.400	6.418	6.434
20	5.444	5.640	5.774	5.873	5.952	6.017	6.071	6.117	6.158	6.193	6.225	6.254	6.279	6.303	6.324	6.344	6.362	6.379
24	5.297	5.484	5.612	5.708	5.784	5.846	5.899	5.945	5.984	6.020	6.051	6.079	6.105	6.129	6.150	6.170	6.188	6.205
30	5.156	5.335	5.457	5.549	5.622	5.682	5.734	5.778	5.817	5.851	5.882	5.910	5.935	5.958	5.980	6.000	6.018	6.036
40	5.022	5.191	5.308	5.396	5.466	5.524	5.574	5.617	5.654	5.688	5.718	5.745	5.770	5.793	5.814	5.834	5.852	5.869
60	4.894	5.055	5.166	5.249	5.317	5.372	5.420	5.461	5.498	5.530	5.559	5.586	5.610	5.632	5.653	5.672	5.690	5.707
120	4.771	4.924	5.029	5.109	5.173	5.226	5.271	5.311	5.346	5.377	5.405	5.431	5.454	5.476	5.496	5.515	5.532	5.549
∞	4.654	4.798	4.898	4.974	5.034	5.085	5.128	5.166	5.199	5.229	5.256	5.280	5.303	5.324	5.343	5.361	5.378	5.394

SOURCE: Adapted from tables compiled by D. B. Duncan, *Biometrics* 11, 1–42 (1955), and modified by H. L. Harter, *ibid*, 16, 671–685 (1960) and 17, 321–324 (1961).

Appendix H   Correlation Coefficients

The entries in this table are the R-values for distributions with from 1 to 100 degrees of freedom, at 5 values of the probability.

df (k − 2)	PROBABILITY OF A LARGER VALUE OF R				
	0.10	0.05	0.02	0.01	0.001
1	.98769	.99692	.999507	.999877	.9999988
2	.90000	.95000	.98000	.990000	.99900
3	.8054	.8783	.93433	.95873	.99116
4	.7293	.8114	.8822	.91720	.97406
5	.6694	.7545	.8329	.8745	.95074
6	.6215	.7067	.7887	.8343	.92493
7	.5822	.6664	.7498	.7977	.8982
8	.5494	.6319	.7155	.7646	.8721
9	.5214	.6021	.6851	.7348	.8471
10	.4973	.5760	.6581	.7079	.8233
11	.4762	.5529	.6339	.6835	.8010
12	.4575	.5324	.6120	.6614	.7800
13	.4409	.5139	.5923	.6411	.7603
14	.4259	.4973	.5742	.6226	.7420
15	.4124	.4821	.5577	.6055	.7246
16	.4000	.4683	.5425	.5897	.7084
17	.3887	.4555	.5285	.5751	.6932
18	.3783	.4438	.5155	.5614	.6787
19	.3687	.4329	.5034	.5487	.6652
20	.3598	.4227	.4921	.5368	.6524
25	.3233	.3809	.4451	.4869	.5974
30	.2960	.3494	.4093	.4487	.5541
35	.2746	.3246	.3810	.4182	.5189
40	.2573	.3044	.3578	.3932	.4896
45	.2428	.2875	.3384	.3721	.4648
50	.2306	.2732	.3218	.3541	.4433
60	.2108	.2500	.2948	.3248	.4078
70	.1954	.2319	.2737	.3017	.3799
80	.1829	.2172	.2565	.2830	.3568
90	.1726	.2050	.2422	.2673	.3375
100	.1638	.1946	.2301	.2540	.3211

SOURCE: Abridged from Table VII of R. A. Fisher and F. Yates, *Statistical Tables for Biological, Agricultural, and Medical Research,* 6th ed., 1974. Longman Group Ltd., London (previously published by Oliver and Boyd Ltd., Edinburgh). By permission of the authors and publisher.

Appendix I-1 Rank Totals Excluded for Significant Differences (5% Level)

Any rank total outside the given range is significant.

Number of Judges	Number of Wines										
	2	3	4	5	6	7	8	9	10	11	12
3				4–14	4–17	4–20	4–23	5–25	5–28	5–31	5–34
4		5–11	5–15	6–18	6–22	7–25	7–29	8–32	8–36	8–39	9–43
5		6–14	7–18	8–22	9–26	9–31	10–35	11–39	12–43	12–48	13–52
6	7–11	8–16	9–21	10–26	11–31	12–36	13–41	14–46	15–51	17–55	18–60
7	8–13	10–18	11–24	12–30	14–35	15–41	17–46	18–52	19–58	21–63	22–69
8	9–15	11–21	13–27	15–33	17–39	18–46	20–52	22–58	24–64	25–71	27–77
9	11–16	13–23	15–30	17–37	19–44	22–50	24–57	26–64	28–71	30–78	32–85
10	12–18	14–26	17–33	20–40	22–48	25–55	27–63	30–70	32–78	35–85	37–93
11	13–20	16–28	19–36	22–44	25–52	28–60	31–68	34–76	36–85	39–93	42–101
12	15–21	18–30	21–39	25–47	28–56	31–65	34–74	38–82	41–91	44–100	47–109
13	16–23	20–32	24–41	27–51	31–60	35–69	38–79	42–88	45–98	49–107	52–117
14	17–25	22–34	26–44	30–54	34–64	38–74	42–84	46–94	50–104	54–114	57–125
15	19–26	23–37	28–47	32–58	37–68	41–79	46–89	50–100	54–111	58–122	63–132
16	20–28	25–39	30–50	35–61	40–72	45–83	49–95	54–106	59–117	63–129	68–140
17	22–29	27–41	32–53	38–64	43–76	48–88	53–100	58–112	63–124	68–136	73–148
18	23–31	29–43	34–56	40–68	46–80	52–92	57–105	61–118	68–130	73–143	79–155
19	24–33	30–46	37–58	43–71	49–84	55–97	61–110	67–123	73–136	78–150	84–163
20	26–34	32–48	39–61	45–75	52–88	58–102	65–115	71–129	77–143	83–157	90–170

Appendix I-2 Rank Totals Excluded for Significant Differences (1% Level)

Any rank total outside the given range is significant.

Number of Judges	Number of Wines										
	2	3	4	5	6	7	8	9	10	11	12
3									4–29	4–32	4–35
4				5–19	5–23	5–27	6–30	6–34	6–38	6–42	7–45
5			6–19	7–23	7–28	8–32	8–37	9–41	9–46	10–50	10–55
6		7–17	8–22	9–27	9–33	10–38	11–43	12–48	13–53	13–59	14–64
7		8–20	10–25	11–31	12–37	13–43	14–49	15–55	16–61	17–67	18–73
8	9–15	10–22	11–29	13–35	14–42	16–48	17–55	19–61	20–68	21–75	23–81
9	10–17	12–24	13–32	15–39	17–46	19–53	21–60	22–68	24–75	26–82	27–90
10	11–19	13–27	15–35	18–42	20–50	22–58	24–66	26–74	28–82	30–90	32–98
11	12–21	15–29	17–38	20–46	22–55	25–63	27–72	30–80	32–89	34–98	37–106
12	14–22	17–31	19–41	22–50	25–59	28–68	31–77	33–87	36–96	39–105	42–114
13	15–24	18–34	21–44	25–53	28–63	31–73	34–83	37–93	40–103	43–113	46–123
14	16–26	20–36	24–46	27–57	31–67	34–78	38–88	41–98	45–109	48–120	51–131
15	18–27	22–38	26–49	30–60	34–71	37–83	41–94	45–105	49–116	53–127	56–139
16	19–29	23–41	28–52	32–64	36–76	41–87	45–99	49–111	53–123	57–135	62–146
17	20–31	25–43	30–55	35–67	39–80	44–92	49–104	53–117	58–129	62–142	67–154
18	22–32	27–45	32–58	37–71	42–84	47–97	52–110	57–123	62–136	67–149	72–162
19	23–34	29–47	34–61	40–74	45–88	50–102	56–115	61–129	67–142	72–156	77–170
20	24–36	30–50	36–64	42–78	48–92	54–106	60–120	65–135	71–149	77–163	82–178

Source: Adapted from tables compiled by A. Kramer and published in revised form in *Food Technology* 17(12), 124–125 (1963).

Appendix J Normal Scores

The entries in this table show the conversion of rankings to normal scores. Negative values are omitted for samples larger than 10.

RANK ORDER	SIZE OF SAMPLE								
	2	3	4	5	6	7	8	9	10
1	0.564	0.864	1.029	1.163	1.267	1.352	1.424	1.485	1.539
2	−0.564	0.000	0.297	0.495	0.642	0.757	0.852	0.932	1.001
3		−0.864	−0.297	0.000	0.202	0.353	0.473	0.572	0.656
4			−1.029	−0.297	−0.202	0.000	0.153	0.275	0.376
5				−1.163	−0.642	−0.353	−0.153	0.000	0.123
6					−1.267	−0.757	−0.473	−0.275	−0.123
7						−1.352	−0.852	−0.572	−0.376
8							−1.424	−0.932	−0.656
9								−1.485	−1.001
10									−1.539

	11	12	13	14	15	16	17	18	19	20
1	1.586	1.629	1.668	1.703	1.736	1.766	1.794	1.820	1.844	1.867
2	1.062	1.116	1.164	1.208	1.248	1.285	1.319	1.350	1.380	1.408
3	0.729	0.793	0.850	0.901	0.948	0.990	1.029	1.066	1.099	1.131
4	0.462	0.537	0.603	0.662	0.715	0.763	0.807	0.848	0.886	0.921
5	0.225	0.312	0.388	0.456	0.516	0.570	0.619	0.665	0.707	0.745
6	0.000	0.103	0.191	0.267	0.335	0.396	0.451	0.502	0.548	0.590
7		0.000	0.088	0.165	0.234	0.295	0.351	0.402	0.448
8			0.000	0.077	0.146	0.208	0.264	0.315
9				0.000	0.069	0.131	0.187
10					0.000	0.062

	21	22	23	24	25	26	27	28	29	30
1	1.889	1.910	1.929	1.948	1.965	1.982	1.998	2.014	2.029	2.043
2	1.434	1.458	1.481	1.503	1.524	1.544	1.563	1.581	1.599	1.616
3	1.160	1.188	1.214	1.239	1.263	1.285	1.306	1.327	1.346	1.365
4	0.954	0.985	1.014	1.041	1.067	1.091	1.115	1.137	1.158	1.179
5	0.782	0.815	0.847	0.877	0.905	0.932	0.957	0.981	1.004	1.026
6	0.630	0.667	0.701	0.734	0.764	0.793	0.820	0.846	0.871	0.894
7	0.491	0.532	0.569	0.604	0.637	0.668	0.697	0.725	0.752	0.777
8	0.362	0.406	0.446	0.484	0.519	0.553	0.584	0.614	0.642	0.669
9	0.238	0.286	0.330	0.370	0.409	0.444	0.478	0.510	0.540	0.568
10	0.118	0.170	0.218	0.262	0.303	0.341	0.377	0.411	0.443	0.473
11	0.000	0.056	0.108	0.156	0.200	0.241	0.280	0.316	0.350	0.382
12		0.000	0.052	0.100	0.144	0.185	0.224	0.260	0.294
13			0.000	0.048	0.092	0.134	0.172	0.209
14				0.000	0.044	0.086	0.125
15					0.000	0.041

SOURCE: Abridged from tables compiled by H. L. Harter, *Biometrika* 48, 151–165 (1961).

Glossary

Williams (1975) has emphasized the importance of a universally recognized vocabulary for cider. His list contains many indefinite terms. However, if his panel can differentiate "like mead" from "like honey," these terms appear to be valid. The value of his terms is that they are related to specific chemical compounds, mixtures of compounds, or reproducible artificial standards.

To us it is obvious that the development of a meaningful vocabulary for wines is even more difficult, partly because of the great range of types and qualities of wines and partly because of the entrenchment of terms from several languages and a variety of commercial practices over the years. Ohara (1966) has published a list of over 350 terms (in English, French, German, and Japanese) used in the sensory evaluation of wines. Although many of these terms are self-explanatory, some are too indefinite to be useful.

The definitions that follow will probably not satisfy some connoisseurs, nor are they intended to, even if that were possible. Experienced judges use many more terms with varying meanings than those listed here. These definitions are intended more for the student, as he begins to learn how to evaluate wines critically. The symbols (+) and (−) refer to pleasantness and unpleasantness, respectively.

Words used to describe color have been omitted. We feel that all but the colorblind can develop their own vocabulary. The professional will probably use physical measurements to specify the parameters of color. However, the human eye is extraordinarily sensitive to small differences in colors, and the development of a rational color nomenclature would be desirable.

Some terms have definite chemical meanings, e.g., acetic, mercaptan, and sulfur dioxide. The amateur will be satisfied with semiquantitative sensory evaluations of such factors, whereas the professional will demand quantitative chemical data.

Finally, we would make a plea for less fanciful terms than those so often found in the popular press. Simplicity and clarity should be the initial goals, but above all the terms must have recognizable meanings with respect to the sensory evaluation of wines.

acescence—See *acetic*.

acetic—The odor of acetic acid and ethyl acetate. (−) The threshold in wine is about 0.07 gram per 100 ml, calculated as acetic acid. A less precise word is *pricked*. In fact, a number of words relating to the degree and unpleasantness of the acetic odor in wines are used in the Western European languages.

acidic—See *sour*.

acidulous—Unpleasantly *sour* (q.v.). (−) More or less equivalent to the French *mordant*.

aerated—The odor of newly filtered or bottled table wines. (−) Probably an incipient *oxidized* odor (q.v.).

aftersmell—An odor sensation, part of the *aftertaste* (q.v.). Probably due to the less volatile components of the wine, which remain in or reach the olfactory region after the more volatile components have disappeared. See also *flavor*.

aftertaste—The lingering taste *and* odor *and* tactile sensations that remain after a wine is swallowed. The finest red table wines are characteristically high in this quality. (+) Red table wines with little aftertaste are said to "finish short." (−) Some white table wines have a surprisingly lingering aftertaste, e.g., some Chardonnays and Sauvignon blancs.

alcoholic—See *hot.*

aroma—The odors of wine that originate in the grapes (muscat, Sauvignon blanc, Concord, etc.).

aromatic—A distinctive odor usually found in wines of certain varieties. A more general term than *spicy* (q.v.).

astringent—The puckery *tactile* sensation. (−) Particularly noticeable in young red table wines. *Harsh, rough,* and *tannic* are related terms. The opposite, usually achieved by fining and aging, is *smooth* (or, less desirably, *soft* or *velvety*). Not to be confused with *bitter* (q.v.).

bacterial—An omnibus term for off odors from bacterial action. Better to specify the responsible bacterium, if possible. (−) See also *acetic, butyric, geranium-like, mousy.*

baked—The caramelized odor of sweet wines that have been heated too long. (−) In California sherries and other baked types of wine it is normal. (+, if not too accentuated) *Cooked* seems to be nearly the same. In certain types the undesirable odor of excessive baking is called *burnt.* See also *raisin.*

balanced—Primarily the taste sensation of wines in which all the tastes are present in their proper proportions. (+) Used especially for the balance of the *sweet* and *sour* tastes (q.v.). It may also be used for the relations of the odorous components to each other. *Harmonious* has a similar meaning, perhaps with a more pleasant connotation, and includes odor. *Unbalanced* is the opposite. (−)

biacetyl—Difficult to characterize the odor, and individuals vary in sensitivity. Present in oxidized red wines. At low concentrations (1–3 mg per liter) it may add complexity (+) but at higher concentrations it is certainly undesirable (−). (This compound is also called diacetyl.)

bitter—A lingering taste sensation. (Usually −) Contrary to some enologists, it is not confined to red table wines. It is partially masked by high sweetness. A number of compounds, if present in sufficient amounts, can give the bitter taste.

bitter almond—The odor of cyanide, resulting from poor filtration of wines treated with potassium ferrocyanide (this treatment is illegal in the United States); rare. (−)

body—The tactile sensation differentiating low-ethanol from high-ethanol wines. The presence of sugar often makes this differentiation difficult. *Full-bodied* would be more alcoholic, and *thin* (q.v.), less alcoholic.

bouquet—The odors of wine that originate in fermentation, processing, or aging, particularly after bottling. (+) European writers often do not distinguish bouquet from *aroma* (q.v.).

brilliant—Free of suspended material.

burny—The pain sensation in the nose; often found in *hot* wines (q.v.). (−)

butyric—From butyric acid, due to bacterial action; rare. (−)

caramel—The odor of heated sweet wines, as in some California sweet sherries. (− or +, depending on the type) Similar to *baked* and *maderized* (q.v.). (−) The odor of the usual grape concentrate is very similar.

carboned—In wines treated with too much carbon. (−) See *oxidized.*

clean—A very much overworked term intended to describe the absence of defects. It is probably better to describe the actual sensations perceived. *Bland* and *neutral* (q.v.) are words of similar meaning, perhaps of a less pleasant connotation. The term *common* falls in the same category. It is not much of a compliment to a wine to describe it as clean. *Vinous* (q.v.) may be better.

clear—The slight haze of a few suspended particles.

cloudy—Colloidal haze and particulate matter.

cloying—An excessively sweet wine, usually also too low in acidity. (−) See also *unctuous.*

coarse—Although this is intended to describe an unbalance of flavor components, it is so weighted down with various other meanings that it is best avoided. The French *corsé* and the Spanish *basto* have different and more favorable connotations.

complex—The juxtaposition of several odors. (+) The great desideratum of quality. However, only those with some experience in the sensory evaluation of wines should use the word.

cooked—See *baked.*

corky or corked—A moldy odor from moldy corks; once recognized, never forgotten. (−)

delicate—A much misused word; used differently by professionals for still and sparkling wines. (+?) Avoid it.

dry—Absence of the sweet taste. Some wines that should be dry are not. (+ or −, depending on the type of wine) Less experienced consumers tend to prefer slightly sweet wines if they do not know they are sweet. Unwary experts have also been fooled.

dull—Definite colloidal haze.

earthy—An unpleasant odor perceived *in the mouth;* difficult to recognize or describe. (−) May not be related to soil.

elegant—A quality judgment. We try to avoid such terms, but one does need a few words of approbation and condemnation. Other favorable words that are used but can't be adequately defined are *breed, character, delicate* (q.v.), *distinguished, fine, great, noble, stylish,* and the like. (+) See also page 204.

faded—More or less the same as the French *éventé.* Incipient *oxidation* (q.v.).

fermenting—The odor of fermenting yeast: possibly sulfides. (Usually −, but a trace of this odor in neutral, young, sparkling and still wines may not be objectionable) See also *fresh.*

finesse—This word needs a rest, along with *delicate* and *elegant* (q.v.).

finish—See *aftertaste.*

flat—Lack of sour taste. (−) See *sour.*

flavor—Odors that are released from the wine as it warms up in the mouth; these "in-mouth" odors reach the olfactory region by diffusion and through exhalation.

flinty—We confess that this flavor (odor?) has never come our way. Perhaps *metallic* (q.v.) would do as well. Best to avoid it.

flowery—An odor, particularly in young white table wines. (+) Related words such as *fragrant, perfumed, scented,* etc., are best avoided unless you know what they mean.

foxy—The methyl and/or ethyl anthranilate odor of *Vitis labrusca* grapes and wines made from them. (+ or −, depending on what you are used to)

fresh—The odor of young wines; perhaps a further stage of *fermenting* (q.v.). (+, or − if too pronounced)

fruity—The grape-like odor, particularly of young wines. Possibly associated with good acidity. (Usually +) There is a refreshing character about a cool, fruity wine. Keats had the right idea:

O, for a draught of vintage! that hath been
Cool'd a long age in the deep-delved earth.

full-bodied—See *body.*

gassy—The tactile (and often visual and even auditory) sensation of carbon dioxide escaping from a wine. *Piquant* may be an incipient state of gassiness, but avoid it as a quality judgment.

geranium-like—The odor resulting from bacterial activity in wines containing sorbic acid. The revealing compound is 2-ethoxy-hexa-3,5-diene. (−) See Crowell and Guymon (1975).

grapy—The same or similar fruit-like odor discussed under *fruity* (q.v.).

green—The odor of wines made from unripe grapes. (−) Often but not necessarily associated with the high-acid sour taste, but it is not a taste.

green olive—The odor of Cabernet Sauvignon. See Amerine and Singleton (1965). Some experts call this the black currant odor.

hard—Uncertain meaning; perhaps high-acid and high-polyphenolic wines are hard. (−) Avoid it. *Dureté* in French.

herbaceous—An odor, particularly of some varietal wines, suggesting the odor of herbs. It is (+) if from the variety and not

too pronounced, but (−) if from nongrape ingredient(s) or spoilage.

hot−A fiery sensation, possibly pain, in the mouth or nose. (−) Probably due to higher-than-normal ethanol content together with low sweetness. See *baked* for a similar odor. *Bite* may or may not be a related term.

hydrogen sulfide−See *sulfide.*

leafy−The odor, particularly of some young wines. (−) See *stemmy.*

lees−The odor of wines left too long on the lees. (−) Most objectionable in low-acid table wines stored under warm conditions. *Mercaptans* (q.v.) may be present.

maderized−See *baked.* We believe most such wines are also *oxidized* (q.v.).

mature−The overall sensation, particularly in red wines, of a wine that gives no evidence of being too young or too old. (+) *Ripe* has a similar meaning.

mellow−Another word that means different things to different people. If it refers to the sweet sensation, why not say so? Sometimes it may mean soft; so, say *soft.*

mercaptan−The objectionable odor of methyl and ethyl sulfides. (−)

metallic−Few wines have enough metals in them to affect taste or texture directly. More likely, metallic is the sensation of low-ethanol, dry, high-acid white wines or of high-polyphenolic, astringent red wines. (Usually −)

mildew−The fungus odor of wines made from heavily mildewed grapes. (−) Rare in California. Not to be confused with *moldy* (q.v.).

moldy−The odor of wines made from moldy grapes or stored in moldy containers; easy to recognize. (−)

mousy−The bacteria-induced odor of wines, usually those made from late-picked grapes or low-acid musts. Very disagreeable once you learn to identify it. (−)

musty−Often used by "connoisseurs," but what does it mean? Avoid it unless you know what it means. We don't.

naive—Used for wines of little merit, by persons who presume—but lack—knowledge.

neutral—A wine lacking distinctive or recognizable character. *Vinous* says the same thing and is to be preferred. See also *clean*.

nose—A pretentious word for odor. Try to avoid it.

nutty—Use *woody*. Webb and Berg (1955) use it for madeira-like, i.e., *baked*.

oaky—See *woody*. Contrary to some books, California baked wines (sherry and sweet sherry) do not have a woody or oaky flavor (with rare exceptions).

off—An undesirable odor (rarely taste). *Odd, sophisticated,* and *spoiled* have similar meanings. (−)

oloroso—Spanish sherries that have not undergone a film-yeast stage during production. They vary in color from light amber when young to a dark amber when aged. They also vary in sweetness.

overaged—*Oxidized* usually serves as well. See also *faded* and *rancio*.

overripe—See *raisin*. It may be worthwhile differentiating the overripe odor from the raisin odor, if you can.

oxidized—In wines, mainly the odor of acetaldehyde. In table wines it is (−) but it is often (+) in dessert wines. *Rancio* (q.v.) is a related, if not the same, odor. *Maderized* is a heat-induced, oxidized odor with a more or less *caramel* character (q.v.). *Overaged* is nearly the same, but often with woody overtones. *Biacetyl* (q.v.) may be present.

palatable—Another word of uncertain meaning when applied to wine evaluation. Probably about the same as *pleasant*. (+) If *palatable* must be used, it should be for tastes. *Pleasant* could then be kept for odors. Probably best avoided anyway.

peppery—An odor occasionally found in California white table wines. The origin is not known. It may be related to a certain concentration of sulfur dioxide. (−)

petroleum—An odor we are happy not to have found in wine. We can think of circumstances in which it might occur, however (shipping wine in petroleum-contaminated containers, mixing wine with compressed air containing oil, etc.). (−)

pleasant—See *palatable.* A favorable odor, but it's hard to define its parameters. (+)

pungent—Best avoided, except perhaps for flavored wines.

raisin—The odor of semi-dried or wholly dried grapes. The same or a similar odor is present in wines made from overripe grapes. This can be (+) in wines made from very slightly shriveled grapes (*passerilage*), such as red Burgundies. It is surely (−) when it is due to dried grapes. It is also (−) in many wines made from grapes grown in very warm climates, such as some from Algeria and Morocco, and occasionally even from the Rhône. *Sunburned* (−) may not be the same odor.

rancio—The special and distinctive odor of old, oxidized, high-ethanol, usually sweet, red wines. (+ for special types)

reduced—The odor of wines in a chemically reduced state; related to *yeasty* or low *hydrogen sulfide* odor. (−) The color of white wines with this odor is usually very light.

resin—The turpentine odor of retsina wine (+) or of non-retsina wines inadvertently contaminated by being placed in containers that previously contained resin-flavored wines (−, except for those who have acquired a taste for it).

ripe—See *mature.*

rough—The astringent, tactile sensation, *not* the bitter taste. The Italian *aspro* comes close.

rubbery—The odor of some wines made from high-pH musts. Also called the *Fresno odor* or *rubber boot* odor. (−) See Brown (1950).

salty—The taste, rare in wines. (−) Perhaps acceptable in low concentrations in old, very dry flor sherries. (+)

sauerkraut—A lactic odor in wines that have undergone an excessive malo-lactic fermentation.

sharp—Probably best limited to *acetified*, or an early stage thereof. See *acetic*.

smooth—The opposite of *astringent, harsh,* or *rough.* Similar terms are *soft, velvety,* and possibly *feminine* and *sensuous. Supple* also seems similar. Avoid these similar terms.

soft—Not quite the same as *smooth.* Used in Europe for slightly sweet wines. Best avoided. A soft wine is more than just one lacking tannin: a higher-than-normal ethanol content seems essential. (Usually +)

sophisticated—The foreign odor of nongrape or unauthorized ingredients, intentionally or unintentionally added to a wine. (−)

sour—The acid taste. Should not be applied to high-acetic acid wines. The opposite is *flat* (q.v.). Wines made from green grapes will be sour. See also *tart.*

sour-sweet—A disagreeable taste, sometimes associated with the activity of lactic acid bacteria in sweet wines. (−)

spicy—A distinctive odor, particularly of some varietal wines, e.g., Gewürztraminer. (+, or − if too pronounced or deficient)

stagnant—Wines placed in containers that contained stagnant water acquire this unpleasant odor. (−)

stemmy or **stalky**—The reported odor of wines made from musts containing fresh stems; possibly related to the *leafy* odor. (−)

sulfide—The disagreeable odor of hydrogen sulfide; usually includes the *mercaptans* (q.v.). (−) About 1 to 5 parts per billion seems to be the threshold.

sulfur dioxide—An off odor, always to be criticized. (−) About 100 mg per liter seems to be the threshold in table wines, but this varies with the composition and age of the wine.

sweet—The taste. (+ or −, depending on the type of wine) A very sweet wine may be *cloying* (−), a less sweet one, unpleasantly *sweetish* (−). See also *dry.*

sweetish—An unpleasant sweet taste, often in low-acid wines. (−)

syrupy—A very sweet wine, particularly one that is low in ethanol. (−)

tart—A pleasant, sour taste in young wines. (+) See *acidulous* and *sour*.

thin—Lack of body. (−) *Watery* is a related term. *Meager* is a similar but superfluous term.

tired—See *aerated, oxidized,* and *vapid.*

ullage—Occurs when wine casks are not kept full, or when bottles leak. The wines are then usually *oxidized* (q.v.), hence the oxidized odor of such wines. (−)

unctuous—The unpleasant texture of an overly sweet wine. (−) Similar to or the same as *cloying* (q.v.).

unripe—See *green.*

vapid—A mildly oxidized odor. See Webb and Berg (1955).

vinegary—The odor of acetic acid and ethyl acetate. (−) Always objectionable.

vinous—Without a specific, distinguishable aroma. *Clean* and *neutral* are similar terms.

watery—Same as or very similiar to *thin* (q.v.). (−)

woody—The odor of wines stored too long in oak containers or in too new, improperly conditioned containers. A little may be (+), especially in red table wines, but if it is recognizable it is considered (−).

yeasty—The odor from fermenting yeasts, possibly the same as *fermenting* (q.v.). (−)

young—The fresh, fruity, unoxidized, and very slightly yeasty odor. In some young white table wines it is (+). More often it is (−), especially in red or aged table wines. *Fresh* is as good or better a term.

Unfortunately, existing wine terminology abounds in words and phrases that have little or no clearly definable meaning with respect to the sensory evaluation of wines. Some such terms are acceptable if used judiciously by experts when *they* know exactly what they mean. Many other terms cannot satisfy even this criterion, and quite a few are simply ridiculous.

It is not our intent to condemn the following terms (although some of them deserve it) for your wine vocabulary, but merely to warn you to use them with caution, if at all. If they *are* used they should be defined as carefully as possible and their meanings should be understood and agreed upon by all the judges on the panel or in the group.

austere
big
bite
breed
chalky
character
chewy
clean
coarse
common
crisp
delicate
delicious
depth (or lack of it)
developed
distinguished
dumb
elegant
empty
evanescent nose
evasive nose
evolved
fat
feminine
fine
finesse
flabby
flashy
flinty (not even for Chablis)
fragrant
full
goaty
great
grip
hard
harsh
heady

heavy
incomparable
intense
lackluster color
lean
light
lithe
little
lively
marrowy
masculine
meager
meaty
medium-dry
mellow
metallic
mild
musky
musty
naive
noble
nose
nuance of mint
nutty
oily
ordinary
palatable
perfumed
piquant
poor
powerful
pricked
pungent
pure
rich
robust
rounded
runny

sap
scented
sec (in sparkling wines)
sensuous
severe
sharp
short finish
sick
silky
small
smoky
soapy
soft
splendid
steely
strong
sturdy
stylish
sugary finish
sunny
superficial
supple
tangy
tender
thick
tired
tough
triumphant
unclean nose
velvety
vigorous
voluptuous
warm
weak
well-bred nose
wet straw (odor)
withered
zestful

It is therefore essential to establish a vocabulary of organoleptic terms—a vocabulary sufficiently rich and precise that each word in the language of enology brings to mind a sensation, just as each word in the language of philosophy brings to mind an idea.

—P. Poupon

Annotated Bibliography

Amerine, M. A., 1969. There really is quality in wines. *San Francisco* 11(10): 38–39.

Amerine, M. A., H. W. Berg, and W. V. Cruess, 1972. *The Technology of Wine Making*, 3rd ed. Avi Publishing Co., Westport, Conn. 802 pp.
Contains section on sensory evaluation.

Amerine, M. A., and M. A. Joslyn, 1970. *Table Wines: The Technology of Their Production*, 2nd ed. University of California Press, Berkeley and Los Angeles. 997 pp. (See pp. 382–385.)
Several score cards are discussed.

Amerine, M. A., and C. S. Ough, 1964. The sensory evaluation of California wines. *Lab. Pract.* 13(8): 712–716, 738.
How wines were judged at Davis and at the California State Fair.

Amerine, M. A., R. M. Pangborn, and E. B. Roessler, 1965a. *Principles of Sensory Evaluation of Food.* Academic Press, New York. 602 pp.
The state of the art and technology as of 1965: Still applicable to many food-evaluation problems.

Amerine, M. A., and E. B. Roessler, 1969–70. The age and acidity of wines aged in wood. *Wine and Food,* No. 146: 120.
    A skeptical look at claims of 100-year old wines.

Amerine, M. A., E. B. Roessler, and F. Filipello, 1959. Modern sensory methods of evaluating wine. *Hilgardia* **28**: 477–567.
    The modern approach; useful methodology and vocabulary.

Amerine, M. A., E. B. Roessler, and C. S. Ough, 1965*b*. Acids and the acid taste. I. The effect of pH and titratable acidity. *Amer. J. Enol. Vitic.* **16**: 29–37.
    Shows how sensitive we can be to the acid taste.

Amerine, M. A., and V. L. Singleton, 1965. *Wine: An Introduction for Americans.* University of California Press, Berkeley and Los Angeles.

Anon., 1973. The ideal wine glass. *Search: Sci. Technol. Soc.* 4(1/2): 4.

Arnold, R. A., A. C. Noble, and V. L. Singleton, 1976. Investigation of astringency in wine—model systems. Submitted to *Amer. J. Enol. Vitic.*
    Distinguishes between bitterness and astringency.

Associazione Enotecnici Italiani, 1975. Il primo congresso nazionale dell' O.N.A.U. *L'Enotecnico* 11(10): 21, 23.
    A new score card.

Bayonove, C., R. Cordonnier, and P. Dubois, 1975. Étude d'une fraction caractéristique de l'arôme du raisin de la variété Cabernet- Sauvignon: mise en évidence de la 2-méthoxy-3-isobutylpyrazine. *Compt. rend.* **281**: 75–78.
    Identifies a revealing compound.

Berg, H. W., F. Filipello, E. Hinreiner, and A. D. Webb, 1955*a*. Evaluation of thresholds and minimum difference concentrations for various constituents of wines. I. Water solutions of pure substances. *Food Technol.* **9**: 29–37.
    Basic data on taste and odor sensitivity.

Berg, H. W., F. Filipello, E. Hinreiner, and A. D. Webb, 1955*b*. *Ibid.,* II. Sweetness: the effect of ethyl alcohol, organic acids, and tannin. *Ibid.,* 138–140.
    Factors affecting the sweetness sensation.

Bradley, R. A., 1953. Some statistical methods in taste testing and quality evaluation. *Biometrics* 9(1): 22–38.

Broadbent, J. M., 1973. *Wine Tasting: A Practical Handbook on Tasting and Tastings.* Christie Wine Publications, London. 54 pp.
    The European wine merchant's point of view. But how can one be sure the differences reported are real?

Brown, E. M., 1950. A new off-odor in sweet wines. *Proc. Amer. Soc. Enol.* 1950: 110–112.
Astute observations about the nature and source of an off odor in California wines.

Buxbaum, W., 1951. Weinbereitung nach Punkten; ein Mittel zur Qualitätssteigerung und Absatzförderung. *Deut. Weinbau* 5: 596–597.
Early use of a score card for wine evaluation in Europe.

Cloquet, J., 1906. *L'Art de la dégustation des vins.* Lébeque, Brussels. 70 pp.
Includes a vocabulary of appropriate terms.

Cochran, W. G., and G. M. Cox, 1957. *Experimental Designs,* 2nd ed. John Wiley, New York. 611 pp.

Crowell, E. A., and J. F. Guymon, 1975. Wine constituents arising from sorbic acid addition, and identification of 2-ethoxyhexa-3,5-diene as source of geranium-like off-odor. *Amer. J. Enol. Vitic.* 26: 97–102.

Daepp, H. U., 1968. Zur Weinbeurteilung mittels Sinnenprüfung-Beeinflussungsmöglichkeiten und Methoden. *Deut. Weinbau Jrb.* 1968: 197–213.
Practical advice on modern procedures for sensory evaluation of wines. Generally follows U.S. practices.

Durac, J., 1974. *Wines and the Art of Tasting.* Dutton, New York. 241 pp.
Includes a number of practical tests, but terms used are poorly defined.

Fisher, R. A., and F. Yates, 1974. *Statistical Tables for Biological, Agricultural, and Medical Research,* 6th ed. Longman Group Ltd., London (previously published by Oliver and Boyd Ltd., Edinburgh). 146 pp.

Foster, D., C. Pratt, and N. Schwartz, 1955. Variations in flavor judgments in a group situation. *Food Research* 20: 539–544.

Gale, G., 1975. VIII. Are some aesthetic judgments empirically true? *Amer. Phil. Quart.* 12: 341–348.
They are.

Got, N., 1955. *La Dégustation des vins; classification et présentation; l'art de déguster et de présenter les vins.* Perpignan. 236 pp.
A general and gentle discussion of procedures for the sensory evaluation of wines. Useful terminology, but how does one measure the significance of the results?

Hagenow, G., 1969. Color-Odor-Sapor: zur Geschichte der Weinbereitung und der Weinkultur. *Deut. Weinbau Jrb.* 1969: 195–200.
How sensory evaluation of wines has evolved in Europe.

Harries, J. M., 1973. Complex sensory assessment. *J. Sci. Food Agric.* **24**: 1571–1581.
   Advanced statistical procedures.

Hennig, K., 1950. Ein neues Verfahren zur Punktwertung von Wein und Schaumwein. *Deut. Wein-Ztg.* **87**: 171–172.
   An early example of scoring wines in Germany.

Hinreiner, E., F. Filipello, H. W. Berg, and A. D. Webb, 1955*a*. Evaluation of thresholds and minimum difference concentrations for various constituents of wines. IV. Detectable differences in wines. *Food Technol.* **9**: 489–490.

Hinreiner, E., F. Filipello, A. D. Webb, and H. W. Berg, 1955*b*. *Ibid.*, III. Ethyl alcohol, glycerol, and acidity in aqueous solution. *Ibid.*, 351–353.
   Further studies on sensitivity to wine constituents.

Jones, F. N., 1958. Prerequisites for test environment; in *Flavor Research and Food Acceptance*, A. D. *Little, Inc.* Reinhold, New York. 391 pp. (See pp. 107–111.)

Kare, M. R., 1975. Changes in taste with age—infancy to senescence. *Food Technol.* **29**: 77.

Kielhöfer, E., 1949. Die Beurteilung der organoleptischen Eigenschaften des Weines und ihre Auswertung, insbesondere bei kellertechnischen Versuchen. *Weinbau, wiss. Beih.* **3**: 262–271.
   Use of sensory evaluation in controlling cellar operations and price.

Kiermeier, F., and U. Haevecker, 1972. *Sensorische Beurteilung von Lebensmitteln.* J. F. Bergmann, Munich. 101 pp.
   A review of the important methods used for evaluating foods. More than 1100 references, including 21 on wine.

Klenk, E., 1972. *Die Weinbeurteilung nach Farbe, Klarheit, Geruch, und Geschmack,* 3rd ed. Verlag Eugen Ulmer, Stuttgart. 172 pp.
   Factors affecting wine quality, mainly of German wines.

Lake, M. E., 1969. *The Flavour of Wine: A Qualitative Approach for the Serious Wine Taster.* Jacaranda, Milton, Queensland. 60 pp.
   Instructive but highly subjective.

Lehrer, A., 1974. *The Semantics of Wine Tasting or In Vino Veritas.* Center for Advanced Study in the Behavioral Sciences, Palo Alto, Calif. 61 leaves.
   The meaning of words used to describe wines and the lack of agreement among individuals regarding their interpretations.

Maga, J. A., 1974. Influence of color on taste thresholds. *Chem. Senses Flavor* **1**: 115–119.
   Color does have an effect.

Marcus, I. H., 1974. *How to Test and Improve Your Wine Judging Ability.* Wine Publications, Berkeley, Calif. 96 pp.
    A number of simple and useful tests that can easily be done at home and that will provide fun and profit for the serious student.

Mareschalchi, A., 1974. *La degustazione e l'apprezzamento dei vini,* 5th ed. Casa Editrice S. A., Fratelli Mareschalchi, Casale Monferrato. 200 pp.
    Mainly the subjective concepts of fifty years ago, but with some modern ideas.

Marie, R., D. Boubals, and P. Galzy, 1962. Sur la degustation rationnelle des boissons. *Bull. OIV* (Office International de la Vigne et du Vin) **35**: 756–787.
    Use of analysis of variance and block designs for sensory problems.

Marteau, G., 1953. Recherche de la qualité par l'examen des vins. *Prog. Agric. Vitic.* **140**: 281–289, 310–314.
    Encourages attention and memory and deplores suggestion.

McBurney, D. H., 1974. Are there primary tastes for man? *Chem. Senses Flavor* **1**: 17–28.
    There are.

McBurney, D. H., and L. J. Moskat, 1975. Taste thresholds in college-age smokers and nonsmokers. *Percept. Psychophysics* **18**: 71–73.
    No differences found.

Meyers, D. G., and H. Lamm, 1975. The polarizing effect of group discussion. *Amer. Scient.* **63**: 297–303.

Ohara, Y., 1966. A guide to terms used in the sensory evaluation of wines. *Bull. Research Inst. Fermentation (Yamanashi)*, No. 13, 63–94.
    From several languages, including Japanese.

Osterwalder, A., 1948. Von Mäuselgeschmack der Weine, Obst- und Beerenweine. Eine Erwiderung. *Schweiz. Z. Obst- Weinbau* **57**: 397–399, 420–421.
    His ideas on the microbiological origin of the mousy odor.

Ough, C. S., and G. A. Baker, 1961. Small panel sensory evaluations of wines by scoring. *Hilgardia* **30**: 587–619.
    Shows clearly the uncertainty inherent in score cards of more than 10 points.

Parker, G. H., 1922. *Smell, Taste, and Allied Senses in the Vertebrates.* Lippincott, Philadelphia. 192 pp.
    An early discussion of thresholds.

Paul, F., 1964. Die technische Durchführung der organoleptischen Beurteilung von Weinen. *Mitt. Rebe Wein,* Ser. A (Klosterneuburg) **14**: 197–209.

Application of modern procedures to sensory evaluation of wines. Considers that 15 is the minimum number of tests on a given wine for testing for significance.

Paul, F., 1967. Die "Rangziffernmethode," eine einfache Möglichkeit für den organoleptischen Vergleich zweier oder mehrer Proben. *Ibid.*, **17**: 280–288.
Use of ranking in wine evaluation.

Pirsig, R. M., 1974. *Zen and the Art of Motorcycle Maintenance: An Inquiry into Values*. William Morrow, New York. 412 pp.
Philosophy of making quality judgments.

Puisais, J., R. L. Chabanon, A. Guiller, and J. Lacoste, 1969. *Précis d'initiation à la dégustation*. Insitut Technique Vin, Paris. 90 pp.

Puisais, J., R. L. Chabanon, A. Guiller, and J. Lacoste, 1974. *Initiation into the Art of Wine Tasting*. Interpublish Inc., Madison, Wisc. 95 pp.
The 1974 edition is a translation from the French edition, with some additions. There is also an Italian edition. Useful on the physiology of the senses.

Rankine, B. C., 1967. Formation of higher alcohols by wine yeasts, and relationship to taste thresholds. *J. Sci. Food Agric.* **18**: 583–589.
Only isoamyl alcohol is present in high enough amounts to affect odor.

Rankine, B. C., 1971. Panel evaluation by tasting tests. *Aust. Wine, Brew. Spirit Rev.* **89**(4): 34, 36.
How to make up solutions in wine for threshold tests.

Rankine, B. C., 1974. Wine tasting and judging. *Food Technol. Australia* **26**: 443–453.
Describes the "expert" wine judgings that are a feature of the Australian wine industry and gives suggested general specifications for wine types.

Rankine, B. C., J. C. M. Fornachon, and D. A. Bridson, 1969a. Diacetyl in Australian dry red wines and its significance in wine quality. *Vitis* **8**: 129–134.
The difference threshold in wines was 1 to 1.3 mg per liter.

Rankine, B. C., and K. F. Pocock, 1969b. Phenethanol and *n*-hexanol in wines: influence of yeast strain, grape variety, and other factors; and taste thresholds. *Ibid.*, 23–37.
Thresholds varied from 30–200 and 4–30 mg per liter, respectively.

Ribéreau-Gayon, J., 1973. Recherche des relations entre les caractères sensorials des vins rouges et leur composition. *Conn. Vigne Vins* **7**: 79–92.

Emphasizes the effects of the senses on each other and the balance between tastes, and suggests various correlations between composition and sensory responses.

Ribéreau-Gayon, J., and E. Peynaud, 1966–69. *Traité d'oenologie*, rev. ed. Librairie Ch. Béranger, Paris. Vol. 1, 753 pp.; Vol. 2, 1065 pp. Contains section on sensory evaluation.

Roessler, E. B., and M. A. Amerine, 1973. The "age" of Madeiras. *Amer. J. Enol. Vitic.* 24: 176–177.

The law of compound interest has not been repealed!

Schrodt, W., and L. Jacob, 1966. Die statistisch erfassbaren Wechselwirkung bei der technischen Weinprobe mit Wiederholungen. *Mitt. Rebe Wein*, Ser. A (Klosterneuburg) 16: 357–369. Use of appropriate statistical procedures for determining significance in sensory evaluation of wines.

Schwacke, 1935. Warum schmeckt warmer Wein saurer als kalter? *Wein Rebe* 17: 123–124.

Warm wine tastes more acid than cold wine because it is more ionized; so he says.

Scriven, L. E., and C. V. Sternling, 1960. The Marangoni effects. *Nature* 187: 186–188.

A historical review.

Singleton, V. L., H. A. Sieberhagen, P. de Wet, and C. J. van Wyk, 1975. Composition and sensory quality of wines prepared from white grapes by fermentation with and without grape solids. *Amer. J. Enol. Vitic.* 26: 62–69.

Bitterness is distinguished from astringency.

Stone, H., K. Sidel, S. Oliver, A. Woolsey, and R. C. Singleton, 1974. *A Scoring Method for Sensory Evaluation of Materials*. Stanford Research Institute, Menlo Park, Calif. 31 pp.

Application of computer programming for analyzing sensory data.

Troost, G., 1972. *Technologie des Weines*, 4th ed. Verlag Eugen Ulmer, Stuttgart. 931 pp.

A general review (pp. 594–627) of the best methods for sensory examination of wines.

Troost, G., and E. Wanner, 1962. *Weinprobe. Weinansprache.* Verlag Sigurd Horn, Frankfurt-am-Main. 63 pp.

A general summary of the sensory evaluation of wines in Germany.

Van Wyk, C. J., A. D. Webb, and R. E. Kepner, 1967. Some volatile components of *Vitis vinifera* variety White Riesling. 1, 2, 3. *J. Food Sci.* 32: 660–664, 664–668, 669–674.

The aromatic constituents of the variety identified.

Vedel, A., G. Charle, P. Charnay, and J. Tourneau, 1972. *Essai sur la dégustation des vins.* S.E.I.V. Mâcon. (Not paged.)
Some suggestive ideas regarding the relation between words and the influence of odor persistence on quality.

Von Sydow, E., H. Moskowitz, H. Jacobs, and H. Meiselman, 1974. Taste-odor interaction in fruit juices. *Lebensm. Wissensch. Technol.* 7: 18–24.
Shows that there is an interaction.

Wald, A., 1947. *Sequential Analysis.* John Wiley, New York. 212 pp.

Webb, A. D., and H. W. Berg, 1955. Terms used in tasting. *Wines & Vines* 36(7): 25–28.

Williams, A. A., 1975. The development of a vocabulary and profile assessment method for evaluating the flavour contribution of cider and perry aroma constituents. *J. Sci. Food Agric.* 26: 567–582.
Useful vocabulary, some of it applicable to wines.

Wilson, C. W. M., 1972. The pharmacological actions of alcohol in relation to nutrition. *Proc. Nutr. Soc.* 31: 91–98.
Use of statistics in analyzing results.

Wine Institute, 1974. *California Wine Type Specifications,* rev. ed. Wine Institute, San Francisco. 8 pp.
Very general definitions of California wine types.

Yoxall, H. W., 1972. *The Enjoyment of Wine.* Michael Joseph, London. 200 pp.
Sensible advice on wine appreciation and evaluation.

Index